Electrics
and Electronics
for Small Craft

John French

Electrics and Electronics for Small Craft

Second Edition

John French

ADLARD COLES LIMITED
GRANADA PUBLISHING
London Toronto Sydney New York

Published by Granada Publishing in
Adlard Coles Limited, 1973
Second Edition 1981

Granada Publishing Limited
Frogmore, St Albans, Herts AL2 2NF
and
3 Upper James Street, London W1R 4BP
Suite 405, 4th Floor, 866 United Nations Plaza, New York, NY 10017 USA
Q164 Queen Victoria Buildings, Sydney, NSW 2000, Australia
100 Skyway Avenue, Toronto, Ontario, Canada M9W 3A6
61 Beach Road, Auckland, New Zealand

Copyright © John French 1973, 1981

ISBN 0 229 11612 4

Typeset by V & M Graphics Ltd, Aylesbury, Bucks
Printed in Great Britain by
Fletcher & Son Ltd, Norwich

Granada ®
Granada Publishing ®

For Rebecca

Contents

Illustrations

Foreword

When John French approached me with the request that I write a foreword to this book, I must confess that I was rather daunted. To contribute to a work so complicated and technical as describing electronic and electrical equipment for small craft seemed beyond me.

Yet the fact remains that every yachtsman in this day and age gets more and more involved with such instruments and equipment. Even the pure sailing yacht has a battery of instruments to measure wind strength and direction, efficiency and speed through the water, to mention the first that come to mind.

I think that most owners or skippers when confronted with these sophisticated instruments are somewhat confused, and pretend to understand because they do not want to appear ignorant. Here is a chance to put all that right and to put things in their true perspective: to understand not only what a piece of equipment is for, but to be able to use it to its full potential and to the best advantage.

A glance at the chapter headings will show what a wide range this book covers. I can think of nothing that has been omitted. A mine of information, it is just what is needed for the professional skipper or the weekend yachtsman. I congratulate Mr French in putting together a book covering such a wide field in a manner readily understood by the practical yachtsman or fisherman.

Foreword to Second Edition, 1981

The rapid development of new techniques in the field of electronics is something that the average man – and perhaps especially the yachtsman – has some difficulty in grasping. The impact of the microprocessor on marine electronics is to allow much more sophisticated equipment to be installed in small craft such as sailing yachts and motor cruisers, that are more compact, efficient, and much more economical on electric power.

John French has revised his excellent book to take account of this new technological expertise, which affects every piece of equipment that we have come to accept as aids to our navigation and the efficient sailing of our yachts, as well as enabling us to install further equipment that previously was too cumbersome for the space available.

It is for us to take advantage of these developments in the new technical age. Used properly, they can make life easier, so long as we remember that they are aids and do not displace basic good seamanship.

Sir Alec Rose

Preface

Whatever it is that takes men to sea for their leisure is captured for me in the words from Milton's *Samson Agonistes:*

> *but here I feel amends, the breath of heaven*
> *fresh blowing, pure and sweet with dayspring born,*
> *here leave me to respire.*

Perhaps it is that boating is such an agreeable escape; so that I can reconcile this ideal with reality and my own personal vocation, I have tried to write a practical book about some of the electronic and electrical equipment available to yachtsmen and other operators of small craft. It is a trifle historic in places, which I trust will add to the interest.

There is a profusion of problems associated with introducing electronics to a marine environment; also, as the boat gets smaller the problems seem to get bigger. Fitting and obtaining good results from electronic equipment can in many cases become both difficult and expensive, in some instances from a lack of general information. What I have written deals with principles, operation and installation on a practical level. This, I hope, will provide information to enable the boat owner to select his electrical and electronic requirements against a better background. Also some of the answers to problems with existing equipment may be found in the appropriate chapters.

Introduction

Each year more people discover the enormous pleasure of boating, and the world of small craft steadily expands. To service the increasing demand the industry is going through a period of considerable growth. Associated with this is a trend towards more extensive instrumentation, much of which is now built in as standard equipment.

Although some of the equipment described may be considered to be beyond the average yachtsman's pocket, I am sure that in the next few years advances in development being carried out at the present time will reduce the cost of a fair number of equipments to the point where they can be fitted on even the smallest cruising yachts.

One of the major marine problems is satisfactory installation, as even the best equipment is only as good as the standard of its installation. All marine work carried out to a good standard is expensive, and if you have not paid for a proper job by investing the right amount of time or money, you will certainly pay later when it fails and ruins something else in the process. A boat in which everything has been fitted correctly holds its value well, as any surveyor is able to take this sort of thing in at a glance. For example, it may be hard to accept that the cost of properly fitting a small craft echosounder could considerably exceed the initial cost of the instrument. Some manufacturers claim that installation is a 'simple' or 'fifteen minute' job, and certainly in these circumstances it is not surprising that many yachtsmen smart at the fitting charge. I have yet to encounter any piece of marine equipment that I can install and check in fifteen minutes.

The electronics industry and the small boat industry have grown up alongside each other, and during the last twenty years a specialised small craft electronics section has emerged, producing a wide variety of instruments. In the early years the equipment available in the UK was sparse and mainly associated with communications. A certain amount of government surplus equipment was in use, largely held in place by string and the owner's optimism. Fantastic feats of navigation or communication were attributed to such rigs, especially over a large gin in the safety of the yacht club. Inevitably all of the early equipments used thermionic valves, and for operation from the boat's low voltage supply some suitable voltage convertor was employed. This usually took the form of a vibrator for small loads or a rotary convertor for larger requirements. Such devices had a power conversion efficiency of about 40% when in good condition. As the initial load requirement was comparatively high, it could be said that all such equipments, no matter how simple, created a considerable battery drain.

To illustrate this point, in the 1950s a well engineered small boat echosounder would have consumed about 5 A at 12 V, whereas a present day equivalent will consume about 100 mA at 9 to 12 V, and give the advantage that at this level of consumption 20 to 30 hours of intermittent use could be obtained from a small dry battery. Thus an improvement so far as power requirements are concerned to the order of 50:1 has been achieved. For the larger users of power, e.g. transmitters, refrigerators, radars, etc., the use of static invertors —equivalent to a vibrator but with transistors instead of the vibrating reed to create the current reversals—gives a typical conversion efficiency of 85%. Extensive transistorisation and the use of integrated circuits has considerably reduced the physical bulk and power requirements of marine equipment, and at the same time these technological advances have been crucial in getting much better value for money in terms of performance.

I have mentioned earlier the economics of installing sophisticated electronic equipment effectively. As this work is usually extensive, I have had a twinge of concern that when confronted by some of the work involved the tendency may be to skimp it. I can only recommend that if it does look a bit mountainous in certain cases, where perhaps a fair amount of refitting is necessary to accommodate a particular equipment, the whole job be undertaken slowly and step by step, if necessary spread over all the wet weekends in the season. The rewards for this sort of patience are great satisfaction and faith in the equipment. For the boat owner who has spent much and sometimes gained little, apart from an hour or so's novelty tuning in an unbearable level of electrical interference on the new direction finder which is lucklessly sited and subject to enormous errors, I hope my humble effort will make some contribution in a practical way to this very transient moment of pleasure being usefully extended.

INTRODUCTION TO SECOND EDITION 1981

It is hard to think of a subject embracing a wider range of technology, which makes it at once both irresistible and exciting to try to look into the future of an industry so full of change.

Microprocessors

One hears much about the microprocessor, that seemingly all-powerful little finger-size computer that will control our lives (or so we are told by those who confuse memory with intelligence). In fact it is a very useful device for extending man's intelligence and it would have been far more extensively applied by now, had it not happened that those who introduced it to the electronics industry described its functions in a new jargon which camouflaged techniques known for years. Certainly the greatest influence on boating electronics in the course of the next decade will be brought about by the application of microelectronics. This will bring within the grasp of designers information displays and signal processing techniques which would have been unthinkable in the past, due to cost or complexity. Low cost is essential and, with microelectronics, it is only achievable with volume production; it is therefore a certainty that a domestic micro-processor with a useful size of 'on chip' memory will find application in small boat equipment. Without exception, all aspects of marine electronics would be much improved by the introduction of control loops supervised by computed data. Among designers of automatic pilots, it has long been acknowledged that comparison of rates of change rather than of absolute proportion lead to a more fluent synthesis of what the human helmsman achieves. It would be possible to run through a program of measurements and instructions at (typically) 1000 times per second, including stabilisation of autopilot hoodwinking manoeuvres such as tacking, because the system would have tight control of course rather than tight control of rudder.

Many equipments are of the measuring type, i.e. depth, windspeed, waterspeed, etc., and the availability of better processing circuitry means that the designer is able to apply a wider range of principles to solving particular problems. For example imagine a new concept in windspeed transducers; the designer finds that it performs at its best when the output signal is in a form unusable by conventional meter displays without a degree of complication too expensive to find a market, and in this situation the design would have to be shelved. By applying a microprocessor, however, it would be possible not only to produce the signal conversion required but also to derive additional outputs in the form of computed parameters, such as rate of change of windspeed. To the observes, all parameters seem to be measured simultaneously; what in fact happens is that the microprocessor repetitively cycles through a series of sequential events, each step taking but a small fraction of a second.

Taken to its logical conclusion, a computing link between wind, water and compass systems becomes feasible; and the immense improvements can then be easily imagined.

Opto-electronic Displays

A light along the sea, so swiftly coming,
Its motion by no flight of wind is equalled,
And when therefrom I had withdrawn a little
Mine eyes, that I might question my conductor,
Again I saw it brighter grown and larger.
Dante's Inferno, translated by *Henry W Longfellow*

In the future semiconductor displays will have a considerable impact on the way electrical information from instrumentation is presented. There are various forms of display, some using light emitting diodes while another type controls the refractive characteristics of a liquid crystal substance; examples of this type are now commonly encountered in pocket calculators and wrist watches. The simple echosounder will lose its motor and rotating arm, and acquire an array of light emitters that are electronically scanned sequentially, producing a display almost identical in appearance. Sailing instruments with expensive moving coil meters will increasingly compete with liquid crystal displays, indicating direct and computed parameters in a form clearly visible both in brilliant sunlight and at night with a small inbuilt light source. Probably the most exciting prospect is the advent of the first solid state radar display. The technology exists at this time to produce such a display, but as yet it is not an economically viable proposition for manufacture.

The cathode ray tube used in radar and sonar displays fulfils two roles: memory and display. The solid state counterpart will be a fine dot matrix, and it will need a separate memory. This will mean that the display will not fade between each circular sweep but will simply be updated on a dot by dot basis in a radial fashion. This idea will no doubt appeal to all those familiar with conventional radar. As such displays have very small front to back dimensions, the bulk associated with today's radar will disappear and a very shallow format will emerge. No mechanical drive will be needed in the display and this will further reduce current consumption; while the low voltage used implies better reliability.

Separating the display and memory function produces all manner of other possibilities which are too numerous to enter into here. It is sufficient to say that the development of radar is far from over.

Change due to Social and Economic factors

Hence we see why all the species in the same region do at last,
if we look to long enough intervals of time, become modified,
for otherwise they would become extinct.
Origin of Species *Charles Darwin*

Some changes become necessary because higher standards are required, as in communications equipment. In order to achieve more channel space, tuning needs to be more accurate and this needs new technology for economic reasons. One classical example of this is the solid state replacement for the mechanical capacitor conventionally used for tuning the radio receiver. For those unfamiliar with the device, it consists of a double series of parallel plates arranged to mesh with each other to a controllable degree, the extent of the overlap determining the capacity. Both it and the coil associated with it are temperature sensitive, which gives rise to tuning drift, and it has a calibrated dial to indicate the operating frequency. In the future this device will be increasingly replaced by

the tiny varicap diode, which is infinitely smaller and cheaper; its capacity is varied simply by applying a small voltage. It is often used in a precision tuning system called a synthesiser, which operates by comparing the diode controlled tuning with a quartz reference; feedback corrects any error. The frequency of operation is usually indicated on an opto numerical display and the effects of temperature on such a system are minimal. Not all advances will be made by applying near miraculous new devices; indeed, for large and expensive vessels, the range of present day gadgets is wide: sonar, stabilisers, gyropilot, inertial navigation, satellite navigation, automatic omega, truemotion radar with 'clear-scan'—in fact all you need is the money to purchase and service the installation. My feeling is that not too many owners are in this bracket and that the majority are, like me, sailing the biggest boat they can afford, with one eye on the future which will inevitably bring specialised small boat versions of complex equipment within reach. Even if we ignore interest on the capital value of the vessel, the cost of insurance, maintenance and moorings is now a substantial annual charge, and it is therefore necessary to look for real economies where they can be found. Due to the ever rising cost of service and installation work I feel that navaids will increasingly become self-contained packages fitted and removed by owners themselves, and in the event of maintenance being required, the owner will simply unplug and return it for service. With most present day equipment this has not been possible, for a variety of reasons such as multi-unit design, weight, external complexity of connection, and so on. I believe that before a very much higher level of technology is reached, this change will have to take place anyway, as the facilities required for more than first-line service will be beyond the economics of a small sales and service outlet.

Existing Technology

I took the oars: the Pilot's boy,
Who now doth crazy go,
Laughed loud and long, and all the while
His eyes went to and fro.
'Ha! Ha!' quoth he, 'full plain I see,
The Devil knows how to row.'
The Rime of the Ancient Mariner *Coleridge*

There are some areas in which industry has failed to apply existing technology, inevitably leaving a wake full of the problems that have beset the previous generation of boatbuilder. It would be good to think that, in the future, all electrical or electronic equipment manufactured for the boat industry would be marked with a clear symbol, indicating that both poles of the supply are totally isolated from the casework and that a formal earth terminal of the DC blocking type is provided. This alone would save money for most boat owners, as many electrolysis problems would be avoided. The problem originated because of the practice of 'marinising' road vehicle equipment when the industry was too small to expect special consideration of its requirements. This is no longer a valid excuse as the small boat industry is a customer of stature, entitled to expect fully insulated equipment from its suppliers as standard and not as an exception. Moreover, if an appliance is capable of generating interference, a suitable suppression kit should be available to a stated standard.

In the last few miles of any voyage, particularly at night in an unfamiliar area, position fixing is rarely attended by over-confidence. The simple MF radio beacon can do much to improve this, and low cost versions are available now having a range of 8 to 10 miles (Adney Automation of Itchener). As the receiving equipment is so simple it is nothing short of amazing that there is any port without a beacon; it becomes even more staggering if you consider that the great Marconi demonstrated a marine radio beacon at Sestri Levante in 1934; for the future one must hope for much better radio identification of harbours and navigation marks, because at the moment we are heavily under using this piece of early technology.

A Question of Size

He had forty-two boxes, all carefully packed,
with his name painted clearly on each:
But, since he omitted to mention the fact,
they were all left behind on the beach.
        The Hunting of the Snark *Lewis Carroll*

Is it not about time that the boat industry evolved a series of standard panel sizes? This is the only way that marine architects, equipment

manufacturers and boat builders will know that what they are designing and building will fit. This would do much to reduce the effort and expense required to mount equipment and would make for better styling of instrument consoles. Considering the present hotch-potch of shapes and sizes, one can only admire the considerable genius displayed by the boat builder in arriving at an aesthetically acceptable layout. This notion has been successfully applied in the light aircraft industry and has been standard practice for some years. Equally the car radio aperture size of 2″×7″ (50×175 mm) produced a revolution in the quality of installation, as tailored fitting kits became available. In the boating industry it would make possible a range of wheel and instrument consoles which would give the customer a higher standard and better value for money; it would also make life much simpler for the builder. I feel that a basic module size which could be stacked horizontally or vertically, would be a great advance on what we have now. For older boats and exceptional conditions, a yoke-mounted module carrier would sustain compatibility. Why not think in terms of the aircraft module size as a starting point? A 2×3 module stack would make a nice radar panel size!

Electronic Tools for Boat Builders

That with a hand more swift and sure
The greater labour might be brought
To answer to his inward thought,
And as he laboured his mind ran o'er
The various ships that were built of yore,
        The Building of the Ship *Henry W Longfellow*

There are many ways in which electronics can assist the boat builder, either in his constant search for higher standards, or in the diagnosis of some problem or other. For example, standards of comfort receive much attention, and reduction of noise and vibration have a high priority. Now, the strobe lamp is a very useful way of making vibrating parts visible to the eye; it is not expensive, and is easy for even someone with no knowledge of electronics to use; it is simply a matter of pointing the lamp at running machinery, rigging or whatever, slowly sweeping the frequency control and watching as vibrating mechanical parts appear to bend backwards and forwards. I regard this as a very useful tool as it makes potential problems visible and experience tells me that boat builders need little guidance when they can see the problem. Meters to measure the effectiveness of sound insulation work are also available and can enable a better assessment to be made on whether the money spent on insulation is cost effective. It is possible to hire this sort of equipment so it is quite easy to have a trial run without spending a lot of money. For more specialised work there are companies who are able to carry out X ray examination of metals. This can be very useful as, with shafts or rigging components, a bad weld or crack can be detected before failure rather than afterwards.

I have touched on just a few details in a vast and changing subject, in which whatever is written is out of date before the ink is dry. With such potential I am sure we shall all be kept on our toes for the foreseeable future.

PART I

1   The Electrical Fabric

The Bellman, who was almost morbidly sensitive about appearances, used to have the bowsprit unshipped once or twice a week to be revarnished, and it more than once happened, when the time came for replacing it, that no one on board could remember which end of the ship it belonged to. They knew it was not of the slightest use to appeal to the Bellman about it—he would only refer to his Naval Code, and read out in pathetic tones Admiralty Instructions which none of them had ever been able to understand—so it generally ended in its being fastened on, anyhow, across the rudder. The helmsman used to stand by with tears in his eyes: he knew it was all wrong, but alas! Rule 42 of the Code, 'No one shall speak to the Man at the Helm', had been completed by the Bellman himself with the words 'and the Man at the Helm shall speak to no one.' So remonstrance was impossible, and no steering could be done till the next varnishing day. During these bewildering intervals the ship usually sailed backwards.

Preface to The Hunting of the Snark
Lewis Carroll

The preface to *The Hunting of the Snark* may seem an odd piece of prose with which to introduce my first chapter; however, as metaphorically speaking the bowsprit does get mixed up with the rudder sometimes, I thought it appropriate for a chapter devoted to the more general details of electrics and electronics afloat.

The finer points of operating and installing this type of equipment in small craft have been extensively looked into over the years by the Royal National Life-boat Institution (RNLI) and the various equipment manufacturing companies in particular. I have tried to translate some of the technical material available into a semi-technical form to make reading as easy and interesting as possible for yachtsmen and other small craft operators. There is now a great variety of equipment available, and to cover the whole range in one volume is something of a task.

To successfully introduce electrical and electronic equipment to the boating environment it is necessary to create a framework of conditions which are the key to satisfactory results. I frequently encounter boat owners who are disappointed with some particular equipment and who have assumed that the marine agent's installation charge included all work necessary to make the new equipment compatible with the boat and all other devices aboard. This is by no means the case. The extent of the work a commercial ship owner has to do at his own expense when fitting electronic equipment would no doubt greatly alarm the average yacht owner, as much of the work has been borne historically by the marine agent. Possibly, due to the nature of small craft work, the borders of who is responsible for what have become somewhat blurred, because the marine equipment agent very often undertakes electrical work, shipwrighting and some mechanical engineering. There are areas where most agents have to limit their willingness to compromise. Typical of such situations is that of securing any skin fitting that may affect the watertight condition of the hull, i.e. echosounder transducers, etc.

Another common cause of misunderstanding between agents and owners is caused by radio in interference suppression, or the lack of it. This particular problem is largely due to the difficulty of securing a position where any manufacturer can say that a particular equipment or piece of apparatus is fully suppressed. All the manufacturer can do is to state the terminal noise figure for the device, and although this figure may conform to, for instance, BS 1597 in the UK, there is no way of being sure that in any given installation the device will not produce an unacceptable level of radiated or conducted noise. Radio interference is a big subject and I have devoted chapter 3 to it. The main point I wish to make at this stage is that effective suppression only starts with the manufacturer of electrical equipment. To be effective, the mechanical and electrical conditions on the boat must reach a basic minimum standard in order to allow electronic equipment to be introduced without creating difficult interference problems. Good suppression equipment is not cheap and can be carried out more effectively during construction; costs often rise dramatically when suppression is added after completion. The level of radiated interference has steadily increased over the years with the wider use of electrical machinery. With the high level of sensitivity available in present day equipments, and the wider spectrum of frequencies in use, we can see and hear interference better than ever.

It will be clear that this is a subject on which there can easily be a great deal of misunderstanding. The boat owner considering installation of any piece of equipment is strongly recommended to reach a clear and firm understanding on exactly what work the supplier is going to do for the price agreed, before placing the order. Surprisingly this is very often not done, with the inevitable bore of claim and counterclaim after the job is finished.

RNLI Practice

These basic marine electronics problems have all been encountered and remedied at some time or other within the RNLI's fleet. The Institution has been kind in providing me with a summary of some details of the development of electronics within the framework of their organisation. The RNLI craft range from 30 to 70 ft in length and this makes for an excellent comparison with most yachts and small fishing boats. The standard required for all

equipment within the RNLI is of course very high and constant efforts are made to improve all aspects of performance as technology advances. Mr Reid of the machinery drawing office has kindly provided details of a typical lifeboat electrical system, and many details on corrosion of materials used by the RNLI, which are listed later in this chapter. The RNLI began fitting electronic equipment many years ago and have accumulated a wealth of experience in small craft electronics. In 1927 the first experimental radio transmitting and receiving apparatus was fitted to the Rosslare Harbour lifeboat. It was of the wireless telegraphy type, which meant that a skilled operator had to be carried as all messages were sent in Morse.

Small Craft Practice

Before we get down to selecting and fitting any particular piece of equipment it will be advisable to consider the basic framework we shall need to create for equipment and boat to live happily together. I think it is easier to see what is required for the electrical system on any particular boat by looking at a wiring layout for a RNLI lifeboat (1.4). It would then be possible for the reader to apply only those details truly relevant to the individual case. Fitting out the electrics and the electronics in different types of small craft means that the layout is going to vary considerably; however if the main points being discussed here are adhered to, sorting out problems when they arise will be greatly simplified. Reference is made to chapters 2 and 3 for the details of radio interference suppression, batteries and charging equipment.

The lifeboat is virtually all electric and built to a very high standard; however the basic rules for this standard need not be expensive to apply to any small craft, particularly if some of the work is undertaken by the owner. It is more a matter of being prepared to take the trouble. Once the groundwork is done the effectiveness of the interference suppression and other similar problems will be greatly increased. Further, unless the groundwork is done it is possible to spend hours and a great deal of money on suppression equipment that will be prevented from fulfilling its job by the installation conditions.

The various parts of the lifeboat electrical

ystem shown have been given a letter key in the diagram, and each component is detailed below ollowing its key.

ALT These units are CAV alternators type AC7, which have a maximum output of 64 A at 27.5 V and are arranged to cut in at 600 r.p.m. Described in greater detail in chapter 2.

SB Suppression box by CAV type 446–24–1 with built-in control board 440–24–2. It is a key item in securing a generating system reasonably free from radio interference. Shown and described in chapter 3.

AMP In order to monitor the charging current from the alternators, two moving coil ammeters are used. The type specified by the RNLI in this application was by McMillan & Co. and scaled 0–60 DC.

JB Many of the junction boxes appearing in the layout are of RNLI design. The most important feature of a marine junction box is that it should be waterproof and for this reason it is generally a cast box with a gasket round the lid. All cable entries are via suitable glands. Conductor bars and clamps are of substantial brass construction.

CB Circuit breakers of the balanced armature type, to obviate 'no fault tripping' when subject to rough weather accelerations. The rating varies according to the loading requirement and many companies supply units suitable for marine purposes in metal cases which may be fitted with an appropriate number of modules to suit the application.

SOC Socket provided for charging the boat's batteries from an external source such as shore supply or portable generator. This should preferably be a non-reversible type and well protected from water.

VOL Voltmeter used for checking system voltage and battery condition. The type shown was a moving coil instrument scaled 0–30 V and made by McMillan & Co.

AMM Ammeter used to monitor the load current. Usually fitted with a remote shunt to avoid heavy loads or voltage drop in the connections to the instrument console.

ES Engine starter button. Sometimes of the lockable type. Suitable units are manufactured by Lucas-CAV.

BIS Heavy duty battery isolator switches made by

CAV, type 134M. These are fitted to enable complete isolation of the batteries for service work or when the boat is idle.

ST Starter motor for main engines.

TS Temperature thermostat for monitoring engine coolant.

PS Pressure switch to monitor engine oil pressure.

P Port

S Starboard

SW A special relay switch to ensure that the battery box fans are always operating when the boat's battery supplies are switched on. If this switch is opened to stop the fans a light shows on the case; it will revert to the closed position automatically when the boat's supplies are turned off at the end of the voyage.

BBF Battery box fan to prevent accumulation of dangerous gases from the batteries. Usually a flameproof type, in the scheme shown an Airmax type X4507/24V.

BAT Lead/acid battery comprising four 6 V units, 145 AH. Dagenite 3PGB11A.

WL A remote warning light panel mounted in the wheelhouse and operating from the temperature and pressure sensors on the engine.

SHL Shelter light, Cooper & Smith type 2422 with 7.5 W lamp.

DR Dimming rheostat for instrumentation lights, 75 Ohms resistance, 1.0 A capacity.

IIL Instrument illumination lights. Arcolectric type SL82. Lamps 28 V, 3.5 W each.

DL 18 W deck light, Simms type TL8102 or LK40.

SIGL 60 W hand signal lamp by T Francis & Son, MK IV.

SL Searchlight by T Francis & Son, Mk III M/13/47.

SOC, AMF Convenience sockets of the Nipham type N662 to enable the signalling lamp and searchlight to be plugged in and used aft, midships or forward.

FL Engineroom fluorescent lights, Easco type C50/24T, one 9 in., 6 W tube.

SNL 7.5 W sternlight

SDL 7.5 W sidelight

SML 7.5 W steaming light

SW3G Three-gang switch unit, 28 V 20 A rating.

SW1 and SW2 Single-switch units, 28 V 20 A rating.

WHL   7.5 W wheelhouse light, Cooper & Smith, type 2422.

RLS   Riding light socket. Sometimes an automatic device is used which has a photo-electric sensor, to switch riding lights on and off at dusk and dawn.

SSO   Switched socket outlet rated 27 V 5 A DC, to enable various ancillary equipment to be conveniently connected, i.e. low voltage vacuum cleaner, electric soldering iron, etc.

BL   Binnacle light

WWU   Windscreen wiper unit or Clearview screen. Sometimes a Wynnstrument straight line wiper is fitted and on other craft a Kent Clearview screen is used.

P & S   Plug and socket, 2 pin 5 A Niphan type N520B & N662.

K   Klaxon hooter

HL   Hand inspection lamp, Walsall conduit type 6988, 12 W.

FLFC   Fluorescent lights for forward cabin, Easco type C50/24T, 6 W, 9 in. tube.

SW2G   Two-gang switch unit rated at 28 V 20 A DC

VF   Hull ventilation fans, Smiths type CBH 2883. It will be noted that out of some of the switched sockets (SSO) a pair of leads is taken, shown terminating in arrowheads. This indicates that a low power lead has been looped into this circuit for convenience—for example the chart table or compass lights. There is nothing wrong with this practice when done with discretion, although in some small craft it is taken to the extent that it becomes the rule rather than the exception. Just above the cabin heaters in the diagram are three fluorescent lights: two of these units are used for aft cabin illumination and the single unit is fitted in the radiotelephone space.

CH   Cabin heater, Smiths type R551, model FHR 5502/17.

SWSP   Switch, single pole rated 28 V 20 A DC.

K   Low voltage electric kettle by Electron Ltd, 24 V 450 W.

R   UHF or VHF radiotelephone

RT   MF radiotelephone

S   Supply for radar or other equipment, when fitted.

A major point to consider is the choice of materials within the hull structure, particularly the wetted area. Especially if the boat is not a new one, check the materials personally or engage a reputable firm to examine the hull out of the water. It will in all probability be necessary to provide protection for the hull or underwater fittings, and this usually takes the form of sacrificial anodes. These can now be obtained with metering facilities which add considerably to the elegance of the system. Details of materials potentials and corrosion control are given at the end of this chapter.

Serious attention should be given to the establishment of a bonding system throughout the vessel to which all electrical equipment, skin fittings, rigging and machinery can be effectively earthed. In every boat there are a number of metallic parts in both the underwater area and the upper structure which should be electrically connected together. This is best done with PVC-insulated copper strip with dimensions of at least 0.05×0.5 in. The linking straps should be kept as short as possible between each connecting point, and where bonding an engine or other large stucture, the lead departing from the point of connection must be taken from the same point as the arriving lead, so that earth currents are not made to flow through machinery if it can be avoided. Do not, for example, link the fuel tanks to the gearbox and the fore side of the engine to the toilet skin fittings. A strap must be run, fixed to a suitable wiring batten, to connect each part of the installation at one point only.

Having created the bonding structure it is necessary to make sure the joints stay clean and tight. This can be helped by making the joints on stand-off insulators, which should be screwed up tight and painted with epoxy-based paint to keep out the salt atmosphere. Make sure to connect up everything metallic in the structure on the basis of 'if in doubt, bond it'.

The bonding system forms part of the interference reducing measures described in chapter 3 and the corrosion control arrangements described later in this chapter. RNLI practice is to connect the bonding system to the protection anodes via their internal connection stud, which is brought through the hull in an insulating bush. This effectively grounds the whole system and makes it anodic to any other metal parts under water.

Thought must be given to the siting and protection of equipment. Care at the time of installation will be repaid many times by providing years of trouble-free operation. Some equipments have been specially designed for exposed conditions; however, I feel that no matter how good any particular make or item of equipment is in this respect, it will not work any better for being subjected to the extremes of its design parameters. As the equipments suitable for exposed positions are the most expensive types, it is bad economy to avoid spending a few extra pounds on spray shields or stowing covers of suitable construction to protect them from the worst of the elements when in use or otherwise. Consider for a moment what happens to the rigging and deck gear in one season; this is specifically designed for exposed positions but it soon loses its appearance. However good equipment is, it still needs to be looked after; even if it never breaks down it will suffer from the effects of weather and quickly become tatty in appearance.

As soon as electronics are introduced we advance considerably the demands made on the electrical system, as we have seen from the RNLI's experience. For years you may have enjoyed satisfactory operation of a small boat electrical system which comprised little else but starter battery, switches and lights sustained by a small dynamo on the engine. Possibly the engine is an automobile engine conversion and often these conversions do not go as far as fully insulating the electrics. Most cars have one pole of the electrical system connected to the engine for economy reasons; however, the conditions on boats are such that it is highly undesirable to connect one pole of the supply to the engine as this will normally be connected via the propeller shaft and other skin fittings to the water. Thus any leakage from the insulated pole would cause the anodic end of the circuit so formed to corrode away in the water. Imagine how frustrating if this anodic end turned out to be the new propeller, as it not infrequently does (1.1). However, these effects go further than is imagined at first sight. The same small leakage currents, even if too small to cause serious corrosion, when acting on the stern gear can cause radio interference by the intermittent contact of the shaft with the stern tube, sometimes erroneously called 'water static'. If we now refer to diagram (1.2) detailing the electrical system of a typical lifeboat, it will be noted that no part of the battery system is grounded to the hull or bonding

1.1   Corrosion

circuit, unless via a DC-blocking capacitor and for a specific purpose.

The existence of an 'earth' can be detected by lamps connected via test switches in series across the supply with the centre point earthed. During pre-trip checks the test switch is made and if both lamps are of equal brightness, no serious earth leakage exists. If, however, one is brighter than the other a leakage exists on the side which indicates a minimum brightness. In the case of a short-circuit to earth, one lamp will come up to full brightness and on the faulty side the lamp will go out. For owners who have boats in which the existing system is grounded and also feel that it would be too much work to change it at this stage, I have made recommendations where relevant under each equipment heading. However, I believe some problems will emerge that may prove difficult to remedy if any amount of equipment is fitted.

Most reputable manufacturers can supply alternative generators and starters on a replacement basis, or conversion kits. If you find that your particular equipment cannot be exchanged for fully insulated types, an auto electrical specialist will usually carry out this work for a reasonable sum.

I suppose there is a tendency for most boats to grow a certain amount of strung-up wiring and fittings because as time goes on all temporary jobs become permanent. Perhaps the start of the season

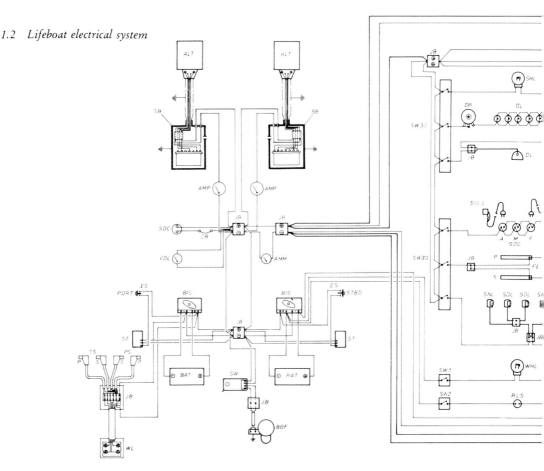

or the purchase of another instrument might provide the opportunity for some tidying up, and in these circumstances a study of the lifeboat circuit (1.2) will show how it should have been done.

Supply circuits

The addition of a separate battery to carry part of the load is by no means unusual where the installation is being extended. Very often in this situation the starter has its own battery which can be protected against accidental discharge although it is charged from the same generator as the general services battery. A very elegant method of achieving this without creating circulating currents can be devised to suit the individual installation by using blocking diodes to obviate mechanical switching. Several circuits are shown in chapter 2.

In the wiring diagram (1.2) the power is fed via a main isolator through switches and circuit breakers which correspond to the maximum rating of the outgoing circuits to lighting, heating, ventilating, radio, etc. It is very important that these switchboards and circuit breakers should be accessibly placed. They should preferably be of metallic construction; if wooden enclosures are used they should be lined with fireproof material. If you are planning a new installation or are making alterations in the distribution system, it will pay to include a few spare circuits for future expansion.

The dynamo or alternator, starter, ignition, batteries, etc. will all need regular servicing and must of course be reasonably accessible. Batteries always seem to suffer in this respect. There is very little pleasure in crawling round the engine to get to dry and corroded batteries. These heavy items should be stowed where they can be safely manhandled; a straight lift out at deck level is to be greatly preferred.

Wiring

Cables must be secured firmly at regular intervals and preferably given some mechanical protection. They may be fastened to a perforated carrier or tray, or placed in galvanised conduit where they are likely to sustain mechanical stress. An excellent scheme in my opinion is to fit PVC cable trunking

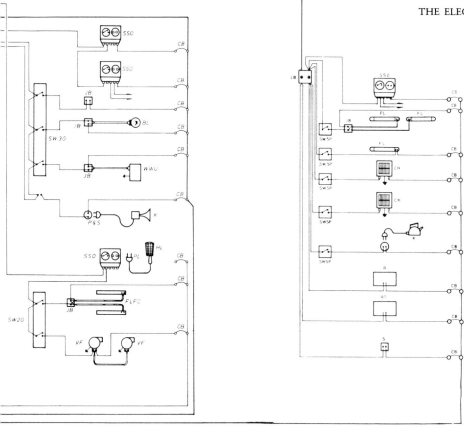

along the fore and aft line in some convenient location. If a piece of strong cord is left in the trunking new cables can be fed through easily without the usual pulling down of cabin linings. From the radio interference point of view, avoid making closed loops in the wiring, such as running leads down each side of the boat to feed equipment at one end. Keep all the wiring as short and direct as possible.

Bear in mind that even if a cable will safely carry a particular current, it may still be most unsuitable for the job. In small craft, in particular with 12 V systems, the cable size is chosen with regard to voltage drop, i.e. both the cross section of the conductor and the length of run must be taken into account. If a cable is run to some remote equipment, even though the capacity of the cable may be well in excess of the current requirements there will be some drop in voltage across the load due to the cable's resistance. If the load is intermittent, for example an autopilot motor, and a second load is connected in parallel at the end of the line remote from the batteries, it will be subject to a varying supply voltage due to the drop caused by the intermittent load. This can give rise to problems if the equipments are at all sensitive to

supply voltage variations. The following tables should be used for guidance with this problem; imperial, metric, and American sizes are given. For marine use butyl rubber compound covered cables, flame-proof braided, are to be greatly recommended. Where PVC insulation is employed attention should be given to the manufacturer's temperature limitations, and the type having flame-retardant polychloroprene (PCP) sheathing should be used.

Where cables are connected throughout the boat's system there is a regrettable tendency to strip back the insulation and twist the stranded conductor around the connecting stud, or if a strip connector is employed it is seldom mounted on an insulated plate, with the result that 'stray' conductors are spread around the connection and failure or leakage occurs. The remedy is to use crimp or soldered terminations; the former are to be preferred where the proper tool is available for compressing the cable grip. Where solder-on types are fitted it is very important to cover the solder with an anti-corrosive paint or to tightly tape over the soldered part of the lug. In a salt atmosphere without some protection there is a tendency for

29

soldered joints to corrode due to bimetallic effects. Termination fittings are available from many companies, such as Hellerman, Amp, Ripaults, Ross Courtney, etc. and may usually be purchased from automobile electrical suppliers.

Corrosion

I have often thought that the average boat owner is a person who is used to responsibility; because of the strain of not worrying at weekends, a boat is acquired so that a spare time worry is available.

Certainly most boats have problems of some sort, often of electrical origin, and particularly in spring when the boating adrenalin begins to swish about, I am asked to solve problems like 'this cooling water pipe corroded away twice during last season' or 'new bolts fitted last year have completely disintegrated', and 'the new propellor I fitted has become very badly pitted again, how can I stop it? I can't afford it'. (1.1).

In practice, the realisation of a good electrical system becomes involved with the compromise between all of the other considerations such as installation of machinery, weight, trim, speed,

British metric size conductors with nearest American equivalents

Flexible cord conductors

Nominal cross-sectional area	No. and diameter of wires	Nominal circ.	AWG	Nominal circ.
mm²	no./mm	cm		cm
0.5	16/0.20	0.987		
	28/0.15			
			20	1.020
0.75	24/0.20	1.480		
	42/0.15			
			18	1.620
1.0	32/0.20	1.975		
			16	2.580
1.5	30/0.25	2.960		
			14	4.110
2.5	50/0.25	4.935		
			12	6.530
4.0	56/0.30	7.900		

Fixed cable conductors

Nominal cross-sectional area	No. and diameter of wires	Nominal circ.	AWG or MCM size	Nominal circ.
mm²	no./mm	cm		cm
			18	1.620
1.0	1/1.13	1.975		
	7/0.40			
			16	2.580
1.5	1/1.38	2.960		
	7/0.50			
			14	4.110
2.5	1/1.78	4.935		
	7/0.67			
			12	6.530
4	1/2.25	7.900		
	7/0.85			
			10	10.380
6	1/2.76	11.850		
	7/1.04			
			8	16.510
10	1/3.57	19.740		
	7/1.35			
			6	26.240
16	1/4.50	31.580		
	7/1.70			
			4	.41.740
25	7/2.14	49.350		
	19/1.35			
			2	66.360
35	19/1.53	69.100		
			1	83.690

Comparison of metric and imperial copper conductor sizes for flexible cables and flexible cords
Flexible cord conductors

Metric			Imperial		
Nominal cross-sectional area	No. and nominal diameter of wires	Nominal diameter of conductor	Nominal cross-sectional area	No. and nominal diameter of wires	Nominal cross-sectional area
mm²	no./mm	mm	mm²	no./in.	in.²
			0.4	14/0.0076	0.0006
0.5	16/0.20	0.93			
0.5	28/0.15	0.93			
			0.65	23/0.0076	0.001
0.75	24/0.20	1.14			
0.75	42/0.15	1.14			
1.0	32/0.20	1.32			
			1.1	40/0.0076	0.0017
1.5	30/0.25	1.60			
			2.0	70/0.0076	0.003
2.5	50/0.25	2.00			
			3.0	110/0.0076	0.0048
4.0	56/0.30	2.60			
			4.5	162/0.0076	0.007

Comparison of metric and imperial copper conductor sizes for fixed cables—circular
Fixed cable conductors (circular)

Metric			Imperial		
Nominal cross-sectional area	No. and nominal diameter of wires	Nominal diameter of conductor	Nominal cross-sectional area	No. and nominal diameter of wires	Nominal cross-sectional area
mm²	no./mm	mm	mm²	no./in	in.²
1.0	1/1.13	1.13	1.0	1/0.044	0.0015
1.0	7/0.40	1.20			
			1.25	3/0.029	0.002
1.5	1/1.38	1.38			
1.5	7/0.50	1.50			
			2.0	3/0.036	0.003
2.5	1/1.78	1.78			
2.5	7/0.67	2.01			
			3.0	7/0.029	0.0045
4	7/0.85	2.55			
			4.5	7/0.036	0.007
6	7/1.04	3.12			
			6.75	7/0.044	0.01
			9.5	7/0.052	0.0145
10	7/1.35	4.05			
			15	7/0.064	0.0225

16	7/1.70	5.10			
			20	19/0.044	0.03
25	7/2.14	6.42			
25	19/1.35	6.75	25	19/0.052	0.04
35	19/1.53	7.65			
			40	19/0.064	0.06

Current rating and voltage drop for flexible cords

Conductor		Current rating	Volt drop per amp per metre	
Nominal cross-sectional area	No. and diameter of wires	DC or single-phase AC, or 3-phase AC	DC or single-phase AC	3-phase AC
mm²	no./mm	A	mV	mV
0.5	16/0.20	3	83	72
0.75	24/0.20	6	56	48
1.0	32/0.20	10	43	37
1.5	30/0.25	15	31	26
2.5	50/0.25	20	18	16
4	56/0.30	25	11	9.6

Current rating and voltage drop for PVC non-armoured single-core cables (1.0–35 mm²)

Conductor		Bunched and enclosed in conduit or trunking			
		2 cables, single-phase AC, or DC		3 or 4 cables, 3-phase AC	
Nominal cross-sectional area	No. and diameter of wires	Current rating	Voltage drop per amp per metre	Current rating	Voltage drop per amp per metre
mm²	mm	A	mV	A	mV
1.0	1/1.13	11	40	9	35
1.5	1/1.38	13	27	11	23
2.5	1/1.78	18	16	16	14
4	7/0.85	24	10	22	8.8
6	7/1.04	31	6.8	28	5.9
10	7/1.35	42	4.0	39	3.5
16	7/1.70	56	2.6	50	2.2
25	7/2.14	73	1.6	66	1.4
35	19/1.53	90	1.2	80	1.0

Ambient temperature °C

	25	35	40	45	50	55
Rating factor for cables having coarse excess-current protection	1.02	0.97	0.94	0.91	0.88	0.77

endurance etc, and is thus a long story. There can be no doubt that the right conditions are more easily created during construction than as an afterthought, so the story starts in the design office before construction of the hull begins.

Galvanic Action

In the course of construction, the first parts of the electrical system that become evident are fastenings, rudder, shaft, screw etc, all these things that seem to have nothing to do with electricity, BUT ... (1.7). If you have doubts about this, take one brass and one steel screw, and immerse them in a jar of seawater while connected to a microammeter. The galvanic current will show quite clearly, underlining the definite existence of the series of galvanic cells that will be present when the boat is complete. If nothing is done to protect the structure in the course of the vessel's life, the current flow will cause the less noble of the metals to dissolve (the anodic metal); also certain salts will be produced by chemical action around each element of the organic couple.

The electrolyte need not be a simple solution, for example any timbers within the construction of the beat will carry enough moisture to become an effective electrolyte. In this case it is also necessary to consider the effect on the timber of the salts generated around the metal parts.

Electro-chemical Decay

The effect of current flowing in saturated timbers can stimulate decay of the grain, in the area affected by the salts produced by metal fittings. These salts may be alkali or acid depending on the type of metal and wood. Alkali is more dangerous to the wood causing the grain to degenerate locally and, in the case of hull fastenings, seepage around the metal begins. When this point is reached, the process is accelerated by the natural movement of the hull, and the fastenings become slack.

The first signs of this sort of decay are the destruction of paint and stopping materials around fastenings, and discolouration where oil or paint exists. Slight longitudinal cracks on the surface of the wood are also a clue. It is important to remember that the chemical attack on timber can still take place within wooden members of a GRP hull, also that the action may be initiated by galvanic currents or by currents impressed artificially on the timber by leakage from the electrical system.

One of the problems with this sort of decay is that it is quite different from the various types of wood rot, many of which are characterised by their fungicidal origin. The development of the decay may be very slow and may have been active for some years before it is discovered. This is easily understood as very few wooden vessels are burnt off every year, and it is only on such an occasion when very close inspection is possible.

Electro-chemical and Galvanic Action in GRP Hulls

Although GRP is now widely used, and is claimed by many to have considerable advantages for small boats, as with all materials used in a marine environment there are points that need watching. For example, few realise that a GRP hull absorbs water during immersion, and that water absorbtion and structural loading are known causes of degradation. It follows that the absorbed water component of a GRP hull is just as good at conducting electricity as water anywhere else. The electro-chemical effects mentioned earlier in this chapter must therefore be in attendance. A typical water absorbtion figure is 1% in weight after three months immersion. This figure includes any that may be taken up by capillary action along fibres and through crazing.

Because of the salts produced where metal fittings penetrate the hull, it is important to apply the same care with installations in GRP construction and with any other material to avoid degradation of the hull or any particular fitting.

Steel Hulls

A better understood situation exists with small steel boats, as a considerable amount of experience exists with larger structures. The steel plating is under attack from itself electrolytically, and must be protected by anodes suitably placed. The hull plating is used as a conductor for the protecting currents, rather than the bonding system in this case. It is still necessary to provide additional protection for dissimilar metal fittings, particularly those operating at elevated temperatures such as exhaust fittings.

I should stress that the hull is only used as a conductor of galvanic currents and that it is important to isolate the battery system completely, so that the hull or fittings cannot become damaged by leakage currents from the boat's electrical system.

Reduction of Electro-chemical Decay in Wooden Hulls

In order to reduce currents flowing within the boat's timbers, the various metal fittings on the hull are connected together with PVC covered copper strip (see also comments under cathodic protection, ch 1 page 36). This process is called bonding; its purpose is to provide a low resistance connection between points that may develop a relative potential. Thus, current that would otherwise flow through the hull material, preferentially flows in the low resistance strip. This is carried to each fitting in turn by a small wiring batten, with joints and junctions made on small insulated stand-off terminals. These may be miniature ceramic types specially made for such applications, or more simply a 5 mm screw with locknuts and washers mounted in a piece of Tufnol or similar material. When jointing is complete, the whole terminal should be painted with an epoxy sealer. It is important to remember that although we may use the bonding system for 'earthing' various things at a later stage, its primary function is practically to eliminate spurious hull currents. It must also not be forgotten that it will affect the activity of materials likely to corrode. This is because the galvanic currents that we have successfully stopped from flowing in the hull by introducing the bonding system, can now flow much more easily without the resistance offered by the hull. As a result the rate at which the anodic end of the galvanic couple will dissolve will increase. It is therefore essential to fit sacrificial anodes and connect them to the bonding system, so that the underwater fittings and the hull are protected as a whole.

When tracing hull potentials with a test meter, it is sometimes difficult to decide whether you are reading a galvanically generated voltage or a battery leakage. The clue is in the magnitude of the reading; refering to the galvanic table in this chapter you will see that all the voltages are of a low order. At the extreme ends of the table, differences are only about 2 volts, and at that level only between the rare simultaneous occurrence of

magnesium and platinum. Readings of up to 1.5 volts should be closely examined with a material difference in mind; when you find indications above the 2 to 3 volt level, there is no doubt that the supply is leaking somewhere. A combination of effects will often be encountered, for example I have recently seen a new vessel with a yellow metal stern tube screwed into a steel hull fitting. The propeller shaft was stainless steel, and water lubricated bearings were fitted at both ends of the tube. The lubricating water used was piped from the engine cooling water outflow with obvious initial economy. Within one working season the yellow metal stern tube caused severe corrosion of the hull at the point of penetration. The cooling water pipe connected the stern gear electrically to the engine, which was in turn connected to one side of the electrical system. As the water injected into the stern tube had been heated by the engine, corrosion of the stainless steel shaft was severely accelerated; by this I mean 7 mm ($\frac{1}{4}$") deep pit holes in a 50 mm (2 in) shaft. The cost of putting all this right is staggering. The latest equipment from corrosion specialists allows constant monitoring of the hull potential and the protective current, and this in my view is to be greatly recommended. Although there is nothing very new about cathodic protection, this new system of control, which makes use of a special reference electrode, does much to eliminate 'black magic' from the fitting of protection electrodes.

The first principles of cathodic hull protection were outlined by Sir Humphrey Davy in about 1824 and the subsequent developments in sacrificial anode systems have become widely accepted by the marine fraternity. Basically the cathodic protection process may consist of either sacrificial anodes which by reaction with the protected material produce their own current, or inert anodes with an impressed current.

In order for corrosion to occur it is necessary to have a metal or metals with a more negative potential in electrical contact with metals of a more positive potential. Both metals must be immersed in an electrolyte if current is to flow from one to the other and corrosion damage occur. Seawater is the most familiar of electrolytes and also one of the more aggressive. It contains a relatively high concentration of salt and covers more than two-thirds of the earth's surface. With a suitable

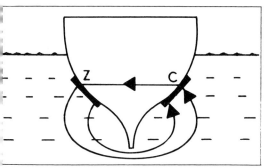

1.3   *Corrosion of dissimilar metals*

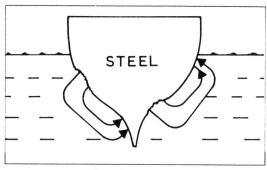

1.4   *Corrosion of similar metals*

electrolyte having anodic and cathodic areas in electrical contact, current will flow from the anode to the cathode. This occurs in two ways: where there are two dissimilar metals in direct contact (1.3) where there are differing potentials on the surface of similar metals (1.4).

Where this situation exists corrosion can occur even with metals of the same type, due to any or all of the following reasons:

Difference in surface: variable paint coating or the adherance of mill scale in varying degree.
Difference in aeration caused by projections and irregularities in the hull.
Electrochemically dissimilar metals: rivets and plating, or weld metal and plating.
Difference in stress: points liable to excessive stress are apt to be anodic.

A series of galvanic cells is created, and since the external circuits are completed through the hull, current flows.

Metal passes into solution at the anodes, but cathodic areas remain unattacked. If very small anodic and cathodic areas are closely grouped, corrosion will be uniform, but if there are small anodic areas surrounded by relatively large cathodic areas more serious pitting will result.

It will be seen that protective current (1.5) from the sacrifical anode ensures that the steel hull is rendered cathodic and therefore is not subject to corrosion damage or metal loss. The anode, which is relatively cheap and easily replaced, can be manufacturer from different metal alloys, namely zinc, magnesium and aluminium, each of which have different characteristics under normal operating conditions.

This simple explanation of cathodic protection does not attempt to describe the great variety of applications in the marine field, neither does it demonstrate the need for careful and well designed cathodic protection schemes if the full benefits of the process are to be realised. For instance, vessels are often slipped and a few anodes arranged around the stern gear. This haphazard use of anodes will obviously have some beneficial effect in the stern area, but may well be either above or below the amount of anode material necessary to provide complete protection. The same is often true of anodes arranged around the hull of a vessel, and it is always essential to ensure that only the requisite amount of anode material is used. The principle which must underlie all cathodic protection schemes for marine craft is that sufficient anode material must be provided to ensure that the hull or area to be protected is rendered cathodic throughout the designed life of the system.

It is obviously important to minimise the corrosion effects caused by the use of dissimilar metals in boat construction and the table given at the end of this chapter gives data obtained under actual service conditions. Once the use of different metals, especially those which are wide apart on the potential scale, has been avoided as far as possible, the corrosion damage which can still occur is that illustrated in (1.4) and which occurs on the surface of similar metals. Steel plates used in hull construction can be very prone to corrosion because of this type of interaction and it will be seen that if the whole underwater area of a steel hull can be rendered cathodic, then corrosion cannot occur.

Cathodic protection

External corrosion damage to the unprotected hulls of all small and intermediate size craft falls, in the main, into two separate categories. Firstly the wastage and pitting of shell plating, weld seams and rivet points which is a common and international problem and can on occasions be most severe, and usually calls for extensive repair work. Secondly a large number of vessels, regardless of size, suffer severe wastage of both cast iron and bronze propellers. Once again, this is a serious problem and renewals or making good the damage can involve considerable expenditure.

It must be remembered also that reduced performance and increased fuel consumption due to a decrease in propeller efficiency or hull roughness regularly occur and that these can be largely avoided if correct use is made of cathodic protection. For instance, a 40% drop in propeller efficiency has been assessed experimentally due to roughness occurring on propeller blades, and it has also been found that 11% more power is required to develop the same thrust from a rough propeller than from a smooth one. These findings refer to only a 'slight roughness' of propeller blades. During these experiments it was also concluded that the roughening was basically of electrolytic origin and electrolytic measures for its suppression might be beneficial. Subsequently this has been proved by cathodic protection experience. On a new steel vessel corrosion-roughening alone could demand some 14% excess of power from the machinery after only two years' service. There would seem to be little doubt that the suppression of hull roughening is as important as suppression of propeller roughening.

Complete control of the corrosion of hulls in seawater can at present only be practically achieved in one way—by suppressing the activity of the galvanic couples which cause corrosion. All underwater corrosion that matters to the boatowner is of electrochemical origin and is caused by the flow of current through sea-water between parts of the structure which are at differing electrical potentials. Causes of potential difference are many—dissimilar metals, differential stresses arising from working, differences in molecular structure, variable surface conditions of the metal, and differences of environment such as those caused by variations in water speed, local turbulence and aeration.

Electrochemical action can be stopped by reversing the flow of current at the anodic areas. Practically this is achieved by making the whole of the underwater part of the vessel's hull into one large cathode by introducing an anode external to the structure and of lower potential than the original complex. The anode is in electrical contact with the hull and current flows through the water from anode to hull, and returns thence to the anode via the metallic path of the hull.

The amount of current and the potential change required about at the cathode to achieve the desired effect will vary in different circumstances. The protected cathode may be the whole underwater structure or some localised part thereof; the required electrical energy may be produced by galvanic means, or it may be taken from the boat's battery or generators and passed through chemically inert anodes: but the underlying principle of corrosion control is the swamping of local galvanic activity by super-imposing a more powerful system, which turns the whole into a non-corroding cathode.

It is essential to ensure that the correct quantity of anode material is used at all times and that the original design data takes into account the vessel's operating conditions, basic hull design kand existing paint coating. Assuming that the cathode protection engineer has been able to give particular attention to these points, there is no reason why the damage to shell plating, weld seams, etc., and the roughening of propeller blades referred to earlier, cannot be avoided.

It is interesting to consider some of the factors involved in the design of such systems. As mentioned above, there are two basic types of cathode protection systems—impressed current and galvanic. Impressed current makes use of flush-fitting electro chemically inert anodes from the boat's electrical system (1.6).

With wooden or fibreglass hulls great care is necessary when fixing the protection anodes. As already stated, wet wood or fibreglass will conduct electricity, and it is possible to find that this has stimulated corrosion of the anode fixing bolts. I recently encountered this in a fibreglass vessel and, in a period of about 6 months, two 10 mm steel bolts were completely cut through within the thickness of the hull. This resulted in the anode

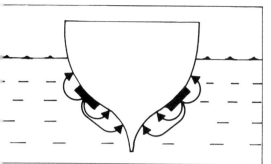

1.5   Sacrificial anode function

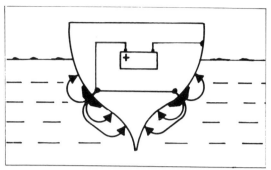

1.6   Impressed current cathodic protection

dropping off and the vessel rapidly filling via the holes in the bottom. The way round this problem is to fix the anodes to the component to be protected, using screws of the same material as the protected component. If a fault then produces a problem, at least it does not leave a hole in the bottom. In my own boat everything including the bolts were cast in the same metal (bronze) at the same foundry as shown in (1.7), this obviates dissimilar metals underwater and goes a long way to reduce future problems.

The rudder stock and gland should be connected together with a short flexible strap as shown; all the metal parts then become part of the protected circuit and radio crackles due to intermittent contact of the two parts are reduced.

1.7   Bronze underwater fittings

Galvanic anode design
During the last twenty years there have been enormous improvement in the basic design of anodes and the careful control and analysis of the alloy itself. This ensures that anode outputs can be

accurately assessed and that the maximum consumption of the anode material is possible. Prior to this time, and even occasionally today, ordinary commercial zinc plate was cut, drilled and bolted to a vessel's hull, mainly in the stern area, with little or no effect. This was often a costly operation in terms of time spent in cutting and machining, but the results could not be worthwhile as simple basic facts concerning galvanic action had been overlooked.

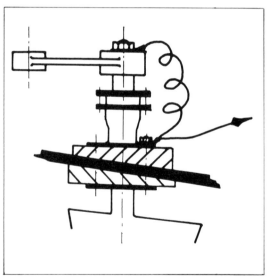

1.8   Bonding rudder stock and gland

It is essential that the anode metal is cast around a non-reactive insert through which electrical contact is made. This can either be achieved by using projecting lugs from the anode insert itself, or by stud-fixing the anode to the vessel's hull by bolting direct to the insert. The photograph (1.9) shows a typical new anode and also a spent one in which the insert can be clearly seen. Both methods

1.9   Zinc alloy sacrificial anodes

are equally satisfactory and ensure the maximum electrical continuity between anode and hull, with the advantage of permitting easy anode replacement without welding.

Galvanic anode materials

In practice it has been found that low-potential zinc anodes, manufactured from the correct alloy, provide the ideal anode material for general use as they give the cathodic protection engineer considerable flexibility in scheme design and the vessel owner the most satisfactory level of protection.

Magnesium alloy anodes, which are manufactured form a high-potential anode material, also have their place in providing protection for certain craft. They are of particular interest where cast iron propellers are being considered.

The use of aluminium anodes can also be considered under special circumstances, but certain shortcomings in some of the various makes available must be satisfactorily resolved before aluminium anodes are considered for general use in seawater conditions. Galvalum aluminium anodes, developed by the Dow Corporation in the US, have been proved under normal working conditions and are the most reliable aluminium anodes at present available.

Propeller and stern gear protection

A well designed cathodic protection system allows for the extra demand placed on it in the stern area of a vessel. The propeller and shaft are of particular importance, although it is true that in some cases, especially when under way, the resistance between the shaft/propeller and the hull is too high to permit effective distribution to this area by the low-potential anodes. This is particularly true of high speed craft, where shaft

slip-ring assemblies can be considered, but for the more ordinary class of vessel a carefully designed cathodic protection system will have immediate benefits in helping to prevent the initial surface roughening of the propeller from which erosion is liable to develop.

In this particular region the use of magnesium anodes is of immense importance, and especially where cast iron propellers are in use. The magnesium alloy propeller boss anode is fitted behind the propeller in direct electrical contact, and is able to provide sufficient current to ensure a high level of protection. Zinc alloy anodes are used with considerable effect in the stern area of vessels, although it is essential that the correct quantity of anode material is employed if the most economic use of these anodes is to be realised. The M G Duff types G-748 (small craft), G-801 and G-802 anodes are particularly suitable for this work: (1.9) shows a typical before and after situation with one of these anodes.

Materials

In the course of fitting or repairing various equipments great care must be taken to select materials that are suitable for use in a marine environment. Much of the following data is used by the RNLI and will help owners to select materials cautiously.

Do

Check the specifications of all materials used. Ensure that correct protection, physical and chemical, is called for and used.

Lubricate all threads, spigots, etc. with the correct lubricants before assembly.

Remember that zinc and cadmium act sacrificially, while they last, and in exposed conditions can soon lose their protective qualities, particularly if scratched.

Remember cadmium's main use in exposed positions is as a lubricant. The cadmium plating of a stainless steel nut will prevent it jamming on a stainless steel bolt or stud. Remember that wood, graphite, asbestos, poor quality chromium plating, bakelite gaskets, scratches and crevices can cause corrosion. Treat crevice attack as a real hazard.

Use glass-filled Macrolon where structural plastic is required and will be subject to moisture or immersion.

Do not

Use materials without checking their potential difference with reference to neighbouring components.

Use asbestos or graphited joints in exposed positions on aluminium assemblies.

Replace stainless steel screws by plated screws on aluminium assemblies.

Leave crevices. All parts should be bedded down using the correct compound, to exclude oxygen and moisture.

Assemble units which are primarily of light alloys or dissimilar metals without correct lubrication.

Use graphited lubricants on or near light alloy components or assemblies.

Chip or scratch any surface whether protected or not. It can cause corrosion of a single metal.

Alter material specifications without justification and checking the physical and electrolytic effects.

Use any screw, nut or component unless it is of the correct material.

Forget that a 'seawater resisting' alloy is only highly resistant to corrosion until subject to normal bimetallic corrosion conditions and moisture.

Use insulating washers and sleeves. Use the correct materials, with compound to prevent the forming of moisture traps.

Use chromium or nickel plated screws unless plating is to BS 1224:1953.

Use cadmium plating (except as a lubricant).

Use nylon in a marine environment if it can be avoided as it is highly hygroscopic and will swell considerably in the course of a few weeks' exposure. Tufnol behaves similarly.

Potentials of various materials in seawater at given temperatures against a calomel electrode

The potential P is negative except where stated, between a calomel electrode and various materials when immersed in seawater at a temperature of T. Data is derived from more than one source. In most cases figures are considered to give only average values. P = volts, T = °C

Material		T (°C)	P(V)
Magnesium (Mg)		25	1.73
Magnesium—2% Manganese (Mn)	(DTD118)	25	1.67
Magnesium—9% Aluminium (Al), 1% Mn, 1.5% Zinc (Zn)	(DTD120)	25	1.58
Galvanised iron (hot dipped)		25	1.14
Zinc plating (electro)	(Plating to BS 1706:1960)	25	1.13
Cadmium (Cd) Zinc solder (71/29)	(DTD221)	25	1.12
Zinc based alloy		25	1.09
Zinc (Zn)		25	1.05
Zinc		26	1.03
Aluminium—4% Zn		25	1.02
Aluminium—1% Zn		25	0.96
Aluminium—12.5-14.5% Zn, 2.5-3.0% Copper (Cu), 0.8% Fe, 0.7% Silicon (Si) (3L5)		25	0.91
Aluminium—4% Mg (solid solution, commercial qualities vary slightly)		25	0.87
Cadmium plated steel (Cd 0.001 in.)		25	0.86
Aluminium—2.25% Mg	(N4)	25	0.85
Aluminium—99.99% min. purity—100%		25	0.85
Aluminium—7% Zn, 2% Mg, 1.75% Cu	(DTD363)	25	0.84
Aluminium—99% min. purity		25	0.83
Aluminium—12% Silicon (Si)	(LM6)	25	0.83
Aluminium—1.25% Mg	(N3)	25	0.83
Aluminium— 4.5-5.5% Mg	(NS6, NE6 or NT6)	25	0.82
Aluminium— 6.5-7.5% Mg	(NS7, NE7 or NF7, also DTD182B)	25	0.81
Aluminium— 10-13% Si	(3L33)	25	0.81

Material		$T(°C)$	$P(V)$
Aluminium—2.5% Si, 1.0% Cu, 0.3–1.4% Fe	(LM7)	25	0.81
Steel, non-stainless—0.5% Mn, 0.20% Si, 0.12% C	(BS 511. 18/26t)	25	0.79
Grey cast iron		25	0.78
Aluminium—2% Cu, 1% Ni, 0.9% Mg, 0.9% Fe, 0.8% Si	(H12.BS1470:1479)	25	0.78
Steel, non-stainless—0.65% Mn, 0.22% Si, 0.20% G (BS.S510) 28t		25	0.78
Steel, non-stainless—0.80% Mn 0.40% C, 0.20% Si (En8) '40' carbon steel		25	0.76
Steel, non-stainless—0.60% Mn, 0.30% Si, 0.22% C sheet strip		25	0.76
Steel, non-stainless—1.0% Mn, 0.40% Ni, 0.25% C (En3) '20' carbon steel		25	0.76
Hot dipped tinned steel		25	0.74
Forged aluminium alloys		25	0.73
Steel, non-stainless—3.5% Ni, 0.80% Cu, 0.70% Mn, 0.45% Mo, 0.30% C, 0.25% Si	(En 27)	25	0.71
Aluminium—4% Cu	(LM 11)	25	0.69
Al/Cu/Mg/Mn alloy	(H 14)	25	0.68
Dural, heat treated and aged		25	0.65
Mild steel		24	0.61
Chromium plate on nickel on steel (Ni 0.0005 in.)		25	0.61
Tinmans solder (A & B)		25	0.56
Tin, electroplated on steel (Sn 0.0005 in.)		25	0.55
Lead (Pb)		25	0.55
Chromium plate on nickel on steel (Cr 0.005 in.)		25	0.53
Silver lead solder		25	0.50
Tin (Sn)		25	0.50
SG cast iron—18–22% Ni, 3% C, 1.5–3% Si, 1.75–2.75% Cr, 0.7–1.25% Mn (type D2)		14	0.47
Steel, stainless, 12% chromium (En56, En56A, En56B)		25	0.45
Chromium plate on nickel on steel (Cr. 000035)		25	0.42
Admiralty brass		25	0.36
Steel, stainless, high chrome (En57)		25	0.35
Brass (60/40)		25	0.33
Gunmetal		24	0.31
Admiralty brass		11.9	0.30
Aluminium brass—76% Cu, 22% Zn, 2% A1		25	0.29
Copper/Nickel/iron—90/10 Cu/Ni, 1.4%		17	0.29
Lead/tin solder (50/50)		17	0.28
Silicon (Si)		25	0.26
Cupro-Nickel (70/30)		25	0.26
Brass (70/30)		25	0.25
Copper/nickel/iron—70/30 Cu/Ni, 0.51% Fe		17	0.24
Nickel alloy, 45%		25	0.23
Copper (Cu)		25	0.22
Copper/nickel/iron—90/10 Cu/Ni, 1.5% Fe		24	0.22
Copper/nickel/iron—70/30 Cn/Ni, 0.51% Fe		6	0.22
Gunmetal tungum		25	0.21
Copper/nickel/iron—70/30 Cu/Ni, 0.51% Fe		26.7	0.20
Steel, stainless, austenitic (En58, En58B, En58C, En58F, En58G)		25	0.20
German silver		25	0.19
Aluminium bronze, Al 10%		25	0.15
Nickel (Ni)		25	0.14

Monel alloy '400'	22	0.11
Nickel '200'	25	0.10
Titanium	27	0.10
Tin bronze, Sn 5%	25	0.08
Silver	25	0.08
Silver plating	25	+0.01
Graphite	24	+0.25
Platinum	18	+0.26

Recommended maximum allowable potential differences: exposed position 0.2 V; interior use 0.25 V

Seawater corrosion resistant light alloys

Alloy	BS spec.	Application
NE5		Light allkoy section for structural members
NE6	BS 1476	
HE30		
LM5		Casting alloy for cast components, etc.
LM6	BS 1490	
LM10		
NS4	BS 1470	Sheet and plating
NS5		
NR5	BS 1473	Rivets

*An approximate guide to bimetallic effects at junctions involving aluminium

Metals coupled with Al or Al alloys	Bimetallic effect
Gold, platinum, rhodium, silver	Attack accelerated in most environments
Copper, copper alloys, silver solder	Attack accelerated in most atmospheres and conditions of total immersion
Solder coatings of steel or copper	Attack accelerated at the interface in severe or moderate atmosphere and under conditions of total immersion
Nickel, nickel alloys	Attack accelerated in marine and industrial atmospheres and conditions of total immersion but not in mild environments
Steel, cast iron	Attack accelerated in marine and industrial atmospheres and conditions of total immersion but not in mild environments
Lead, tin	Attack accelerated only in severe environments, such as marine and some industrial
Tin/zinc plating (80/20) on steel	Attack accelerated only in severe atmospheres and conditions of total immersion

The above metals, especially those at the top of the list, which are generally cathodic to aluminium and its alloys, will cause preferential attack when corrosion occurs.

Pure aluminium and alloys not containing	When aluminium is alloyed with appreciable amounts of copper, it becomes more noble, and when alloyed with appreciable amounts of zinc it becomes

substantial additions of copper or zinc	less noble. In marine or industrial atmospheres or when totally immersed, aluminium alloy suffers accelerated attack when in good electrical contact with another aluminium alloy that contains substantial copper, such as wrought alloys H14 and H15 and cast alloys LM4-M and LM11-WP. The aluminium/zinc alloys being less noble are used as cladding for the protection of the stronger aluminium alloys
*Cadmium	No acceleration of attack on cadmium except in fairly severe atmospheres in contact with aluminium alloy containing copper, and under conditions of total immersion
*Zinc and zinc alloys	Attack on zinc accelerated in severe environments such as marine and industrial, and under conditions of total immersion

*These metals, and especially those at the bottom of this list, are generally anodic to aluminium and suffer attack when corrosion occurs, thereby protecting the aluminium.

Magnesium and magnesium base alloys	Attack on magnesium accelerated in severe environments such as marine and industrial, and under condition of total immersion. Attack on aluminium may also be accelerated
**Titanium	Little data available but attack on aluminium is known to be accelerated in severe marine and industrial conditions and when immersed in seawater
**Stainless steel (18/8, 18/2 and 13% Cr)	No acceleration of attack on aluminium in moderate atmospheres, but attack may be accelerated in severe marine and industrial atmospheres and under conditions of total immersion
**Chromium plate	No acceleration of attack on aluminium when plating is not less than 0.0001 in. thick, except in severe atmospheres, also provided the preliminary nickel coating is in accordance with BS 1224:1953

**These metals form protective films that tend to reduce bimetallic effects. Where attack occurs, the aluminium base material suffers.

The above notes indicate roughly the extent to which bimetallic effects may accelerate corrosive attack when the conditions of exposure favour its occurrence. With the exception of the metals at the end, which form protective films, the list is one of approximately descending order of galvanic effect, the more noble being at the top of the list. The table should be applied only in conjunction with the relevant information given in the table of potentials of various materials.

Wrought and cast materials to be welded together should be of similar composition or of the same types of alloys; castings of high silicon content (e.g. LM6) should not be welded to sheets of high magnesium content (e.g. N5, N6).

Erosion-corrosion of corrosion resistant materials

Most corrosion resistant metals receive protection from the formation of a 'passive' surface coating of an initial corrosion product; e.g. aluminium and stainless steel form extremely thin oxide films at high water velocities, particularly when air is trapped in the water. If this coating is disrupted electrochemical action known as erosion-corrosion is initiated. Under such conditions marked corrosive attack can occur, e.g. on copper inlet pipes where water velocity exceeds 3 ft/sec. (2⅓ m.p.h.).

The protective coating of materials in contact with light alloys

Steel and cuprous components can be coated, steel by hot-dipping or sheradising zinc coating processes; most materials by spraying with aluminium, aluminium/zinc or zinc coatings by the Schori process, or by electrodeposited coatings of zinc, cadmium or tin/zinc (80/20) to BS 1706: 1951. It should be noted that the zinc and cadmium coatings can act sacrifically, only preserving as long as the protective coating remains intact. When the coatings can act sacrifically, only preserving as long metal, electrolytic attack will commence. For exposed components, a sprayed metal coating gives better adhesion for protective paints than hot-dipped or electro-deposited coatings.

Corrosion of a single metal

Electrochemical action can be responsible for the corrosion of a single metal. Scratches and crevices due to badly bedded joints forming pockets where salt water can lie are liable to suffer this form of corrosion. *All* metals and alloys, including stainless steels, can be attacked given suitable conditions.

Corrosion of light alloys in contact with nonmetallic materials

The majority of timbers have a very slightly acid reaction and are harmless when dry, but may cause significant corrosion when wet and in prolonged contact with aluminium. All timber in contact with aluminium should be painted with zinc chromate primers, aluminium paint or a good quality bitumen paint before assembly with the aluminium component imperfectly seasoned timbers in particular need painting to prevent the effect of acid wood saps and resin at the content surface. Impregnated wood should be painted, as the nature of the impregnating medium (often copper based) is not always known. 'Z' or tin/zinc-coated steel, or preferably a correct grade of stainless steel, should be used for fastenings.

Gaskets and jointing for aluminium assemblies

Many commercial gaskets and jointing sheets contain graphite, asbestos or a mixture of both. Examples of graphite impregnated seals are Walkerite, Lion and Hallite, asbestos forming a basic ingredient of these and also of Klingerite and Mastite jointings. The above will attack aluminium alloys due to the high negative potential between carbon(graphite) and aluminium and alkali attack from asbestos, due to damaged or damp gaskets. For high temperature seals in aluminium assemblies sheet aluminium or aluminium laminate, e.g. Plexeal, should be used. Sheet jointings such as

Walkerite can be replaced either by Golden Walkerite which is a non-graphite base, or Walkerite which has been specially ordered from the manufacturers with a non-graphite finish. It should be remembered that these modified Walker gaskets contain a high proportion of asbestos. Kautex are synthetic or natural rubber and cork compounds and are satisfactory for use with aluminium. Aluminium is unaffected by plastics unless they have deteriorated or become spongy and hold water.

Surface preparation prior to painting aluminium

An anodised surface is satisfactory as a painting key, although rather costly for such a purpose. Less costly treatments developed specially as pre-treatments for painting, such as Alocrom, are usually simple chemical dips followed by rinsing in water and drying, Suitable anodising specifications are:

BS 1615:1958
DTD 910   Full marine treatment to be specified
DTD 915A

It should be noted that the coating thickness of normal anodising in between 0.00685 and 0.013 mm (0.00027 and 0.00055 in.).

Tracing Electrical Faults

As it is not possible to do electrical work without access to the insides of various types of equipment, I stress that high voltages are very often present during operation. In transistor equipment these voltages are generally of a lower order; however, if you are doubtful about your knowledge in this respect, it is better to call in an engineer than to run the risk of shock.

Once you have decided to get involved with electrical or electronic equipment, work will become much easier if you master the technique of measuring simple electrical quantities. I would suggest you obtain a small multirange testmeter and, with its basic instructions, apply it to your problem largely by following the pictures in this chapter. Apart from those who like looking after everything on their boat, the cruising yachtsman often finds himself doing the job, as the local electrical witch-doctor either does not have a suitable bone for the job in hand or is away visiting his mother-in-law.

I would not want to convey the idea that a faulty piece of equipment should immediately be taken to pieces. Indeed, there are few worse places to service electronic gear than on a small boat. However, much will be saved if you can establish for yourself that the supply is electrically sound where it enters the equipment, and that simply by connecting the supply you will not cause damage by reverse polarity, fire, electrolysis, and so on. If you reach this standard, you are in a position to land any piece of faulty equipment for return to the manufacturer, where it can be serviced under the best conditions at a minimum of cost to yourself.

Selecting a Testmeter

There are many small multirange testmeters on the market in most countries, many of which originate in Japan. Because it is not likely to be used very often, probably not more than 4 or 5 times every season, there is no justification for spending very much, but it should provide at least the ranges of measurement detailed here.

AC volts	DC volts	DC current	Ohms
5	0.5	10 u/A	0–10k × 1
10	5	2.5 mA	0–10k × 100
50	25	25 mA	0–10k × 1000
100	50	500 mA	0–10k × 10,000
500	250		
	500		
	1000		

If you do buy a more expensive type, you would expect it to have higher DC current ranges of say up to 10 amps, and some provision to measure AC current. In general, higher voltage ranges for both AC and DC will also be provided. If you keep a meter on the boat, seal it with a dessicant in an airtight polythene bag.

The Units Measured

The electrical units that can be measured directly with the simple meter shown are

1. Volts (V) = electrical 'pressure'
2. Amps (A) = electrical 'amount': volume or quantity: current
3. Ohms (Ω) = resistance, or degeneration of flow
4. Watts (W) = volts × amps: power consumption

Only the first three are measured directly with the test meter; the fourth may be derived when needed from separate measurements of voltage and current. The quantities all interrelate in Ohms' law as: resistance (ohms) = volts ÷ amps or in real figures as an aide-memoire, 1 = 1/1 or 8 = 32/4. Knowing any two of the three quantities, the other can be worked out if required. This is equally true of the formula: watts = volts × amps.

Familiarization with the Test Meter

If test meters are new to you, try the following exercise, not forgetting to read the instructions for your particular meter. I have assumed a 12 V system for the sake of clarity, but the methods hold good for any value of supply voltage.

Measurement of Voltage
Set the meter to the 0–25 V range. Measure the voltage at the boat's battery terminals: connect the negative lead to the negative (—) battery terminal and the positive lead to the positive (+) terminal. The meter will now show the battery voltage. If at any time you attempt to measure a completely unknown voltage, set the meter to its highest range and work downward, range by range, until a readable deflection of the needle is obtained (1.10).

Measurement of Current (amps)
Set the meter to 0–500 mA. This test is carried out by making the current to be measured flow through the meter. For an exercise, use a miniature lamp and connect neg meter lead to battery neg, positive meter lead to lamp, and positive battery lead to lamp as shown in (1.11). Be careful to use a

1.10   Testing for voltage

small lamp of, say, nominally 0.3 A rating, as many small test meters do not have high current ranges. This test is not as frequently required as voltage resistance testing (1.11).

1.11   Testing for current

Measurement of Resistance (ohms)
Although it is not often necessary to measure absolute resistance, generally speaking small meters have a number of ohms ranges. One of the most useful is the lower range, as it can be used for continuity testing, e.g. fuses, lamps, cables, earths, etc. For use on these ranges the meter has an internal battery which provides a small current to pass through any object connected to the meter terminals (1.12).

The current flowing through the device or circuit under test is measured on a special scale calibrated in ohms, so that the value of the resistor can read directly. To retain the calibration accuracy when the voltage of the internal battery falls, the meter is first set up by connecting the two test meter leads together and adjusting the needle to zero ohms on the scale. If the test leads are now separated and connected to the small lamp used for the last test, the meter will read the cold resistance of the lamp (1.13).

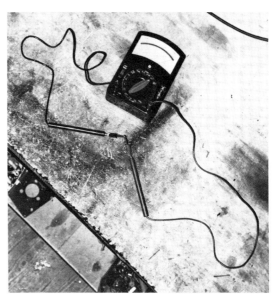

1.12   Testing for continuity

By this point, if you have worked through these four tests as an exercise, you will have functionally carried out all that is needed for simple electronic tests on your boats.

Checks with the Test Meter
Polarity
If when attempting to measure voltage with your meter, the needle moves off the scale to the left (1.14), reverse the leads and the needle will then move to the right onto the scale (1.15). In this way

1.13   Testing for resistance

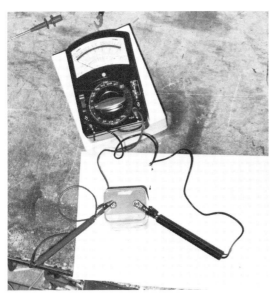

1.14   *Polarity reversed*

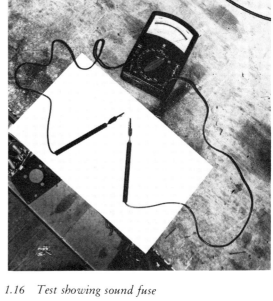

1.16   *Test showing sound fuse*

it is possible to establish positive from negative between two leads, even if they have the same colour. When the meter gives a reading in the correct sense, the positive side of the device you are testing is the one to which you have connected the positive (red) meter terminal.

Fuses
Select the lowest ohms range and set the meter to zero as may be necessary, see above. If the fuse is

now connected between the meter terminals as in (1.16) and it is sound, the meter will read full scale as shown. If on the other hand the fuse has ruptured, the meter will show an infinitely high resistance (1.17).

Measuring the Supply Voltage at the Equipment
Connect the meter as shown in (1.10) with the equipment operational. Always take the reading where the supply cable enters the equipment, with

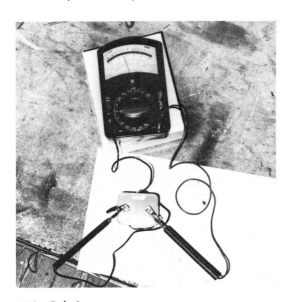

1.15   *Polarity correct*

1.17   *Test showing ruptured fuse*

1.18   Identifying particular core

and without the engine running. Voltage drop in the wiring will begin to show in this test.

Voltage Drop on Cables

Where it becomes necessary to measure the precise voltage drop across a particular length of cable, it is clearly necessary to have all the load carried by the cable switched on. By connecting the meter with one meter lead to either end of the cable under test, a voltage reading will be obtained indicating the drop across the length tested. Don't forget to double it to allow for the return conductor loss. By hooking on a heavier cable the improvement can be measured.

Cable Continuity

Sometimes it becomes necessary to identify particular cores in a multiway cable; 1.18 shows how this can be carried out using the ohms range on the meter. It will often be necessary to extend one of the meter's leads for this job.

Electrical Tests without a Meter

Where a minimum of equipment is available, the spare lamp for the navigation lights will give you a means of carrying out a few simple checks. Fitted with a pair of leads this can be used roughly in the same way as the meter, lamp brightness being used as a guide to quantity. Continuity tests can be out on cables etc. by connecting a lantern battery in series. If a fault is of the 'continuous fuse blowing' type, putting a lamp of similar rating to the equipment in series will stop the fuse blowing and enable you to trace the short circuit. From my school days I remember that polarity can be determined by sticking a lead from both terminals into a potato! It will turn black around the positive pole due to metallic salts passing into solution. Almost any other wet, light-coloured starchy material will do the trick.

2 Batteries, Starters and Charging Equipment

Thou art the sun of other days;
They shine by giving back thy rays.

John Keble

Since batteries were first used for marine purposes there has been one type readily available to yachtsmen. This is known as the fully discharged or flat battery. Perhaps with the hope of preventing the proliferation of the species, we should look at the requirements and performance of the lead/acid or alkaline batteries that are now commonly used for marine purposes. There are various advantages for each of these batteries, and various classes within each type are designed for different applications. For example, engine starting duties are very different from those of general services.

Before deciding how big the battery will need to be for any particular requirement, there are a few general rules which if considered before fitting out, or even during the winter layup, for a modest outlay and a bit of work will do much to make the boat safer, worth more, and less prone to irritating failures. The obvious is frequently ignored when stowing batteries; for instance, it is by no means uncommon to find four heavy duty batteries stowed outboard of each engine where they will necessitate an unholy amount of industry even to top up. While small craft are of necessity volumetrically well packaged, they are also intended to be capable of giving pleasure to their owners. It should be possible to gain virtually instant access to the boat's batteries from a cockpit or deck position so that they can be removed without invoking a heart attack. All batteries are heavy and need removal in the winter for storage, and should therefore lift out with the minimum of lost skin from knuckles, to facilitate easy removal to the quay. The battery stowage should be separated from the engine-room or compartment

and be well ventilated either by natural draft of by electric fans, which must be flameproof. The bottom of the compartment should have a lined tray for the units to stand in, to take up any spillage of electrolyte that could damage the hull. This tray should be made so that it can be replaced easily from time to time, not built into the hull. If the battery compartment is a top opening type, do not make it so small that you are unable to fit a bigger battery if needed, and even then allow something for getting the bigger unit in and out. Loose battens should be provided under the batteries to allow a rope end to be dropped round for lifting them out. Stowage wedges, blocks and clamps must also be provided to prevent movement of the batteries when the boat is under way.

As both lead/acid and alkaline batteries release oxygen and hydrogen due to electrolysis in the water component of the electrolyte, it is very necessary to ventilate the battery compartment to prevent a dangerous buildup of these explosive gases. This has become an absolute must in modern craft as most are fitted with alternators with high rates of charge and discharge which produce quite high gassing rates.

The basic rules of battery care and use are:

Properly constructed and ventilated stowage.
Site batteries so that they can be serviced or remove at deck level.
Position stowage to achieve the shortest possible cable run to the starter motors.
All connections clean, dry and tight, with a smear of petroleum jelly.
No switches, relays or fuses in the battery

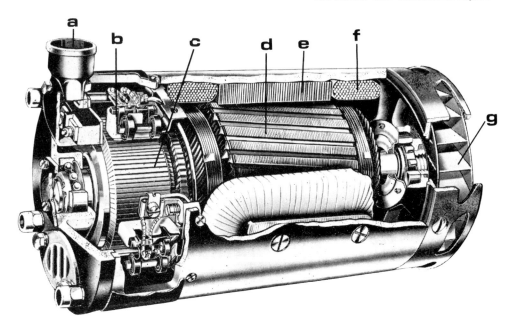

2.1 *Dynamo*
  A *Cable entry*
  B *Brush gears*
  C *Commutator*

D *Armature*
E *Pole piece*
F *Field winding*
G *Cooling fan*

compartment.
A steel or GRP tray for alkaline types.
A lead or GRP tray for lead/acid types.
Ventilation fans should be flameproof.
An air inlet must be provided below the level
of the batteries.
An air outlet (vent) from above the batteries to
a position above deck level (not to be confused
with an inlet for salt water and spray).
Do not use lead/acid batteries and alkaline
batteries in the same location if it can be
avoided, and keep separate hydrometers for
each type as even a small amount of acid will
seriously degrade the alkaline type.
Note: lead/acid battery hydrometer checks
state of charge; alkaline battery hydrometer
checks state of electrolyte.
These two types of battery, lead/acid and alkaline,
have an extensive history and a highly involved
chemistry; however, I have given this in a very
much shortened form.

Lead/Acid Types

The lead/acid batteries we take so much for
granted today originated probably with a secondary
cell invented by Gaston Planté around 1860; it
consisted of two electrodes formed from plates of
soft lead and immersed in a solution of sulphuric
acid. Emil Faure further developed the idea about
1880 by first coating the plates with red lead.
Subsequently antimonial lead alloy cast into grids
with oxide paste fillers brought the forerunner of
today's excellent lead/acid batteries to an advanced
state of development.

The chemistry of the charge/discharge cycle is as
follows. In a fully charged cell, when current flows
oxygen is freed from the negative plate due to
electrolytic action, and its surface, due to acid
attack, tends to become converted to sulphate of
lead. Simultaneously hydrogen is released by
electrolytic action at the positive plate; this
becomes oxidised and attacked by the acid and
tends to become coated with sulphate of lead. In
the course of this action, part of the acid is
removed from the solution and the specific gravity
drops. The acid in a fully charged cell will be about
1.28; when discharged this will have fallen to about
1.115. Given this chemical evidence we are able to
use a hydrometer to establish the state of charge.
During the recharging cycle the above events are
reversed; hydrogen is deposited at the negative

plate, reconverting the lead sulphate to metallic lead. The positive plate is reconverted to lead peroxide and the sulphuric acid is released into solution, returning the specific gravity to 1.28.

The open circuit voltage of a fully charged lead/acid cell is about 2.2 V, and about 1.8 V when discharged. If discharged below this point both positive and negative plates become sulphated and the efficiency begins to drop. This will also occur if the battery is left uncharged for a period of two or three months, due to self-discharge losses.

Lead/acid batteries are available in 6 and 12 V units with capacities up to about 300 ampere hours (AH). Units above about 150 AH are often built into wooden cases for marine applications; however the batteries commonly found on small craft are similar in appearance to the automobile type and are supplied in tough rubber or plastic cases. Due to the number of lead/acid batteries manufactured for the motor car industry the capital cost of this type of battery is very low by comparison with the alkaline type. The same lead/acid AH capacity can be stowed in about half the volume in about half the volume required for an alkaline battery, although the life expectancy of the latter is about four times longer.

One of the problems with boat batteries is that they are often left unattended for sometimes several weeks, and this often does much to reduce their life. In order to keep a battery in good condition, it needs to be charged and discharged regularly. During layup time this is sometimes a problem, as all types of battery lose their charge while standing unused at the rate of about 1% per day at 60₃F; at higher temperatures the loss is even greater. It is therefore important to see that batteries are removed and serviced during the layup period.

The battery's condition, as distinct from its state of charge, may be established by the use of a heavy discharge meter. This device presents a heavy load to each cell, and for accurate results the battery must also be fully charged while measuring voltage. A cell in good condition will hold its voltage for about 10 sec.; a rapidly falling voltage indicates a weak cell. Care should be taken when using a heavy discharge meter after a period of charging, to avoid ignition of the hydrogen released in the charging process.

Particularly violent explosions have been known to occur when precautions have not been taken in this respect. I recall taking a battery off charge some years ago and on picking it up a jumper lead fell off the battery charger above me—the infernal thing exploded in my hands and acid ran down my legs into my shoes. The most amusing part of the incident was the affect of the acid on the socks I was wearing; they were of some synthetic material which just vanished as the acid touched it, and in no time at all my socks had been removed without taking my shoes off! Should you be so unfortunate, the procedure is to discard any clothing that might hold the acid and apply plenty of water. If possible use sodium carbonate (or baking soda) to neutralise the acid. Apply this to the skin with plenty of water as it gets hot as it works.

The capacity of a battery is usually quoted at the 10 hour rate; for example, if a 250 AH battery is discharged at 25 A, it will sustain its output for 10 hours. At higher currents its capacity decreases, and vice versa to some extent. It is possible to recharge modern batteries very quickly, but the temperature rise and the ambient temperature must not combine to produce a battery temperature in excess of 43°C (110°F). The correct rate of charge can be established as follows: divide the battery capacity in ampere hours by the charging time in hours and multiply this by 1.4 to allow for a battery efficiency of 70%. The charging time should be taken as 10 hours.

$$\text{Charging current} = \frac{\text{Battery capacity in AH} \times 1.4}{10 \text{ hours}}$$

a typical example:

$$\frac{100 \text{ AH}}{10 \text{ h}} \times 1.4 = 14 \text{ A for 10 hours}$$

With a modern regulator for the generator or alternator, the charging current will commence higher than 14 A and slowly taper off until the battery is fully charged.

Alkaline Batteries

Generally these are of the nickel/cadmium type, although occasionally a nickel/iron battery is found. The nickel/iron cell was invented by Edison and the nickel/cadmium type by Junger. The active materials in these cells are disposed on steel plates of special construction. The active material in the positive plates is nickel hydroxide, and in the negative plates is fine iron or cadmium dust, depending on the type of cell. The electrolyte is potassium hydroxide with a specific gravity of 1.2 approx., which does not vary with the state of charge. The outer case of the cell is steel and is therefore 'live', and it was usual to package five cells in a wooden crate to make up a 6 V unit, although nickel/cadmium batteries in two grades up to 120 AH can now be obtained in plastic containers.

Discharge reduces the nickel hydroxide on the positive plate to a lower form of hydroxide, and on the negative plate oxidation of the cadmium or iron occurs, producing the appropriate hydroxide. When charging the reverse occurs. The nickel/cadmium cell has a fully charged voltage of 1.7 V and the nickel/iron cell 1.85 V.

The nickel/cadmium type of cell is particularly suited to marine use as it will withstand long periods of idleness: a fully charged battery will retain its capacity for several months without attention. Of the three classes of alkaline cell, the nickel/iron are not the most suitable type and will rarely be found in small craft; the nickel/cadmium high performance type should be used for engine starting, and the normal resistance type for general services. In smaller craft, of course, the latter may also be used for starting.

Alkaline battery capacities are quoted at the 2 hour rate for high performance cells and at the 5 hour rate for normal types. The normal charge requirement for the latter is arrived at by multiplying the battery capacity by 0.2 and charging at that rate for seven hours:

$$100 \text{ AH} \times 0.2 = 20 \text{ A for 7 hours}$$

When calculating the charging requirements the figures are again multiplied by 1.4 as in the case of lead/acid cells; e.g. after a discharge of 10 AH a charge of 14 AH is required to restore the original state of charge. Higher rates of charge may be employed; however the battery temperature is again important and should not be allowed to rise above 45°C (113°F).

Battery Requirements

To determine the battery size or capacity required for a particular vessel, many factors must be reasonably assessed. For example if the vessel is a pilot cutter on call 24 hours a day in all weathers,

the allowance made for its radar and radio aids will be much higher than for a yacht of similar size with identical equipment. This assessment must be made realistically by the owner, and by way of illustration an example of a possible small boat's requirement is shown below.

A 30 ft sailing yacht with 12 V system and a 2 litre inboard diesel auxiliary could average over 24 hours:

Four 12 W cabin lights for 8 hrs	384 watt hrs
Four 12 W navigation lights for 4 hrs	192
3 W echosounder for 24 hrs	72
100 W PEP R/T, with DF receiver on continuously and with 2.5 min. traffic reports in 24 hrs	120
Sundry small intermittent loads averaged over 24 hrs	100
	868 WH

As the system is 12 V, $\dfrac{868 \text{ WH}}{12 \text{ V}} = 72$ AH approx.

Allow for starter	90 AH
Battery capacity required	180 AH approx.

The amount of equipment can be varied to suit the particular vessel, and where engine starting is to be considered it is a good plan to consult the engine maker for a figure for starting loads only. If this is in excess of 100 AH, use a separate battery for starting purposes and charge it via blocking diodes later in this chapter.

The figures above have been based on a period of charge during each 24 hour period to sustain the battery capacity, and this will generally be possible at sea. However, if for some overriding reason charging can only take place every 48 hours, for example, then twice the battery capacity will need to be provided.

Generating Equipment

In order to provide primary power at sea, the main engines are normally fitted with generators, or more recently alternators with integral rectifiers. These machines are required to provide sufficient output over a wide range of engine speed and load conditions. A choice is generally made between a generator and an alternator if the vessel is a new construction; however, it has become very popular to leave the DC generator on an existing installation to service the starter battery only, and to provide a new alternator driven from another power takeoff on the engine to balance the load of general services.

The generator capacity may be established from details of the load and charge rates. If we look again at our simple 30 ft sailing boat with a 12 V system:

Four 12 W cabin lights	4 A
Four 12 W navigation lights	4
3 W echosounder	0.25
R/T averaged	2.0
Sundry small loads averaged	2.0
	12.25 A

We can ignore the 0.25 A as this would not be significant in the total load.

You will remember that the calculated battery capacity in this case was 180 AH. This means that as established earlier for lead/acid batteries we will recharge at the 10 hour rate which will work out as follows:

$$\frac{180 \text{ AH}}{10 \text{ hours}} = 18 \text{ A charging current}$$

This figure must be increased by a factor of 1.4 to allow for the battery efficiency, thus: $18 \times 1.4 = 25.2$ A. Adding to this 12.0 A for the running load, $25.2 + 12.0 = 37.2$ A gives the maximum current the generator must provide to sustain the services and battery.

Dynamo versus Alternator

Generating enough electricity for the boat's requirements often has to be considered at several stages of a small boat's life as the demands of its owner change, or perhaps when the boat changes hands and a refit is undertaken.

The Dynamo

Most of us are familiar with the DC dynamo, (2.1) which is used extensively and, until in recent years when the alternator appeared on the scene, was the means employed to produce electricity for general services and for charging batteries. On present day marine engines one can still choose to have a dynamo fitted; the factors to influence this choice may not be readily discernable and for this reason I will try to make clear what each type does.

Electricity is generated when a conductor moves in a magnetic field, and this condition is achieved

in the dynamo by placing a coiled conductor on a rotor which is mechanically coupled to the engine. Surrounding the rotor (or armature) is a field winding, so called because with its static assembly of ferrous material it creates the magnetic field that the conductors on the rotor move within.

When the engine is running the small amount of residual magnetism in the stator assembly creates a weak field for the armature conductors to move through. A correspondingly small output is produced within the armature; however, as the field is connected in parallel with the armature at the moment of starting, this small current flows through the field winding, so increasing the magnetic field to which the rotor is subject. This process is regenerative and the output voltage is limited by the constants of the machine, the load, the regulator and the speed of rotation, which must reach a certain minimum for the buildup of the magnetic field to be initiated.

The arrangement of the machine is such that the output current must be collected from the rotor via a rotating switch called a commutator. This is essential so that a direct current output is obtained. The commutator consists of radially disposed copper bars, insulated from one another, to which the armature conductors are connected and having a smooth circumference upon which brushes may run to collect the generated current. It is from this rotary switch that the familiar radio interference comes; this characteristically is continuous and builds up as engine speed increases.

The dynamo has been able to reach a very advanced level of development due to its use in motor cars over several decades and it is very economical to produce. Its advantages could be summarised as follows:

Economically priced
Simple construction
Relatively easy to suppress RI when in good condition
Difficult to damage even in fault conditions.

Its disadvantages have to be qualified, but are:

Low output at low speeds. It is not possible to run a dynamo at very high speeds because the stress on the rotor windings and commutator would be unacceptably high. With the dynamo, the rotor

2.2   *CAV marine alternator*
A Sliprings
B Brushgear
C Cable entry
D Rotor

E Drive shaft
F Stator
G Diode rectifiers
H Ball race

windings are heavy ones to carry the whole of the output current. It may well be that for your purpose extensive tickover speeds are not customary, and it could therefore be perfectly adequate in this respect. The whole of the output current passes through the brushes, which produces a finite brush and commutator life. This may not be very important for a weekend yachtsman. Due to its maximum speed of rotation large outputs from this type of machine demand a frame of considerable bulk, this again is not relevant if you only need a small output.

The alternator

The major difference between the dynamo and the alternator is that the exciting winding or field winding rotates and the output windings are located in the stator assembly. The effect of this is that only about 5% of the output current has to be passed via rotating contacts, in this case slip rings, to the rotor assembly. This makes the rotor simple, small and easy to balance, and capable of being rotated at much higher speeds by means of a suitable drive ratio to the engine. Copper slip rings are mounted on and insulated from the shaft to which the rotor coils are connected. With this arrangement wear on the brushes is considerably reduced. The output from the stator windings is AC and to uni-directionalise the current, that is to convert it into DC, a number of rectifier diodes

are used. These diodes, as I have explained earlier, are simply one-way valves and equate with the commutator in the DC machine. The buildup of electrical energy takes place in exactly the same way as in the DC dynamo. The advantages of the alternator could be summarised as follows:

Smaller than the dynamo for the same power output
Higher speeds attainable due to simple rotor, which enables cutting-in at lower engine speeds given the correct drive ratio
Low brush wear even at high speed because of low rotor current and slip rings.
Its disadvantages are:
More expensive than the dynamo
Radio interference is more difficult to suppress
Rectifier diodes can be damaged by the battery connections being reversed inadvertently when stationary, or by open circuiting the machine when it is running.

A high quality CAV marine alternator is shown in (2.2).

Surges

It is as well to get a clear picture of what this term implies. Imagine the dynamo or alternator running in a steady state and charging the batteries. At some stage an interruption of the circuit takes place, the effect of which is for the machine, now left under no load conditions, to produce a voltage surge, which may be many times the nominal battery voltage. By far the most common cause of this is loose or dirty battery terminals.

If equipment is connected on the generator side of the break, it will be subject to the surge and can be damaged. With alternators, the surge can be large enough to cause damage either to the rectifier diodes within the unit or the regulator. I recall one incident where a well meaning watchkeeper turned off the battery isolator switches, because it was thought that the batteries were being overcharged. The effect of this was to blow every lamp, including the navigation lamps, on the boat; leaving everyone in pitch darkness in the middle of the North Sea.

In order to prevent such surges taking place, it is necessary to protect the alternator and the load with an advance field switching battery isolator (units of this type are available from CAV Ltd); the principle is that the field of the machine is wired via a separate pole of the switch, and this is mechanically arranged to break before the main contacts carrying the alternator output. The output of the alternator is thus virtually zero at the instant of break.

It has been said that the DC dynamo does not give problems with surges on the supply, however, I can assure you that if such a machine is open circuited when in operation, a surge of about ten times the nominal supply voltage will appear, although it must be said that as most dynamos have quite modest outputs and are rotated at relatively low speeds, such surges have not in practice given rise to many problems.

Spikes

One of the effects of making and breaking any electrical circuit is to produce very short impulses, which are often referred to as 'spikes'. The precise nature of the circuit may either diminish or enhance the spike; capacitive circuits normally have the former effect and inductive circuits normally the latter.

Very often such spikes are destructive and, although this may not prove too disastrous on very expensive equipment with superb input filtering, or on older units using valves, with transistorised equipment, particularly the lower cost type, a

hazardous condition exists.

In some instances the cure may be to add capacitance across the circuit giving rise to the problem. It should however be remembered that if contacts are involved that capacity will shorten the contact life and a better solution may be to install a 10 W Zener diode with an operating voltage about one and a half times the line voltage and connected in parallel with the offending machine. The Zener diode should have a 1 ohm non-inductive resistor fitted in series, in order to protect the machine in the event of the device breaking down. The better quality marine voltage regulators embody a spike suppressor; however they are not universally fitted. Where this sort of damage is suspected its cause can be traced with the aid of a storage oscilloscope. As the work is quite involved however, and beyond the scope of the average yachtsman, specialist advice should be sought.

In the past, spikes were thought to emanate only from generation equipment, it is now generally acknowledged that the load and wiring may be equal contributors.

Blocking Diodes

These very useful circuit elements are so called because they block the flow of current in one direction only and have only two terminals. They are very reliable and can be better understood if they are regarded as one-way valves. The diagrams (2.3, 2.4, 2.5, 2.6) show some of the configurations that can be used. The arrowhead in the diode symbol indicates the direction of the current flow.

In (2.3) the diode allows the generator to charge both battery S and battery P. However if P becomes discharged the diode will prevent current flowing in a reverse direction from battery S. Such protection is desirable for engine starting applications.

Scheme (2.4) shows two generators coupled to charge one battery, enabling charging to take place irrespective of whether one machine is idle. This precaution is not necessary when alternators having integral rectifiers are fitted.

Scheme (2.5) shows a configuration which could represent port and starboard generators charging their respective batteries. The auxiliary generator is connected via diodes in order to prevent circulating currents between the two batteries. The

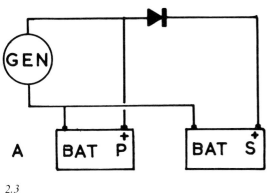

A

2.3

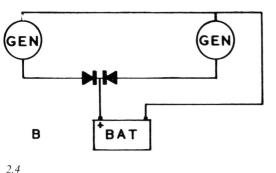

B

2.4

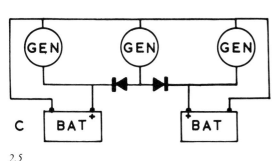

C

2.5

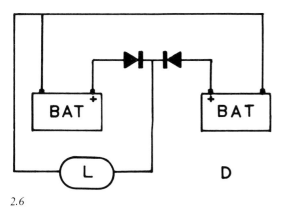

D

2.6

arrangement would allow both batteries to be charged simultaneously from a single auxiliary and discharged by separate loads.

Scheme (2.6) shows two batteries connected via diodes to a common load, which enables both batteries to be used without creating circulating currents which would dissipate the charge. These circuits give an idea of the many possible arrangements which can be created to suit individual requirements. The diode units may be obtained from a number of suppliers, for example CAV Ltd, who manufacture a conveniently packaged device for marine applications. Much manual switching and a fair amount of wiring can be saved by careful application of the units.

Regulator Units

The regulator most familiar to everyone is the vibrating reed type used in association with the dynamos of most cars. In a small bakelite box it houses the reverse current relay (or cutout), and a similar looking coil and armature which possess voltage and current sensing windings so that the output of the machine can be regulated by interrupting the field current to suit conditions of load and speed. It is this device that produces radio interference which may be identified by slowly increasing the engine revs. When a critical output current has been reached a terrific clattering noise is usually audible on the radio; it will get faster as speed is increased beyond the critical point and disappear at charging currents below this value.

Solid state regulators such as the CAV 440 are now produced for alternator control. These units intercept the alternator field for control purposes as the mechanical unit does, but transitors and diodes are used to sense current and voltage. As the alternator has one-way valves (diodes) in its frame it does not suffer from reverse current problems and does not need a cutout. The reverse of this problem may occur however—it may be that someone will connect the batteries in reverse polarity at some stage and very heavy current will flow through the machine, usually breaking down the diodes as a result. Polarity sensing relays are available now to prevent damage under these conditions, which are I think rare in occurrence.

For all types of regulators where electronic equipment is likely to be used, it is essential to fit the appropriate screened and suppressed unit (chapter 3). The screened case should be connected to the boat's bonding system with a suitable insulated strap and the unit sited as close as possible to the machine it controls. The cables between the filter unit and the dynamo or alternator should be screened and carefully connected via the glands, with the screening securely connected where the leads enter.

Tracing Faults

One question arises from time to time as the owner looks down at the engine and scratches his head. Is it the dynamo/alternator or the control box/regulator that does not work? Firstly, whenever you have either unit serviced it is much better to take both items along to an accredited dealer and have them tested and set up together. Secondly, if you are at sea or otherwise compelled to diagnose the problem, I suggest as follows:

1. Make sure nothing obvious like a fuse, circuit breaker or, with some alternators, the warning lamp is defective.
2. Disconnect the system wires from the alternator of dynamo, leaving the terminals on the machine free.
3. Connect a lamp across the main positive and negative terminals and a short length of wire to the field terminal.
4. Run the engine at about 900 r.p.m. for an alternator and about 1800 r.p.m. for a dynamo.
5. Touch the wire from the field terminal on the A, D, or positive terminal for about 20 seconds. If the lamp lights it can be taken that the machine is sound. If no output is obtained touch the field wire on the negative terminal (some machines are connected differently inside) and test again.
6. If no output is obtained in either case, suspect the machine itself and investigate brushes, internal connections, etc. With the dynamo these are made visible by removing the band on the end of the machine.

It may be that if the machine builds up in the above conditions without a regulator, the lamp you are using might blow, so be ready to remove the field wire again if it is important to preserve the lamp.

Where an 'extra' generator of either type is to be fitted. Do not fit it with a puny drive; a $1\frac{1}{2} \times \frac{3}{8}$ in. aluminium pulley on the shaft of any generator is just not enough in terms of frictional area. Fit belts and pulleys to the manufacturer's specification, which may involve tandem belts for the larger machines. A minimum pulley diameter for the generator end is about 3 in. or 75 mm, even if this means fitting a larger diameter pulley on the engine. If the drive is not substantial slip will occur as the machine loads up and full output will not be achieved; also the belt will wear quickly. When allowing for generator loading on the engine rating about 3 BHP for 1 electrical h.p., i.e. 746 W, is required.

When a dynamo has not been used for a long period, the residual magnetism drops to a low level and the machine may not excite immediately. If you have not encountered this situation before, it is at first quite puzzling as everything looks sound, and tests indicate that everything should work although no output can be obtained. Well tried methods of overcoming this are, first run the engine up to top speed for 30 seconds or so. If this fails, run the engine at about half speed and with a flying lead momentarily connect the battery positive (+) terminal to the dynamo positive (+) terminal. This has the effect of connecting the dynamo directly across the battery and, if nothing else is wrong, the machine will excite and pull the cutout in. This method has the advantage that the machine will excite with the correct polarity.

I have never encountered this problem with alternators or dynastart units, as in the former case the higher speed means that a little magnetism will go a long way, and in the latter case pushing the starter button puts an immense amount of magnetism into the frame.

Dynastart Units

Many small engines are fitted with a starter-dynamo composite which has heavy duty series field windings for starting, and parallel windings for battery charging. By far the most irritating thing about these units is that I have never seen one with both terminals insulated from the frame. Clearly for marine use this job needs to be done at an early stage if problems are to be avoided. When used on small diesel engines there is often insufficient inertia to swing through the first compression after pushing the start button. Do not hold the button in until it eventually heaves over, the field coils will overheat and quite quickly a condition known as 'fault by user participation' will occur. Release the button and let the engine run back and try again, or use the exhaust valve lifter.

Having stated the only disadvantages I am aware of, I must say that I believe the demand for simple and compact units must increase, my own boat is fitted with one and I am very pleased with it. The CAV DS418 is of 4-pole construction, two poles carrying the series winding for starting, and two others carry the shunt winding for generation. The construction of these machines is somewhat similar to the conventional generator, and it is usually mounted in the same sort of swinging bracket. When the starter button is pressed, a heavy relay is activated in the control unit, thus connecting the machine to the batteries. In this condition it operates as a compound motor with predominantly series characteristics. When the engine starts, the button is released and, driven now by the engine, it becomes a self-excited shunt generator. As soon as the rated voltage is reached, the regulator begins to maintain a rate of charge to suit the state of the battery. Typical wiring for a 12V system is shown in (2.7), and (2.7a) gives an exploded view.

Auxiliary Generators

Some sort of auxiliary power unit will make life more bearable in many ways, particularly for the weekend yachtsman. Often something is left on or a fault occurs when the boat is unattended, or for some other reason the batteries are low. Even without a mishap of any sort it is rather wasteful to burn main engine hours and fuel just to charge the batteries.

Necessities of life afloat depend greatly on how big your boat is and how much you are prepared to spend. Some cooking appliances for low voltage use are available, and others can only be used on a high voltage supply from either shore supply or auxiliary plant. I would recommend anyone about to purchase an auxiliary generator to buy a machine with a high voltage AC output, i.e. 240 V AC for UK and 110 V AC for US use. If your

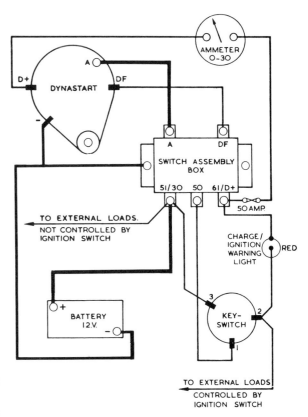

2.7   Wiring set-up for using dynastart

boat is big enough and you intend to fit and use any amount of equipment, the cost of a high voltage alternator is quickly offset by the savings in cost brought about by using standard domestic equipment such as electric blankets, kettles, power tools, cooker etc. It also means that shore supply is easily made use of, as a separate high voltage wiring system is already installed. When connection to shore supply is made I strongly recommend the use of an isolating transformer, which should be of the type fitted with an earthed electrostatic screen between the primary and secondary windings. Contact with the live side of 240 V mains when on board surrounded by virtually ideal earth conditions is far from being the best way to secure ripe old age. The screen is necessary because there is enough capacity between the windings of a large transformer to pass considerably in excess of fatal current. The transformer should preferably be mounted ashore, even if in a portable weatherproof housing, so that the mains wiring never enters the boat. The size of the transformer will depend on

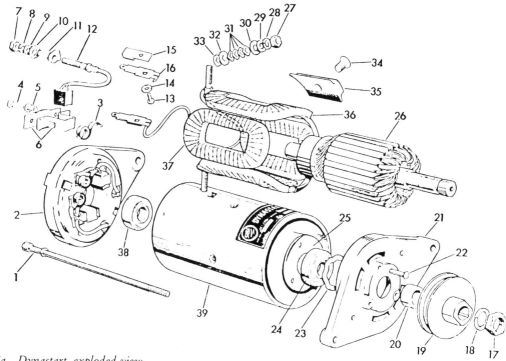

2.7a *Dynastart, exploded view*

1 *Thru-bolt and washer (2)*
2 *Commutator end cover*
3 *Brush spring (2)*
4 *Brush holder rivet (2)*
5 *Rivet insulator (2)*
6 *Brush holder and insulation(2)*
7 *Brush terminal nut (2)*
8 *Brush terminal nut lockwasher (2)*
9 *Brush terminal nut washer (2)*
10 *Brush terminal insulating washer (2)*
11 *Brush terminal insulator (2)*
12 *Brush terminal*
13 *Spade (F1) terminal rivet*
14 *Spade (F1) terminal insulator washer*
15 *Spade (F1) terminal insulator*
16 *Spade terminal*
17 *Pulley nut*
18 *Pulley nut lockwasher*
19 *Pulley*

20 *Spacer*
21 *Drive end cover*
22 *Bearing retainer rivet (3)*
23 *Spring washer*
24 *Ball bearing*
25 *Retainer plate*
26 *Armature*
27 *Field terminal stud nut*
28 *Field terminal stud lockwasher (2)*
29 *Field terminal stud washer (2)*
30 *Field terminal stud insulating washer (2)*
31 *Field terminal stud insulator (8)*
32 *Field terminal stud insulating washer (2)*
33 *Field terminal stud washer (2)*
34 *Pole shoe screw (4)*
35 *Pole shoe (4)*
36 *Series field coil set*
37 *Shunt field coil set*
38 *Ball bearing*

the load, which you will have to calculate, but it is not difficult to keep these requirements within reason. My own feeling is that 3 kW will suffice for all but the largest boats.

One common complaint with auxiliary power units is that they make a lot of noise, often at times when it would be nice to have the boat quiet. Vibration and soundproofing is rather expensive, for example the 10 kW equipment shown (2.8) is in a sound reducing enclosure which adds roughly 20% to the price. For many smaller craft it would not be economic. This diesel generating plant is one of those produced by GM Power Plant of Ipswich.

Further advantage can be taken of a high voltage supply to replenish the batteries via a constant voltage charger (such as the Constavolt). Unlike a conventional charger, it senses the battery voltage and reduces the charge rate as the battery recovers. Its output may be divided using diodes as outlined in this chapter, so that where shore supply is available all the batteries can be charged simultaneously and silently. From a practical aspect of high voltage supply, consider the working improvisations on a two speed electric drill clamped in the boat's bench: vice, lathe, sander, saw, grinder—all available at sea.

Electric Starters

Modern marine starters are complex devices as can be seen in (2.9). The greatest care must be taken to ensure the correct type of battery, cabling of adequate cross section, and proper terminating lugs, for otherwise good performance will not be achieved. Battery manufacturers often recommend the provision of separate batteries for engine cranking. The effects on the starter motor caused

by an inadequate battery can be serious. It is probably generally realised that cranking speed is critical from the engine starting aspect; however, it should also be realised that it is also critical, because the starter motor is a series type to give maximum torque at the lowest speed. If the voltage applied to the starter is low the speed is also low; the current becomes excessively high, producing a condition that can be guaranteed to reduce starter motor life.

The CAV starter shown in (2.9) operates as follows:

When the starter switch is pressed, current flows through the windings of the relay and closes the relay contacts, thereby energising the operating solenoid. The magnetic field of the solenoid draws the sliding plunger axially forward, bringing the pinion nose into mesh with the engine flywheel teeth . At the same time a first set of contacts mounted on the plunger closes, and current, limited by a resistance incorporated in the starter, passes through the windings, cuasing the armature shaft to rotate slowly.

The pinion, prevented from rotating by the flywheel teeth, is then drawn into full engagement by the action of the helix and the slowly rotating armature. Just before the fully engaged position is

2.8 *Soundproofed auxiliary generator*

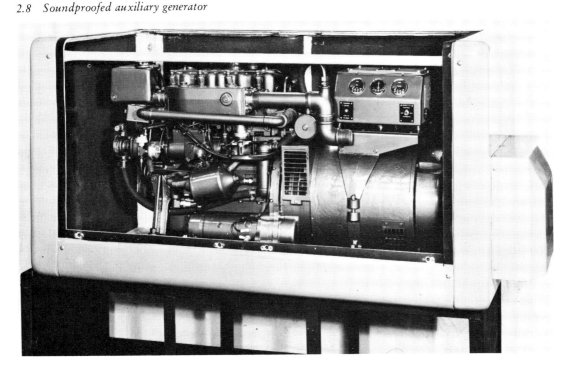

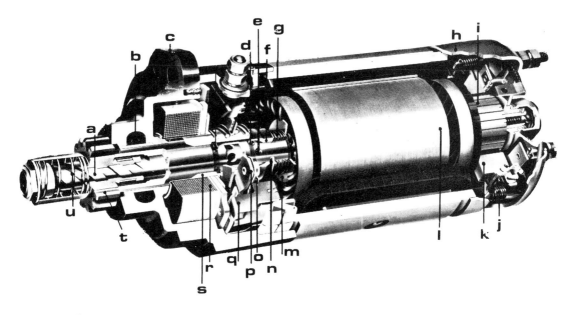

2.9   *CAV electric starter*

A *Helix*
B *Lubricator*
C *Drive and shield*
D *Overspeed balls*
E *Locking balls*
F *Locking collar*
G *Lock collar spring*
H *Commutator and shield*
I   *Commutator*
J   *Brush spring*
K *Brush holder*

L *Armature*
M *Trip collar*
N *Trigger arm*
O *Trigger spring*
P *Second contact*
Q *Trigger assembly*
R *Solenoid assembly*
S *Solenoid plunger*
T *Pinion assembly*
U *Pinion return spring*

reached, the collar carried on the pinion sleeve trips the trigger operating the second contacts. When the contacts are made, the resistance is short circuited, and full current passes through the field and armature windings. Full starting torque is exerted only when the pinion is properly engaged, and thus the risk of damage to pinion and flywheel teeth is minimised.

As the pinion sleeve moves forward, the locking balls in the sleeve drop into the shaft dimples, and the lock collar travels over them, as already described. The pinion cannot be ejected prematurely, but will remain in mesh until the starter switch is released, or the overspeed mechanism operates. This is necessary when starting compression-ignition engines, as spasmodic engine firing might otherwise cause ejection before the engine is running properly.

A return spring is fitted on the forward end of the pinion, to assist disengagement and to prevent the pinion wandering towards the flywheel whilst the engine is running.

Faults in Operation

If the starter does not function, or is sluggish or intermittent in operation, check that the battery is in a satisfactory state of charge, and that all cable connections are clean and tight. A defective starter switch, badly worn starter brushes, or tampering are possible causes of failure. If, after these points have been checked, the starter still fails to operate then the starter should be removed for internal examination, which should be entrusted to the nearest CAV Depot or Agent.

Difficulty in smooth engagement between starter and flywheel starter ring may be caused by dirt in the helix of the armature shaft, preventing free pinion movement. In this case the starter should be removed from the engine, and the helix thoroughly cleaned with paraffin and then smeared with a small quantity of grease.

Very little servicing should be necessary with this starter, but I suggest that the following maintenance procedures be undertaken at regular intervals, the length of which are dependent on operating conditions. Before removing the starter or taking off the commutator cover, the outside of the starter should be thoroughly cleaned.

Brushgear

Remove the commutator cover, and ensure that the brushes are free in their holders by pulling gently on the brush leads. If a brush is inclined to stick, remove it from its holder and clean the brush and the inside of the holder with a a clean cloth, moistened in petrol or carbon tetrachloride. Be sure to replace the brush in its original position, so that the curvature of its contact surface accurately conforms with the commutator periphery. When insulating sleeving is provided on the brush leads, see that it has not become burnt or charred, thus creating the danger of short circuits.

Replace the commutator cover, ensuring that the yoke windows are fully covered, and that the cover fixing screw is at the bottom of the starter when the starter is mounted on the engine. This is most important, as fuel oil and water may enter the machine if the cover is not correctly positioned.

Commutator

If the commutator surface is dirty or discoloured, it can be cleaned with a fine grade of glass paper (do not use emery cloth or carborundum paper). In cases where the surface is badly pitted or grooved, the armature should be set up in a lathe and the commutator skimmed. Such work should be carried out by skilled engineers. The commutator must not be undercut otherwise brush dust tracking may occur.

Solar energy

The means by which solar energy is applied

depends on the type of vessel and its work. One can imagine all manner of loading requirements, ranging from a busy pilot cutter whose daily work involves enough running time for the batteries to be fully charged, right through to a sailing vessel in a round the world race carrying as little as possible.

In motor craft, the solar energy unit will provide only a fraction of the power instantaneously available from the main electrical system, however this small output is sustained over long periods and will keep everything topped up when the vessel is left unattended. The choice is between solar cells, windmills and watermills, the first having no moving parts and output limited by daylight, and the others having moving parts and a 24-hour output.

Whilst in sailing vessels the problem of electrical power generation can be significantly reduced, the solution in any particular case will depend to a large extent on whether you are racing or cruising. Obviously careful selection of all the electrical equipment is a first step. If racing, photovoltaic cells are the obvious answer as they cause no drag, and the weight of conventional fuel can be reduced by more than the weight of the solar cell array. An alternative suitable for longer cruising voyages is a towable generator, such as the Aquair 50 equipment which uses a water turbine towed by 20 metre of 10 mm braided line. The drag is about 5 kg at 3 knots, 10 kg at 5 knots, and 15 kg at 7 knots. There is also an optional wind drive kit,

2.10 Wind generator

consisting of a 66 cm (26 ins) aerofoil blade unit. Output averages 2.5 amps at 12 volts in either mode of operation. A wide range of wind and water generators are available and your precise requirements will have to guide you; the unit shown here is marketed by Ralph Howe Marketing Ltd. of Poole in Dorset, England (2.10)

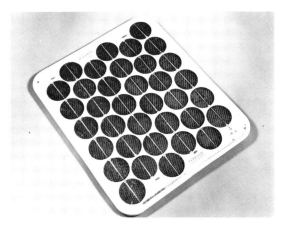

2.11 Solar panel

Solar cell arrays are commercially available from Ferranti Electronics of Oldham. Their MST 300 (2.11) is already in use on buoys, beacons, and all manner of other unattended installations. The cost of a single unit is comparable with small windmills, but as production levels improve it may well drop. The standard panel measures 562 mm by 476 mm (22.5 in. by 19 in.) on the face exposed to the sun, and it is only 10 mm thick (0.4 in.). The output is nominally 15 watts, and units may be connected in series or parallel, using suitable diodes to suit your particular installation. The weight of each panel is about 4 kg (9 lbs); it is weatherproof and will operate from -30°C to +80°C. I have no doubt that these units will find considerable application in small boats. The input voltage will vary with the light falling on the cells but, as all good quality marine instruments have internal regulators, this is not likely to be a great problem. The power demand of instrumentation has dropped with each decade of design, and a solar device such as the MST 300 must surely have a great future.

Power Conversion

Where a high voltage auxiliary is out of the question for one reason or another, one possible answer is to use a convertor or invertor. I should explain these terms, which have degenerated by usage to refer to the same thing in many cases. A convertor (or converter) is an electrical device for transforming power having certain characteristics to a different form, for example 110 V DC to 110 V AC. It could also refer to a device with a low voltage input, say 24 V DC, having the same output. The term convertor is thus very wide, covering devices that carry out power conversion of any kind by any means, whether as a rotary machine or with solid state devices. Invertors (or inverters) are devices that perform similar functions; however, strictly speaking these functions should be performed by sequentially inverting the supply voltage.

Many applications can be found on small craft for equipment of this type. For instance some particular piece of instrumentation may only be available for a 24 V DC input, and if the boat's supply is 12 V this may prove something of a problem. Convertors or invertors are now available which enable conversion to be carried out with an efficiency of about 80%. This type of solid state convertor has in the past been associated with failure, primarily because of the low voltage ratings of the transistors used and the spikes that could be caused by fast current transients within both the boat's wiring and the inductive elements of the convertor. There has been, therefore, a tendency for manufacturers to retain rotary convertors in some instances. While rotary units are more rugged in some respects, their efficiency even when in the peak of condition is something in the order of 40%. Clearly this more than doubles the current required from the primary power source to operate any particular equipment through the convertor. Just as rotary convertors are available with AC or DC inputs, outputs, operating frequencies and phases, the solid state versions also have these facilities. Cost and complexities vary considerably, and clearly the more demanding the load requirements the more expensive the convertor or invertor becomes. For many purposes a very simple invertor will provide all the necessary power and a waveform that will not unduly affect performance.

A typical example of this is an invertor designed for battery charging or intermittent operation of power tools.

When the load is reactive, as an induction motor for example, special precautions need to be taken. These conditions may cause the current to lead or lag behind the voltage, with the result that excessive current is drawn and efficiency drops or damage occurs within the switching transistors. The normal practice is to correct the power factor of each load to better than 0.85. Many service departments do not have a means of measuring power factor; however satisfactory correction can be made with the aid of a simple service oscilloscope. A low value resistor, say 1 ohm, is connected in series with the load to be corrected and the X deflection system of the oscilloscope connected across this resistor. The Y amplifier is connected in parallel to the load. The gains of the X and Y axes are then adjusted to give a trace at roughly 45°. The shape of the trace will be roughly an elipse where the convertor has a sinewave output, and a distorted parallelogram where the output is a squarewave. Where the load is inductive, capacitance is progressively added in parallel with the load until the minor axis of the trace is virtually a straight line. With overcorrection, the trace will invert and the minor axis dimension will again increase. The ideal trace is a single line at 45°, indicating that current and voltage are perfectly in step, i.e. unity power factor. For purely resistive loads (heaters, lamps, etc.) this correction is unnecessary. Radio interference may also be a problem with converters of all types; this is dealt with in chapter 3 and should be approached as in (3.9).

Power Consumption

As an aid to the assessment of the system requirements so far as the overall power consumption is concerned, the table below will give fairly accurate working figures.

Power consumption typical of present day equipment

Echosounders

Small neon type	1 to 3 W (own battery or boat's supply)
Meter indicating	0.5 to 3 W
Small paper recorder	2 to 6 W
Semi-commercial paper recorder	10 to 50 W

Direction finders

Portable receiver, battery operated	Less than 0.5 W
Fixed receiver, boat's supply	1.0 W
Automatic DF, Portable	3 W
Automatic DF, fixed receiver and loop	6 to 120 W

Automatic pilots

Control electronics only		1 to 3 W
Electric drive units	$\frac{1}{10}$ h.p.	120 W
	$\frac{1}{8}$ h.p.	168 W
	$\frac{1}{6}$ h.p.	240 W
Hydraulic spool valve controls		25 W

The average consumption for automatic pilots under working conditions is roughly one-third of the steering consumption, thus 3 W control

circuit, plus $\dfrac{120}{3}$ = 40 W average

Radar

3 kW commercial equipment	240 W
3 kW yacht eauipment	50 W or less

Sonar 120 W

R/T receivers 100 to 300 mA

R/T transmitters

DSB		DSB	
120 W	25 W RF	120 W	100 W PEP
200 W	50 W RF	350 W	400 W PEP
400 W	100 W RF		

Met. equipment

Windspeed and direction indicators	1 to 3 W
Facsimile	120 W roughly

Stabilisers

EMI	Less than 6 W (for monitoring)
Vosper	48 W intermittent
Sperry	Less than 6 W (for monitoring)

Compasses

Illumination	Generally less than 6 W
Magnesyn	25 W approx.
Digital	Less than 12 W
Gyro	150 to 200 W

Logs 1 to 3 W

Navigation systems

Omega	50 W upwards
Decca	25 to 100 W
Loran	12 to 50 W
Consol RX	1 to 3W

Pumps
  Roughly 1,000 W per h.p. when in good
  condition

Refrigerators (small, 2.5 cu. ft)
Compression type	48 to 60 W intermittent
	say 15 W average
Absorption type	30 W intermittent
	say 20 W average

Cookers
| Small direct heating | 3,000 W |
| Small microwave | 1,500 W, required for only about 20% of the conventional cooking time |

Water heaters (small)	1,000 W
Horns	60 W
Fluorescent lights	5 to 65 W, dependent on fitting
Oil-fired cabin heaters	40 to 100 W
Pressure water systems	120 to 180 W intermittent, averages less than 15 W

Television
Transistor	25 W
Valve	130 W
Loudhailers	25 W intermittent, very low average

3 Radio Interference Suppression

At length a universal hubbub wild
Of stunning sounds, and voices all confused,
Borne through the hollow dark, assaults his ear
With loudest vehemence; thither he plies,
Undaunted, to meet there whatever Power
Or Spirit of the nethermost abyss
Might in that noise reside, of whom to ask
Which way the nearest coast of darkness lies

Paradise Lost
John Milton

The problem of radio interference suppression has become considerably extended by the great diversity of equipments which are now available for use on small craft. Bear in mind that on any but new craft some equipment will be of older design, and fewer precautions to filter out spurious radiations were necessary when the problem was smaller. I have included under the general heading of RI all forms of random noise irrespective of whether they become manifest via the ship's radio receiver or in some other way. For instance, ignition systems frequently interfere with echosounders, giving rise to random marks. Although some part of the problem may be solved by equipment design, attention to input filters, etc., there can be no doubt that the correct place to suppress interference is at the source. In small craft this means suppressing every piece of electrical equipment aboard and also giving attention to such normally non-electrical things as steel stays and propshafts: in fact anything in the water or moving in the vessel. Radio frequency energy is generated by every varying or interrupted current flowing in a conductor; typical examples occur in generator brushes, ignition systems and regulators.

Interference may not at first appear to be particularly grouped into frequency bands. While it may have a frequency spectrum which has higher amplitude components in a particular group, in general the interfering signal will be able to shock-excite the tuned circuits of any sensitive equipment so that they 'ring' in sympathy at their natural frequency.

Interference must obviously travel from the point where it is generated to the point where it causes problems, and by examining the various methods of propagation we are able to arrive at solutions for each case (3.1). The two most important are conduction and radiation. Conducted RI travels via the ship's wiring and/or structure directly from source to equipment. In the course of flowing through the wiring it will also radiate by using the wiring as an aerial. Perhaps a third type of propagation is induction, caused by running conductors close enough together for their mutual magnetic fields to couple. The level of interference may be greatly enhanced by absorption and re-radiation by metal fittings, wire stays, etc. If these 'aerials' happen to be of a length that is harmonically supportive to the unwanted signal, then the level will increase.

The basic methods employed to reduce interference to an 'acceptable' level are electrical bonding, screening and filtering. I stress the word 'acceptable'; it is rarely necessary, if indeed it is possible to suppress completely all unwanted noise. What is necessary is to reduce it to a level, relative to the wanted signal, where it ceases to be a problem.

The British Standards Institution (BSI) has produced marine standard BS 1597. This covers the permissible levels of spurious radiation of a range of frequency from 15 kHz to 300 MHz. In order for equipment to be sold as conforming to this standard, it must have a terminal noise figure no greater than that shown (3.2). If these levels for both terminal noise and radiated field strength are adhered to, satisfactory operation of electronic devices will be obtained under average conditions at sea.

Electrical bonding is employed to establish a

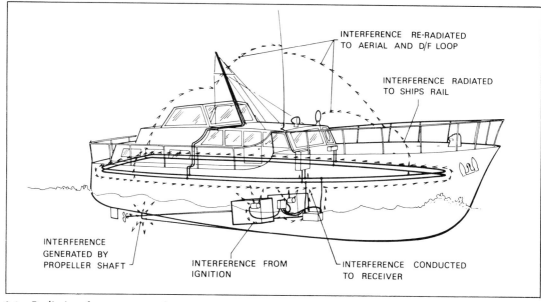

INTERFERENCE RE-RADIATED
TO AERIAL AND D/F LOOP

INTERFERENCE RADIATED
TO SHIPS RAIL

INTERFERENCE
GENERATED BY
PROPELLER SHAFT

INTERFERENCE FROM
IGNITION

INTERFERENCE CONDUCTED
TO RECEIVER

3.1   *Radio interference propagation*

common potential for all the metal parts of the ship. The bonding system will terminate at roughly its central point with a connection to an earth

3.2   *BS 1597 for RI levels*

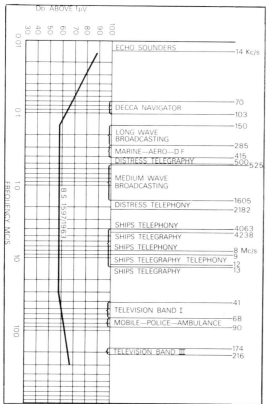

Db ABOVE 1μV

ECHO SOUNDERS — 14 Kc/s

DECCA NAVIGATOR — 70
— 103
— 150
LONG WAVE
BROADCASTING
MARINE—AERO—D F — 285
DISTRESS TELEGRAPHY — 415
— 500 525
MEDIUM WAVE
BROADCASTING
DISTRESS TELEPHONY — 1605
— 2182
SHIPS TELEPHONY — 4063
SHIPS TELEGRAPHY — 4238
SHIPS TELEPHONY — 8 Mc/s
SHIPS TELEGRAPHY   TELEPHONY — 9
— 12
SHIPS TELEGRAPHY — 13
— 41
TELEVISION BAND I
MOBILE—POLICE—AMBULANCE — 68
— 90
TELEVISION BAND III — 174
— 216

FREQUENCY MC/S

B S 1597/1963

plate, which should be positioned as far away as possible from propellers and other underwater fittings. It may also be incorporated within the corrosion protection system (chapter 1). Bonding consists in the main of connecting all metallic objects within the boat's structure with a low-impedance strap, which may be preferably copper strip or a braid of equivalent cross sectional area. This bonding will not be necessary when an aluminium or steel hull is encountered, although even in these cases care must be taken to ensure that each piece of machinery or equipment is grounded, and not partly insulated by wooden pads or paint, particularly when it is supported on anti-vibration mounts which may be electrically insulating as well.

Filtering makes use of capacitors and inductors to produce low or high impedance paths for interference energy. Some filters also make use of a contra- inductive effect which cancels interference; 3.3 shows a selection of general purpose components manufactured by CAV for marine use, to BS 1597. As filters have been known to develop electrical faults, in order to protect the boat's electrical equipment the filter unit will often have its own fuse.

Screening is simply a metallic box around the offending part, for example, the regulator shown 3.3. It is important to remember that if you bring leads through this screening barrier they will act as

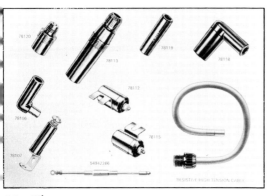

3.3 Filters

aerials both inside and outside the box and thus defeat the object of the box. The answer, if you have to bring a lead through a screen, is to filter the lead where it comes through. The feedthrough filters can be clearly seen on the bottom left of the box (3.4).

More often than not a combination of all three methods is necessary. Some types of interference are obvious and need no tracing; others can be more obscure. Tracking the offending noise can sometimes be achieved by using a portable radio as a means of measuring audibly the improvement or otherwise. For any particular vessel, the degree of RI suppression must be an economical compromise, since both the offending parts and those that are affected are part of the boat's installation. Particular attention should be paid to reducing interference in the regions of 500 and 2182 kHz and 200–400 kHz. The first two frequencies are the international distress frequencies and the last is the band in which most RDF beacons operate. When using RDF, a manual RF gain control is used, which is necessary to achieve a 'clean' null which otherwise would be made very wide by the action of the automatic gain control (AGC). This means that interference will not be reduced by AGC action.

The interference problem is very extensive in small craft and the only way to achieve good results is to go through everything in turn, including many non-electrical items, and make sure it conforms to a basic minimum standard. This is more involved than it at first appears, as unlikely objects are capable of causing severe problems. For instance, I encountered a situation where a luxury yacht had been fitted with stainless steel shafts, bronze

screws and aluminium A- brackets. This potent combination caused enormous interference: one can imagine the owner's chagrin when told of the cost for curing that part of his radio interference troubles. It proved fortuitous for me that the boat was on the slipway. My attention was drawn by the severe corrosion of the stern gear, and with the aid of a penknife I was able to establish the underlying cause of the trouble. An hour or so later and I would have been baffled, as with the ship afloat I would defy anybody to diagnose such a source by listening to the noise on the radio. Sometimes this sort of noise does not come up really strongly until at sea, hence owners' complaints of 'Well it sounds all right when you're here, but when I go to sea it's awful.' Other highly elusive noises that come up when at sea can be caused by oil films in gearboxes and oil pumps; even water pumps have been known to give problems in this respect. These noises, in the case of gearboxes and oil pumps, are caused by static charges building up by friction when the gear wheel is running and becomes insulated by a film of oil. The charge reaches a level eventually where it is able to break down the oil film and in doing

3.4 Screening box

so the discharge radiates RF energy. This can be picked up by sensitive equipment such as echosounders, logs, radio receivers, etc. The cure for these troubles varies from boat to boat, but can in general be alleviated if not always completely cured by either bonding the gearbox or pumps or fitting a mechanical brush which will short out the offending charge before it builds up.

Another point comes to mind while discussing the more elusive sources; suspect everything, even if it is not metal. For example an asbestos rope lining between a deckhead and cabin heater flue gave rise to problems, and when removed, after much head scratching I found that the galvanised flue was reacting with the highly alkaline asbestos. Replacement of the rope lining cleared the problem. I used refractory standoffs to hold the flue clear of the deck head.

I mentioned above the problem of stern gear where dissimilar metals are involved. It sometimes happens that, even with well designed stern gear using the proper materials, interference arises, and this can usually be cleared by a mechanical brush running on the shaft just clear of where it enters the inside of the hull, i.e. at the gland. This should of course be connected to the stern tube.

Interference from an electric motor normally decreases after a few running hours, during which time brushes bed down. The level will of course increase again when the brush and commutator wear and the brush is sufficiently worn to need replacement.

The main causes of interference are created by changes in local electromagnetic fields due to sharply varying currents in a conductor, or sharply varying contact resistance within structures subject to an electrical field. In the first group such things as motors, starters, switches, contactors, bells, rectifiers, tachometers, etc. are likely trouble sources. In the second group the sources are generally confined to loose rails or wire stanchions, anchor and chains, shrouds and other rigging.

Practical precautions should be taken during the construction of the boat to ensure that equipment siting is optimised, and the wiring layout is good. Radiation and induction from wiring is greatly increased when the conductors are allowed to form partially closed loops or when the line and return runs are widely separated. It will be clear that any advantage gained by good siting can be quickly lost by poor indiscriminate wiring. As a guide, the following rules should be applied:

All shrouds, stays and wire rigging must be either bonded to earth, or isolated by strain insulators at each end and the length broken up by insulators at intervals of not more than 5 to 6 metres (15–20 ft).

The use of insulators is recommended as being less subject to troubles than bonding, and in general giving more reliable results.

Pay particular attention to breaking up possible loops in the rigging with insulators or lengths such as triatic stays. This especially applies close to the direction finder aerial.

Where main shrouds have to carry very large stresses it is advisable to connect these to the ship's bonding system rather than use strain insulators.

Avoid the use of wire running rigging.

Rigging can be earthed in fibreglass sailing vessels by connection to the underside of the rigging eyes where they penetrate the hull.

Interference has sometimes arisen due to intermittent electrical contact between rigging, shrouds, chains, rails, etc. where this is close to the radio equipment. Paint or corrosion has partially destroyed the original continuity, which at sea is intermittently made and broken. To clear these problems two possibilities are apparent: connect a bonding wire over the loose point or shackle; insulate the rigging or shackle to isolate it from the earthed fitting.

Insofar as the wiring can bring about an increase in the level of noise, the following notes should be taken into account.

All permanent wiring within 8 metres of any receiving aerial or DF loop should be screened. This may be achieved either by cables with a braided screen and PVC covering, or conduit; also where a metal deck or bulkhead provides suitable shielding.

Flexible cables used to terminate a movable appliance should be screened wherever possible.

Make the wiring for the radio or DF in a completely separate run, keeping clear of radar and autopilot wiring.

Use of a PVC cable trunking will greatly facilitate alteration and addition to the wiring, and at the same time it closely defines the main run of the wiring along the boat.

Screening Cables

Sometimes when wiring is bunched together, the conductors carrying the electrical noise radiate this to the adjacent cables. When this is proved to be the case by connecting temporary leads, it is possible to overcome the problem by screening rather than re- routing the offending lead. One reasonably straightforward way of doing this is to obtain a suitable length of soft copper tube (fuel line type) and slip it over the cable by disconnecting one end; earthing the copper tube completes the job.

Screened cable alone is sometimes unable to provide enough attenuation and in these circumstances it may be necessary to run the screened cable in a metal conduit.

One final note on cables: metallic conduits or cable sheaths should be bonded to any adjacent cable sheaths or conduit, only if experiment proves that this will reduce the noise. Keep all bonding points accessible. Conduit or cable cleats should be a close fit to prevent movement and should be earthed close to the point they are connected to the supply. The metalwork of the appliance should also be earthed, although a series capacitor of 1 μF should be used if the boat's electrical system will thus be earthed.

Having effected as many precautions as are applicable, we are left with a situation which is controllable. Any noise-producing apparatus now introduced may have various noise-reducing measures applied to it and they will be able to operate with maximum effect. One principal method of reducing noise levels is to provide short non-radiating paths for the noise currents by means of capacitors. Another is by the insertion of an inductor or resistor designed to have a high impedance at radio frequencies. Sometimes a combination of the two methods is employed.

The type of equipment and the installation conditions will determine the extent to which the above methods need to be employed. The level of interference created by any particular piece of equipment can only be established after installation. Before committing oneself to a particular equipment, it will pay big dividends to ask for a written definition of the interference suppression measures employed. Any company of repute will have this data available.

During installation it is important to make all bonding joints absolutely sound and to paint them afterwards to reduce corrosion. Where a particular piece of equipment cannot be directly connected to the bonding system, at least two bonding strips should be employed to reduce a possible concentration of earth currents. Screening of units can be used in extreme cases, but in general will not be needed for metal cased equipment.

Capacitors are the most economical form of suppressor and should be of a type that has a very low self-inductance and a very low impedance at the frequency at which trouble is experienced. The CAV components shown (3.3) are to BS 1597, which ensures this. Connecting leads to capacitors should of course be kept as short as possible.

The use of inductors in heavy current circuits is to be avoided wherever possible, as their bulk and cost can become excessive. One particular type that has excellent effects is the toroidal winding with each winding connected in opposition. The point with this type is that the DC component is cancelled by the opposing winding in much the same way as the symmetrical noise elements. Its inductance is therefore maximised.

It is sometimes necessary to enclose suppressors in screening cans in order to achieve maximum effect. Where this is the case, connect the screened enclosure directly to the offending equipment if possible, and employ screened connecting links.

In practical terms I would say that if the basic electrical system in the boat has been well laid out along the lines proposed, and in general accordance with IEE regulations for marine practice, the interference problems will not be difficult to overcome, although some refitting may be necessary. Practical networks and suggestions for a number of equipments are detailed in the following pages.

Ignition Systems on Petrol Engines

Ignition interference is affected considerably by the system layout. In general, the longer the ignition leads, the worse the interference. A reduction of interference is sometimes made possible by mounting the coil on the engine, thus making the lead to the distributor as short as possible. Mounting the coil on bulkhead or under the instrument console is a bad practice, as this produces conditions which allow RF currents to circulate from a wide area. Stray induction can be minimised by keeping the HT and LT leads as far apart as possible. Conductivity of the earth system is also of vital importance.

Sparking associated with internal combustion engines occurs at the distributor and plugs. At each discharge there is a rapid rise and fall of current it is in fact a damped oscillation, unless the circuit resistance is high enough to prevent this. In order to achieve this damped condition resistive type suppressors are introduced. A flame discharge also occurs, which gives rise to a current fluctuation that may be sustained in one form or another for as long as 1 mSec. Part of this energy is radiated and gives rise to an audible click at every discharge; at high speeds these clicks merge to a continuous buzz. The low tension side of the distributor (the contact breaker) may give rise to problems occasionally, although they are normally restricted to cases where the aerial is in close proximity or where extensive wiring radiates this energy.

The energy field from spark ignition systems reaches its highest values in the region of 30–50 MHz and in general frequencies above 10 MHz will be more adversely affected. It should, however, be understood that the extent of any particular interference will not necessarily be limited to equipment operating on similar bands, but that where radiated levels are high enough the circuits of the receiving apparatus will be shock-excited to respond at their own resonant frequencies.

Suitable spacing between source and receiver will often help in reduction of noise level. Some variation will also be caused by the signal polarization (or orientation) and local reflection. In practical boating terms, as far as the ignition

systems of petrol engines are concerned, the only method that will reduce the level of interference substantially is screening. Due to the capacity of the screened components the spark voltage is reduced in amplitude when standard components are used; however, the current when discharge takes place is increased and this tends to pit the points of the plugs so reducing their life. If you have serious problems with ignition interference and the standard remedies of plug and distribution suppressor resistors (3.3) will not acceptably reduce the level, I suggest you write to the engine manufacturer or the ignition system or sparking plug makers, who may have information relevant to your particular power unit. Many light aircraft have small screened magnetos by Lucas to get over the radio interference problem, in fact two on each engine, and although the cure may prove expensive it is certainly possible, if the condition is investigated thoroughly.

Suppression of Generating Equipment

Most small craft now have diesel engines and the biggest problem obviously comes from the main engine generating equipment, which is often running continuously. Some engines will have conventional dynamos with vibrating reed regulators. These machines are generally quite straightforward when in good condition and will respond well to suppression. Check the commutator and brush condition and see that the machine and its electrical terminals are clean. If it should happen to have one output terminal grounded to its case, take the dynamo off and have it converted to insulated return. Reconnect and run the engine, and observe the interference: the dynamo will make a 'fine' background hash which will increase in intensity with engine speed. When the regulator cuts in it makes a pronounced splutter that will increase in repetition rate with engine speed. The two sounds are quite different, and even if you have never heard them on a radio before, you will be able to identify them. The dynamo itself can be suppressed quite satisfactorily by connecting a $1\,\mu\text{F}$ capacitor from each of its output terminals to ground; a third capacitor is connected between positive and negative. The capacitor case is the ground connection and is usually fastened to a bracket on the end plate of the dynamo. The leads to these components must be kept short. The dynamo field connection should not have a capacitor fitted as this will upset the regulator action. The field and output leads from the machine are then carried via conduit or screened cable to the regulator (3.5). The cable should be properly supported on a suitable batten, and a bonding strip run parallel (3.6).

If your existing regulator is an unfiltered, non-screened type, CAV manufacture a screening box that can be used to enclose it (3.7). This box has all the necessary filtered feedthroughs. If for any reason production units will not suit your needs, special components are available to manufacture a box to your requirements. ITT Electronics, South Denes Rd, Great Yarmouth, Norfolk produce a range of RI filters that would considerably simplify construction. I stress that to make up an effective screened enclosure is much more involved for the layman than it may at first appear. It is highly likely that only a partial cure will be effected as internal layout and screening is usually required, and the average boat owner does not have the specialised knowledge and facilities.

Alternator suppression

Alternators have proved more difficult to suppress with standard components than conventional dynamos, as the rectifier diodes produce a considerable level of harmonic energy which breaks through into most electronic equipment. The only satisfactory remedy is to fit the machine with a special screening cowl and place the regulator within a suitable enclosure containing filters and a surge limiter. The CAV unit shown with the lid removed in (3.4) is the only proprietary device available at the moment in the UK. Wiring diagrams for single and parallel operation are shown in (3.8). I have fitted several of these units and find no difficulty in achieving a quiet installation. Before these units became available a very considerable time had to be spent on each installation, making special filter units on a one-off basis and always at breakneck speed as the boat was often at the handing over stage before anyone had realised that the problem existed. My advice is to buy an alternator and its associated regulator that meets the radio interference requirements of

3.5   *Screened lead and feed-through*

3.6   *Screened cable and bonding strip*

3.7   *Screening box for regulator*

BS 1597. This is not cheap, but I have found it effective.

Suppresion at Source

Often a piece of electronic equipment can cause interference which will affect some other instrument—for example the echosounder may produce clicking noises on the radio receiver. Reference to the maker of the offending equipment may produce some assistance which will help, but as each installation has its own peculiarities, very likely you will have to employ a specialist or have a go yourself. When you have isolated the offending equipment, whatever it is, use the step by step diagram as a guide; the terminals are the supply terminals to the noisy equipment (3.9).

Before doing too much work, it is as well to check that its case is earthed and that all basic precautions (see above) have been taken. Given that everything is installed correctly, the sequence for suppressing noise (3.9) is:

A Disconnect boat's supply from the equipment and run locally on a small temporary battery with short leads. If interference is reduced, supply line filters will help.

B Is equipment metal cased—if so, is it bonded to ground?

C Connect a 1 μF capacitor between the terminals.

D Connect a 1 μF capacitor from each terminal to ground.

E Insert chokes in series with the supply.

F Completely screen the equipment and use feedthrough filters.

G If screening alone will suffice, try lining the case with cooking foil, which should be connected to earth.

H Run the equipment mechanically free of its mountings and see if a change in orientation or siting helps. Refit if necessary.

The chokes (E) should be of the double wound type; suitable units can be fabricated as shown (3.10). The wire gauge depends on the current drawn by the equipment to be suppressed and the sizes given below will cover most small craft loads. The wire should be Lewmex insulated copper and wound with 20 turns parallel on a $\frac{3}{8}$ in. (10 mm)

3.8   *Alternator suppression circuits*

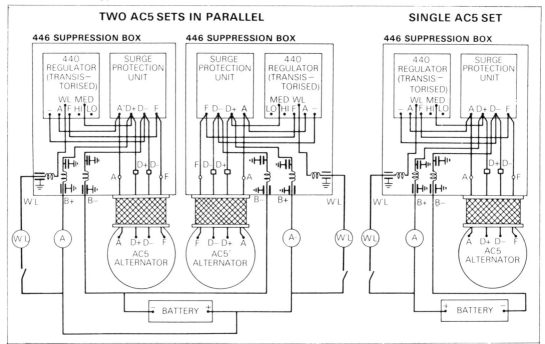

Current	Wire gauge	Ferrite rod length	
A	SWG	in.	mm
1	23	1.5	40
2	20	2	50
5	17	3	75
10	14	4	100
15	12	5	130
20	11	6	150
25	10	6	150

Compatibility

It is by no means unusual to find several major pieces of equipment in quite a small wheelhouse, and mutual interference frequently results. Radar often produces interference due to the high energy pulses, with very fast rise and fall times inherent in the circuitry. It is not just a question of making sure that energy is not radiated; the radar equipment must also be prevented from picking up excessive amounts of radiation from radiotelephones and other transmitters on board.

Various government specifications exist which shed light on the problem. The European Standards concentrate particularly on terminal noise (the measurable interference voltage which appears on the power lines at the radar terminals), and compliance is compulsory. The American FCC specification concentrates mainly on the absence of measurable radiated noise, and again compliance is compulsory. In the UK, compulsory regulations cover both radiated noise and terminal noise, but only refer to vessels of over 300 tons; however, limits indicated in BS 1597, in association with the code of practice B5, are effective guidelines for industry.

Siting to minimise Radio Interference
When fitting the scanner unit, it is important to keep it and the associated cables as far as possible from the radiotelephone aerials and any power lines. It may be necessary to refit some parts of the aerial installation to achieve something like 2 metres (6 ft) spacing. The mutual coupling transfer of power from one circuit to another falls off in proportion to the inverse square of the spacing, so clearly this can make a great deal of difference to the level of interference. The likelihood of interference on the radar from the vessel's radio transmitter will also be minimised.

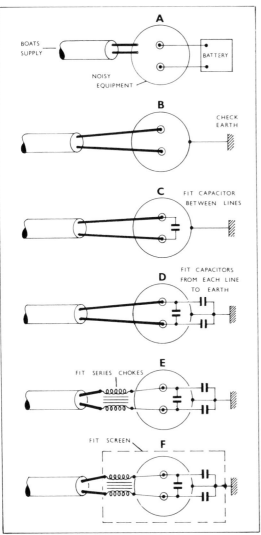

3.9   *Suppression at source*

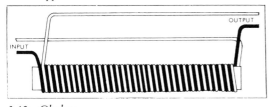

3.10   *Chokes*

ferrite rod of the type used for portable radio aerials. These can be obtained inexpensively from any radio service shop. They can be cut by nicking with a file and breaking over a sharp edge. The whole assembly can be finished by slipping it into a piece of polythene sleeving and dipping it in synthetic varnish.

Direction Finders

It is important to apply the same rules on spacing to the direction finder loop aerial and its downleads. When checking for interference, don't forget to rotate the loop or goniometer, as the DF aerial is just as directive to interference as it is to a radio beacon.

The effect of the radar installation on the direction finder calibration must also be considered. The radome itself will not usually cause significant errors, but gantries or other supports might. Any metalwork at or above the height of the loop will begin to affect it at distances of about 2-3 metres (7-8 feet), particularly with VHF direction finders.

Effects of Interference

Radar interference on the radiotelephone, on both MF and VHF, will usually appear as a high-pitched whine corresponding to the pulse repetition frequency of the radar. Radiotelephones rarely interfere with the radar, but the effect is for bright radial lines to appear, particularly at the instant the 'Press to talk' switch is made, and also at modulation peaks, for example when whistling into the microphone. Radar interference on echosounders has an effect which varies depending on the readout system used by the echosounder in question. The paper recorder type produces a herringbone pattern; the flashing light type produces a fine series of flashes which can rotate clockwise or anti-clockwise; meter or digital types will generally read zero.

Where an echosounder is showing interference, a similar approach is required, disconnecting and re-routing the supply and transducer leads in turn. Sometimes it is advantageous to borrow a transducer of similar type, so that the best cable position and transducer site can be found. Some installations will become very time absorbing.

With any make of equipment, no matter how carefully it is made, or indeed no matter how tight the radio interference specification which it passed, there will be some particular installation which enhances radiation from one equipment to another. If you examine the manufacturer's installation data, various requirements are specified which have been found to give satisfactory results in a test installation, and it is essential to carry out this work. These recommendations, however, assume that the vessel already has a sound electrical system and, if this is not so, you could wind up with a certain amount of interference until it is brought up to standard.

Make sure that any curative measures which you adopt will not earth (ground) either pole of the electrical system. If there is any likelihood of this, mount the equipment on insulating pads and connect to earth via a 1 µF paper dielectric capacitor which has no leakage or polarity problems, so you will avoid increasing the level of electrolysis in the course of reducing interference.

It is often a good plan to connect new equipment with temporary leads to get the siting right, then fix a temporary earth to establish what is required; when all is satisfactory, the wiring can be permanently installed with a minimum of pulling about.

Earthing

Particularly in fibreglass boats, makeshift earth planes can be created by spreading cooking foil of the aluminium type inside the hull below the water line. If a permanent earth of this type is required, it is better to use thin copper sheet, or foil covered with a thin layer of fibreglass, as aluminium will quickly corrode. The foil can be terminated by bringing one edge 50mm (2 in) up a bulkhead and passing a bolt through it. Although such an earth is in theory insulated from the water by the hull, the distributed capacity between the foil and the water is large and it is an effective earth.

Even after choosing the site, earth point and cable disposition carefully, you may still have a problem. If a radio receiver is affected, try resiting a makeshift aerial or screening the download. If the interference is just as strong with the aerial removed, connect the offending equipment to a portable battery with short leads, so that it is completely isolated from the boat's supply. If the interference is reduced, it is probably being conducted via the boat's wiring, and external filtering may be necessary, in which case you can proceed as in (3.9) and (3.10) or ask the equipment manufacturer to recommend a suitable filter.

Noise and Vibration

Excessive or unnecessary noise is distressing to

most people; certainly it impairs personal efficiency I recall fitting a 2 MHz radiotelephone some years ago for a professional client. After a few weeks, I heard from him to the effect that he had been unable to use the equipment due to unbearable radio interference. I arranged for a trip at sea with him and, as we set off, the throttles were opened and as RPM increased just about everything in the boat went through its own resonance; at normal cruising speed the level of noise was considerable. When it came to making a link call, the poor man was so stressed that he could not concentrate his thought sufficiently to speak. Clearly, someone used to working in a quiet environment would be at some disadvantage with unfamiliar functions to carry out. The boat in question was from a reputable builder but it dated from a period when one expected to be drowned by engine noise. In a practical sense the description 'interference' was correct and, as small craft must intimately mix people and machinery, suppression of acoustical noise and vibration has a similar importance to that of suppressing electrical noise. In recent years there has been a greater awareness of the effects of noise and a closer study made of methods of reduction, including the development of suitable noise and vibration level meters.

Vibration and its effect

This term embraces all those manifestations of stray mechanical energy which can cover a frequency range from less than one cycle per second, the beat frequency between two engines for example, to ultrasonic frequencies such as wind noise.

Apart from considerations of physical comfort, which is in itself quite important from the fatigue aspect, actual structural damage can occur. It is by no means uncommon, for example, to encounter an hydraulic pipe between two points of high mechanical activity; sooner or later a crack will appear at a high stress point, and under hydraulic pressure of about 1000 psi a spectacular rupture takes place. In my case, for some obscure reason, this has always seemed to happen a few minutes before the ship was supposed to leave port, and repairs were therefore panic-stricken measures involving replacement of pipework in an area which had just been sprayed with hydraulic oil—it gets into everything including self!

Often vibration will cause unexpected movement of some parts of the boat's gear and, when examining such problems, one should not forget the effect that gravity will have on any component subject to vibration. For instance, a valve with a simple lever handle will always be biased toward the handle-down position; where larger components such as cooking gas cylinders are installed, it will be found that the regulator and hose have the same effect without suitable restraining clamps; under the influence of vibration, the cylinder can be lifted clear of its stowage by the odd fraction of a millimetre, and gravity will rotate it so that any assymetrical weight is downwards. On the subject of butane gas installations, two obvious hazards are often overlooked. The first is that the half metre or so of solid pipe left for connection at the cylinder end of the installation is a prime candidate for failure due to fatigue, and should obviously be clipped down right to the union, which should also have a mounting flange. The second point is that gas taps should have a circular handle with a symmetrical weight distribution, so that vibration is less likely to rotate the valve.

Suppression

Noise and vibration can be likened to electrical interference in many ways, although it is stray mechanical energy rather than electrical energy. It travels by the conduction or radiation of mechanical pressure waves, and the best place to suppress it is at the source.

Mechanical suppressors are again analogous to their electrical counterparts; they are (a) a high mechanical impedance in series with the source, which is equivalent to the radio suppressor choke, and (b) a low decoupling impedance in parallel with the source which is equivalent to the radio suppressor capacitor. Preferably, these impedances are applied at the source but they may also be sited at the point where the undesirable noise is experienced. Careful attention in the design of the offending part can do much to reduce the problem.

Vibration in Rigging

On sailing boats the rigging and spars can produce considerable amounts of vibratory energy under the influence of the wind. This often gives rise to those seemingly unaccountable failures of the masthead light, the cure for which is to move the position of the light up or down an arms length, in the hope of moving from a vibration maximum (antinode) to a minimum (node).

Consider for a moment the use of rod rigging fabricated from solid bar—a popular extra in recent years. Energy will be imparted to the rod by the wind, some of which will excite various waves within the rod, and a standing wave pattern will be established in exactly the same way as a string on a musical instrument behaves. Along the rod, regular areas of high and low amplitude will appear. The energy is dissipated mainly by pressure waves radiated in the air and by causing other cyclic movement of the points the stay is attached to; both means of dissipation create noise. Any mechanical structure is tunable mechanically as a moments thought on how conventional musical instruments work will underline. Mechanical losses are also present in all mechanical contrivances which of course includes rigging. Put as simply as possible, in any vibrating component, the ratio of the losses (mechanical resistance) to the springiness (mechanical reactance) will determine the amplitude of the vibration at resonance. It therefore follows that we would look for the effects of vibration more closely in solid rod rigging than in more 'lossy' multi-stranded rigging wire.

It will be as well to clear our minds on what 'resonance' is. Any mechanical structure will resonate at several frequencies, and in practice these states can be observed quite easily; if a series of pressure waves is made to impinge on a particular mechanical component, and the frequency of the waves is made to sweep from zero Hz up to say 100 kHz, at certain specific frequencies the weight, size and shape of the components will be in sympathy with the applied wave, to such an extent that the component will vibrate in coincidence with the exciting wave; the first frequency above zero where this occurs is called the fundamental resonance.

Above this frequency other resonances will be found, some more pronounced than others, which are called harmonic resonances. If we consider for one moment a vibrating component of a rectangular form, it will have resonances sympathetic with its width, length and thickness. As an exmple, a shroud would have a fundamental resonance of a few Hz at most, although it would probably oscillate on at least two

harmonics due to the presence of spreaders.

Effect of Resonance

Under conditions of resonance, quite small amounts of energy can produce substantial amplitudes of cyclic deflection. So far we have established that, due to its length, it can excite in a great number of ways, and that it will not need much energy to excite considerable deflection at the resonant frequencies.

The design protection open to us in this situation is that we could discover the natural resonances of the stay, it would thus be possible to position spreaders or provide absorbers to reject dominant resonances. In modern boats many parts of the structure are exposed to the elements, which makes them susceptible to vibration, for example alloy booms, spinnaker poles, masts, etc; below deck, engine control bars and propellor shafts come to mind. Some of these components are of light alloy construction (such as magnesium or aluminium alloys) which coincidentally are excellent conductors of noise. It has long been understood that bar section stays can be subject to metal fatigue and failure; also that this dangerous condition is most difficult to detect by visual inspection. Modern X-ray techniques can be used to advantage for examining such high-stress fabrications; indeed it is surprising that such inspection is not carried out more often, as considerable experience is at hand in the petrochemical industry. Particularly among the racing fraternity, mechanical failures are by no means uncommon.

Vibration in Sheet Materials

Apart from the manifestation of vibration in solid sections discussed so far, a common effect of surface waves can be seen on sheet materials, such as fuel and water tanks and, on fibreglass hulls, between bulkheads. These are important from the unit life aspect; for example, badly welded tank seams can be cracked by vibration, whilst stress is a known factor in reducing the life of fibreglass laminates, and thus resonances in the hull assume importance.

For reduction of noise and vibration there are tools to assist. The stroboscope is a good example of a practical boatyard tool: if used outside it is

Stroboscopes sample the position of a vibrating object, and allow its movements to be viewed by presenting the samples at a rate below the point where continuity masks the problem.

The strobe lamp is used simply by pointing it at the area to be examined. The frequency of the strobe is then swept, increasing very slowly from zero and, as coincidence between the vibrating object and the strobe is approached, a slow beat frequency appears which makes the objects appear to vibrate in slow motion. I think that an appreciation of the possible damage can be made instantly when using this test, as objects that one has been absolutely certain are solidly fixed, can be seen flapping about in an incredible way.

Much more data could be supplied by the manufacturers of major noise sources, such as engines. Attention to defining the nodal points and making sure that any mechanical connections—mountings, shafts, exhaust pipe, water connections, controls, linkages—emanate from such points would do much to reduce the problem. A published noise analysis for each type of engine would also facilitate more effective design for engine compartment insulation.

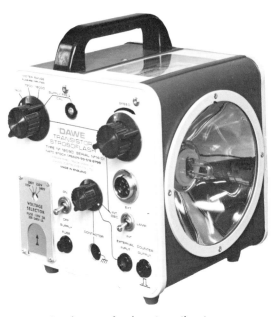

3.11   Stroboscope for detecting vibration

best to work at dusk, so that the reflected light can be seen to best effect. (3.11)

Even when the amplitude is large, vibrating objects appear to be perfectly still, due to the continuity of vision of the human eye.

3.12   Anti-vibration mountings

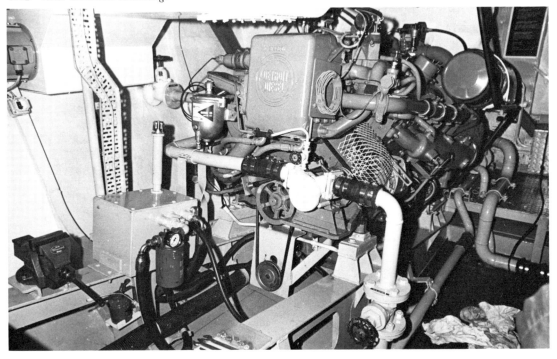

3.13   Shaft and coupling

Anti-vibration Mountings

This type of unit is available in a variety of design, and it should be carefully selected to suit the particular application; see example shown (3.12). The principle of these mounts is diametrically opposite to accepted practice for engine mountings, in that the engine has freedom of movement relative to the vessel. A means of limiting the ultimate movement is necessary and is sometimes included within the anti- vibration (A/V) mount unit. When mounted like this, the engine's vibratory power will be decoupled from the hull, and therefore its *apparent* deflection amplitude will increase; at some stage you may have heard someone say 'Oh, we fitted A/V mounts, but the engine vibrated more than before'. Well, so it should; it's an encouraging sign, meaning that power which was being used to shake the boat is now being restricted to the engine to a greater extent.

Now that we have an engine flexibly mounted, it will be obvious that the mounting is capable of producing its own resonance. If we are not careful, in fact, the mountings could resonate at the engine rotational frequency or at one of its harmonics, which is the part of the energy spectrum where the

highest levels are attained. Close consultation is therefore required between manufacturers of the engine and anti-vibration mounts. The lowest frequencies are the hardest to suppress and, in general terms, the isolation is zero at a frequency 1·4 times the resonant frequency of the mounting. As frequency increases above this point, isolation also increases, the higher frequencies being reduced in power by a factor of about one hundred. Obviously the engine bearers in the hull affect the situation; from the vibration point of view, the best place to mount the engine is where its bearers can be rigidly fastened on the keel, because this provides a high-mass energy sink of great value. Fitting anti-vibration mounts under the engine is of course only part of the problem; the shaft must be coupled using a resilient coupling such as the unit shown in (3.13), are suitable arrangements made for the propeller thrust to be taken in the stern tube. Flexible couplings must also be fitted to the fuel, exhaust (3.14), and water connections, and also to any hydraulic pipes for stabilisers, autopilot, steering or winch pumps; the engine controls (throttle and gearbox) must also be isolated.

3.14   Flexible coupling for exhaust

Noise Suppression

Much akin to the suppression of vibration is the suppression of noise. However, in this respect, the stray energy which assaults our ears is being launched as pressure waves through the air from various devices such as engines, etc. Wherever the noise originates, it will be made worse by anything solidly connected to it, as this will help to radiate the acoustic energy. Successful noise reduction is often complex as it involves many structural and operational necessities, such as an adequate means of aspiration for the engines. Undoubtedly the first consideration is to establish the path the noise is taking into the required quiet area.

It will obviously not be advantageous to spend a lot of time and money insulating the engine room, where the biggest part of the noise is originating via some part of the structure, via ventilators or exhausts.

Unless quantitive measurements are taken, using a sound level meter, the improvement or otherwise of any work done will be impossible to assess. It is important to use only meters with a dB-A scale factor, as this type has an intensity/frequency curve comparable to the human ear. This is clearly important, for you could spend a lot of time reducing noise that cannot be heard. By temporary fixing of insulation material over discrete areas around the noise source, the improvement can be measured. These measurements are quite good enough for practical boatyard work.

Noise control enclosures are available from some manufacturers for specific equipments, for example (2.8) shows a GM auxilliary fitted with such an enclosure. As the work involved is often extensive, I suggest that where possible noise control be embodied in the original design, as retrospective fitting is even more expensive and rarely as effective.

Part II

Introduction

Small boats are complex products in a hostile environment. Even when everything within the structure is as it should be, the vessel still has to be navigated accurately.

Consider for a moment the period from daylight to darkness: *above deck* equipment is subject to a reduction in temperature, say, of 15°; then at some point the pilot will turn on the boat's heater, and the equipment *inside the boat* will become subject to an increase of, say, 10°. Now, equipment like radar, which is half in and half out, is thus being heated at one end and cooled at the other. The story continues; as darkness descends, various lights are used; the heating equipment will make some noise or vibration; the extra current drain will change the demand on the alternator and affect the regulators; higher currents alter the magnetic field associated with the wiring; and so on, ad infinitum. The crackles and bangs on the boat's radio equipment used to be called 'radio interference'; now that we have so much more equipment to interact mutually, it rejoices under a new name: 'electromagnetic compatibility'. Our boating gear needs to be more than compatible in an electromagnetic sense; it must also be compatible with all the other physical properties of the hull, environment and other equipment— probably the ultimate compatibility is the financial one. Microelectronics has brought better value for money but, outside this, labour intensive installation and service costs continually rise and must be considered part of the price tag. The way round this problem is to purchase equipment that is designed to be returned by the owner periodically for servicing, such as the Autohelm automatic pilot or the Aptel direction finder; even the latest radars are designed so that the owner can remove the units for dealer service.

Display of Information

Before going on to discuss specific equipments, most of which will be used to produce information for the navigator, it is useful to consider factors that influence the display. For example you could easily spend a lot of money on an impressive looking digital display, only to find that a simple scale is easier to read and divides the price tag by two. I do not imply that digital displays are in any way undesirable, I simply stress that it is better to consider each function, and to select a display to suit it. Apart from general purpose displays it is rarely a matter of choice, as such things as radar and sonar have specialised presentations.

For most equipments, the choice is made at the date of purchase, and if you get it wrong at that stage you are stuck with it. There are two types of digital display each with its own characteristics, so with this in mind let us think about the properties of three types: moving coil meters, light emitting diode digital display, liquid crystal digital display.

Moving coil meters

An excellent level of development has been reached which is easy to read in all light levels, the construction and principle of operation is well known and simple, and it does not create radio interference; the current consumption is generally low, typically 100 μA. The reliability is excellent, but the cost is always rising as meters are assembled by hand. For some applications the meter will hold its place indefinitely, indeed as a left-right indicator it is hard to think of anything better.

Light emitting diode displays

The semiconductor age has brought us light emitting diodes (LED), which can be formed into various shaped displays. The most common type is fabricated from small chips of gallium arsenide phosphide, which emit light when a current is passed through them. These dots are covered by a plastic lens and formed into such shapes as the application demands; a typical standard function being the seven segment numeral indicator. This is now used extensively in electronic equipment, however, it consumes much more current than a moving coil meter, typically 100 mA per numeral.

The electronic drive circuitry may produce harmonically rich radiation from the fast-switching elements controlling the display; this often gives rise to radio interference. The packaged unit is however hermetically sealed and, when used properly, is very reliable.

Liquid crystal displays

This type has the advantage that the current consumption is low, and in this respect it compares favourably with the moving coil meter. Solar powered wrist watches use this principle, which exploits the ability of some substances to change their refractive index when subjected to an electrical charge. A typical display is produced by enclosing a liquid crystal substance between two glass plates, on which electrodes have been etched to correspond in shape with the character required. Leads from the electrodes are brought through the hermetic seal which encloses the device for connection to the drive circuitry, in much the same way as for LED displays. The device does not generate light within itself as do other types of display, but depends on producing a well defined and controllable difference in the transmitting ability of the crystal within the area of the character to be displayed, making use of reflected ambient light. For night use a small internal light source is provided. Radio interference is still possible, but is generally at a lower level, as the current required to operate the devices is low.

Selecting the Display

It is helpful to consider these various displays in relation to the functions they might fulfil in a marine situation. When steering by hand with a conventional compass, one takes a point to hold and generally the eyes assimilate the rate at which the card is turning and not the absolute number of degrees by which it has turned. I believe that it is easier to follow a rotating card for this application than a continuously changing static three digit display. Imagine a drift to port, instinctively one makes a correction in the right sense with a card or pointer. In the same situation a digital display would successively indicate, for example, 333—332—331—330—329 and so on; I would then have to think about a number. This illustration holds good for all the circle-based aids to navigation that a small boat carries.

Now take a completely different function—the frequency of the radiotelephone receiver or transmitter, for example; what better indication could you have than a clear digital display? There are equipments where both displays can be used to advantage, such as the automatic direction finder, indicating frequency by digits and bearing by a rotating scale. With echosounders a digital indication would seem to be the best general purpose display, but in this application it proves unsuitable, because the physical nature of echosounding demands a display that will allow more than one response to show without obscuring the bottom echo. Separation of the bottom echo to display as a numeral under all conditions is not economically possible for the small boat market. The log also seems a likely candidate for a digital display of speed. However, if an electronic display of distance is used a momentary loss of power can wipe out the distance run figure. Thus the electro-mechanical counter is by no means obsolete.

The type of vessel will also affect the choice, sailing boats may need equipment that will run from internal batteries, powercraft have no such problems as the extra load of the display system would not need to be considered. The choice comes down to roughly four points.

1. Does the display satisfy the operational requirements?
2. Is it economic—are you paying more to get a less effective display?
3. Does it require an excessive amount of power to operate?
4. Will this produce interference on another equipment?

4   Radio Direction Finders

'What's the good of Mercator's North Poles
*   and Equators,*
Tropics, Zones and Meridian Lines?'
So the Bellman would cry: and the crew
*   would reply*
'They are merely conventional signs!'

The Hunting of the Snark
Lewis Carroll

About 1905 Marconi was experimenting with the directional properties of radio aerials, and with the object of finding the bearing of a transmitting station tests were carried out aboard HMS *Furious* on behalf of the Admiralty. During 1907 Bellini and Tosi began their experiments into achieving some degree of directivity with radio signalling, and subsequently the Marconi Co. secured their patents. By the commencement of the 1914–18 war several direction finding stations were being set up for military purposes. Captain H J Round of the Marconi Co., who was largely responsible for this work, contributed greatly to the advances made in radio direction finding technology during this period.

The direction finding system employed two fixed aerials erected at right angles to each other, Each of these formed a separate tuned circuit and consequently tuning and balancing were a critical part of obtaining good results. Both aerials were connected via a goniometer to a receiver comprising one stage of HF amplification, a balanced carborundum crystal detector, and two stages of LF amplification. The valves were the early 'soft' types.

This was roughly the kind of equipment that was employed for the anti-submarine campaign of the period, and was to reveal the movement of the German fleet that heralded the battle of Jutland. The signals from the German fleet were of the 'buzzer' type on about 200 metres. By taking bearings from the direction finding stations established at Lowestoft, Flamborough and Aberdeen it was found that the communication ship *Bayern* had moved into the Jade River, a difference in bearing of only 1.5°. Just after the

end of the battle, a British convoy was navigated across the North Sea in fog, entirely by radio bearings from the Isle of May station.

Direction finding systems were under continuous development at the time and subsequently aperiodic aerials and 'hard' valves appeared. Mr E J Roberts of Boardley & Roberts Ltd at Ipswich was an operator at the Lowestoft station from about 1916 and has given me some very interesting details, all of which lead me to believe that in over half a century we have not really come as far as is imagined. It is easy to imagine that automatic direction finders are relatively recent innovations; however the goniometer of this early DF was motorised for search purposes and the accuracy was about half a degree. I wonder how many small boats fitted with present day direction finders can get anything like this standard of accuracy? I suspect very few, which is rather disappointing if one considers how selectivity, sensitivity, physical size and price have improved since those early times.

The major difference between the early DF stations and present day systems was that the former were land based. The vessel in need of a radio fix had to contact the DF station by radio-telegraphy and ask for a bearing while sending continuously so that two land-based stations could take cross bearings. It was not long before equipment had improved to the extent that it was possible to install the direction finder on board the ship, so that bearings could be taken of fixed transmitting stations ashore and indeed of any other vessel with transmitting equipment. The photographs show early shipborne direction finding aerials. That on the *Royal George* (4.1) was called a

4.1   Early ship's DF aerial system

'pyramid' and the aerial shown in (4.2) a 'birdcage'. It was these very early and very effective arrays that paved the way for the present generation of small craft loop aerials.

A few years ago it was thought by many that the conventional loop aerial would be replaced completely by a ferrite rod or other similar device. However, new equipments using Bellini-Tosi loop aerials continue to appear on the small craft market in both Europe and the US.

The range of equipment available falls roughly into five groups:

1. Hand held direction finder embodying receiver, aerial and compass all in one unit
2. Fixed receivers with 'portable' or 'hand held' loops with or without compass
3. Fixed Bellini-Tosi loop assembly with DF receiver and goniometer
4. Rotating deckhead loop assembly with DF receiver
5. Automatic direction finders

The first two groups have gained great popularity, which is surprising as the more expensive versions of this equipment cost more than a really first class system in group (3), the results from which would be immeasurably better.

Those portable instruments embodying a compass are so easy to read that their deficiencies are easily overlooked. For instance, there are several makes of 'chart table loop' which embody a 50 mm (2 in.) compass. The recommended method of operation is to place the unit on the chart table and take bearings from the compass to transfer directly to the chart. As this entails moving the

4.2   Early 'birdcage' DF aerial

compass and loop about, the probability of large errors is enormous and correction is impossible. Take into account that in this situation there are present the following effects which, if the unit is moved other than about a fixed pivot, are not calibratable:

Compass error
Quadrantal error
Ferrite to compass induction: although this in general is small it will vary with the position, bearing and characteristics of surrounding objects.

Remember that you may be able to read a signal easily and take a bearing from a first class null, but this has nothing to do with accuracy of results. There is a widely held belief that if you use a hand held DF in the same reasonably clear place every time, the errors are not great. I assume this belief originated with some salesman keener on fixing his commission rather than his customers' positions. The 'same place' is for obvious reasons only achievable if the unit is fastened down and pivots about its fastening: just standing in the same position will not do. If you already have a portable unit, make a pivoted clamp to fasten it to the boat and calibrate its compass and the DF aerial—then consider well the errors you will find and how they would effect the safety of navigation.

Instruments in groups 3, 4, and 5 have the advantage of better defined calibration as follows:

Bearings will be derived by reference to the boat's compass; this is corrected and calibrated so first class data is available. Quadrantal or other errors in the DF system may be calibrated and/or corrected: again first class data.
No aerial to compass interaction is possible, as the aerial is non-magnetic, and a healthy distance from the compass.

A calibrated MF direction finder provides the best value for money out of all the electronic navigation aids available to the small craft navigator. Its value is greatly enhanced by the steady increase in the number of local low power beacons, such as those by Adney Automation Ltd.

Errors Associated with Direction Finders

To get the best out of the direction finder, it is necessary to have some understanding of the various errors that can appear, how to recognise them and what to do about them. These errors can be attributed to three distinct causes:

Propagation errors
Installation, including siting errors
Instrument errors

Night effect
The most common error encountered due to effects outside the installation is caused by the effect of skywaves. This is caused by the constantly changing polarization of the wave reflected from the ionosphere. It may be recognised by the null being unstable. The effect generally appears at night only, as during the day the waves are absorbed by the ionosphere and thus do not cause interference. For this reason the error is often referred to as 'night effect'. So that radio engineers can quantitatively establish the effect of waves which are distorted in polarization and arrive at

the loop aerial in a downward inclined direction, a standard wave which descends at 45° polarized with the E plane at 45° to the horizontal is used to check DF aerial systems. With simple loop aerials the error under the above conditions is 35°. These tests are not normally carried out on small craft DF aerial installations as obviously the cost would be prohibitive. The point to remember is that when a minima is indistinct and unstable do not use it, because it is probably distorted by skywave signals and is not reliable.

Vertical error
Sometimes called 'antenna effect', it is brought about by the loop and input system of the receiver being unbalanced. When the DF is being calibrated this effect will become clearly apparent. Its symptoms are that when the aerial or goniometer is rotated into a null, the loop voltages do not exactly cancel: it appears as though a small vertical aerial is also connected to the receiver. This imbalance may be caused by the slight difference in the capacity of the downleads from the loop aerial, also by defective bonding. If this effect remains after checking through the cables, connections and bonding of the aerial system, it is usually overcome by using a balancing capacitor. Commercial equipments very often have a variable control on the receiver called 'zero sharpen'. As the phase of the loop signals may differ from the vertical signal, two possible effects will be noticed. In the first case, if the loop and vertical signals are in phase the minima will remain sharp but will not be 180° apart; and in the second case, if the loop and vertical signals have a 90° phase difference the minima will become indistinct. This type of effect is called a semicircular error because it is cyclic and becomes apparent at the 180° points.

Direction finder errors become alternately positive and negative as the bearing of the signal moves through 360° about the boat. The total error is generally made up of a combination of errors of different types. If these are recognised it will make the process of straightening the calibration curve much easier. The cyclic effects can be classified as follows:

Octantal errors: changes sign every 45°
Quadrantal errors: changes sign every 90°
Semicircular errors: changes sign every 180°

Provided that the equipment has been well designed and the size of the loop represents a small fraction of the wavelength, octantal errors will not be apparent.

Quadrantal errors (QE)

By far the most common, these are due to the presence of conductors such as rigging and other aerials in close proximity to the loop aerials. Bellini-Tosi loops also exhibit this error if the loops are not equal. This particular error arises generally because the signal from the DF beacon also induces currents in the surrounding rigging, etc. which are then re-radiated. At the loop aerial the original signal will have the highest strength and a total field will appear having a direction due to the vector sum of the original signal plus all the subsidiary waves. For practical yachting purposes the loop should be calibrated at a frequency in the middle of the beacon band. The calibration varies with frequency, and sometimes very dramatically between bands. If you are a keen DF type, it will pay dividends to go over the whole tuning range to get a certain knowledge of what is happening. It is a good plan to make deviation graphs for several frequencies where serious differences are encountered, and to this end a specimen blank graph (10.11) is included in chapter 10. Do not regard your installation as complete until you have the calibration chart covering at least the beacon band of frequencies on the bulkhead beside the loop.

Installation and Testing

So far as siting the equipment is concerned, the receiver and loop handle are better placed where the compass can be read easily. The receiver may form part of the R/T and therefore is generally reasonably close to the helm on small craft, for convenience when sailing single handed.

The site for the loop aerial should be as high and clear as possible, on the boat's centreline, and reasonably accessible for maintenance. The length of cable between the loop and the receiver should be kept as short as possible. The site should be free from aerial leads, rigging and large metal masses.

Metal rails and stanchions that are in close proximity must be connected to the boat's bonding system.

Steel rigging and triatic stays in the vicinity of the loop should be broken up by strain insulators. Ensure that an efficient earth bond is provided from the loop aerial to the receiver.

Check that the lubber line on the loop is accurately fore and aft.

Remember that metal window frames are fixed loops in their own right, and keep the DF aerial well clear.

The type of aerial will depend on the particular make of equipment, although the commonest permanent aerial for small craft has proved to be capable of excellent results; however the Bellini-Tosi system allows the fixed aerial to be mounted high and clear, and the associated goniometer may be sited in the most accessible place for navigating purposes, is of course the rotating loop. This type when positioning B-T loops, the cabling should not be longer than 40 ft on small craft. Check that the R/T aerial has no effect by establishing the null position with the aerial connected normally, then connected to earth, and then open circuit. If no noticeable difference is encountered, no further action need be taken. If open circuiting or earthing is required to minimise errors, a switch must be provided for this purpose.

On completion of installation graphical comparison between visual bearings and DF bearings is essential as a final check.

Fitting a rotating loop

In this case the height of the loop aerial is determined by the height of the wheelhouse. Suitable fairing pads are fitted in order that the loop will be vertical when the boat is in normal trim. The exact position will have to be chosen taking into account the operational and siting requirements mentioned earlier. If you have any doubts about the site, before drilling holes in the deckhead make up a temporary jig to hold the loop and then run a quick check to establish roughly the performance. With patience a reasonable site will always be found. It is well worth spending some time on this particular job, as once the errors have been established the calibration holds good for the life of the vessel, providing the surrounding rigging, metalwork, etc. does not change.

After fitting, test the loop for continuity and insulation, preferably with a 500 V 'megger' or similar instrument. The DC resistance of the loop should be less than 2 ohms including cable, and the insulation resistance should not be less than 1 Megohm to earth. Connection may now be made to the receiver. Tune into a strong signal at any of the quarter points relative to the boat's head and note the reading; rotate the loop by approximately 180° to the second null and again note the reading. There should of course be exactly 180° between the two nulls. If semicircular errors exist, they will be clear at this point. These errors are generally caused by direct pickup due to bad earthing of the centre point of the loop. Examine and adjust the earth system to the loop until this error is minimised. Set the loop pointer to zero—this should be at 90° to the frame. However, if the loop frame is distorted the pointer may be offset; check this and correct if necessary.

Again rotate the loop into the null using a station of known position. The loop should then be rotated exactly 90° to bring the sense or blue pointer over the null reading and pointing in the direction of the received station, when the receiver should be switched to the sense position; the S meter reading should now fall. If the reading rises, the loop connections should be reversed. It may be necessary to adjust the level of the sense aerial signal to achieve a good sense indication. The signal from the sense aerial should be equal to that from the loop if the best results are to be obtained, and this can be achieved in two ways:

Adjustment of the length of the sense aerial by the installing engineer. This adjustment will only hold good for one band as all aerials are frequency conscious.

A fixed length of aerial with a potential divider, which is used to tap off an amount of vertical signal to equal the loop signal. Special coupling units are sometimes provided which enable a correct proportion of sense signal to be selected for each band in use.

The adjustment in either case can be made by disconnecting the sense aerial and setting the RF gain to produce an S meter reading on a known station to a convenient level, with the loop aerial swung for maximum. The loop is then disconnected and the sense aerial applied to the receiver. At this stage the aerial or the coupling unit is adjusted to produce an identical S meter reading. Both aerials are then connected to the receiver and optimum sense discrimination will be obtained.

Fitting a fixed loop

The second type of DF aerial is the fixed Bellini-Tosi type which, although more expensive, gives much more flexibility to the installation as the goniometer may be fitted in the most convenient place, possibly close to the S meter and compass. Also, as the aerial does not have to be on the deckhead it can be higher and in the position of minimum error. Obviously a compromise must be reached when fitting such an aerial: for example, at first sight the masthead seems attractive. However, consider the expense and inconvenience of maintenance to anything in this position. Also the leads could be very long and thus more liable to pick up vertical signals on the braiding, which can be irksome to remove.

When connecting the B-T loop, make the same sort of insulation and continuity tests as with the rotating type, adding an insulation check between the fore and aft and athwartships loops. This should read at least 1 Megohm at 500 V. The ingress of moisture by leakage or condensation is a great source of bother in junction boxes and is easily detected with an insulation test. The effect is an unstable null position and noisy performance.

The goniometer associated with the B-T loop is set up using the same procedure employed for a rotating loop. In fact it can be regarded as a rotating loop inside a screened box. Inside this box special coils create an electromagnetic field corresponding to that experienced by the aerial system. This type of unit is available with a quadrantal error corrector, which is set at zero when fitting is complete and advanced or retarded as required during calibration.

Calibration

If, as is generally the case, bearings of a group of known beacons can be taken from the boat's moorings, a rough idea of the probable errors can be arrived at. With a rotating loop quadrantal error correction is difficult, although quite possible in theory: if some object causes a distortion then clearly an identical object geometrically opposite will produce an equal and opposite distortion to cancel the first. In small boats the best policy is to do a good fitting job and thorough calibration, rather than to attempt correction.

To achieve a reliable calibration, it must be known that the test site is clear from error-producing factors such as large sheds, or other structures such as railway lines and metal fences. In estuaries or coastal waters care must be taken to assess coastal refraction. The distance between the calibrating transmitter and the station should be as great as possible, preferably at least a mile, and ideally it should be visible from the ship. For the best results all bearings should be taken with a pelorus; however, where this equipment may not be available for accurate visible observations the use of the boat's corrected compass will allow calculation of the bearing of an invisible station without introducing appreciable errors. Calm conditions are also a must for a good calibration, especially on small craft.

When commencing calibration, sometimes the errors appear inconstant, and the cause of this effect must be tracked down before proceeding as the installation will otherwise prove unreliable. It is generally found to be due to rigging making a variable contact at some junction. The remedy is to bond across all rigging joints and bottle screws with jumper wires and cleats. If this effect is noticed it will be helpful to go around the rigging points one by one to isolate the primary offender for future attention.

If possible correct visual or compass bearings and the DF loop bearing should be taken every 10°, and it is usual to take three bearings and average them while the boat is steadied at each 10° point. This method produces about 36 check points more or less evenly distributed over the 360° scale, and a continuous error curve may thus be plotted. Do not panic if you fluff one set of readings—don't go back, go on to the next 10° point and all will be well in the end. Any one point missing is not serious as by reference to the rest of the curve it will be easy to fill in the missing one.

Remember DF errors appear relative to the ship's head, not the compass. Before drawing the error graph try a different frequency: usually as frequency increases there is a tendency on small boats for the amplitude of the error to increase. If the errors are not a minimum when the loop reading is 0° or 180° relative it is probably due to either the loop being offset from the centreline or some steel halyard or stay disposed to one side of the loop and working as a parasitic aerial.

During the calibration procedure avoid the temptation to rush the operation. At least an hour is required for swinging and this is a rate of about 6° per minute, which is by no means slow. When you consider that you have drawn a reasonably accurate error graph, go through another swing and try to repeat the results; consistency will indicate success and give you confidence in the installation.

Operation

Having calibrated the equipment the procedure for position fixing by radio bearings is very simple (4.3). In order to identify the beacons some knowledge of the Morse code is required. If you are unfamiliar with Morse, write down the call signs of the beacons you need to use together with their code equivalents, and in spare moments tune in on the frequency of your local group. It will not be long before the rhythm of each call sign becomes familiar and readable. Referring now to (4.3) the line RT is the required track for a hypothetical voyage between Lowestoft and the Hook of Holland. During the course of the passage it was established by using the DF that off-track positions K, L, M were reached. Each of these fixes were built up by measuring the radio bearings of the beacons in the area. The exact procedure will vary slightly with each type of direction finder and my explanation must be read in conjunction with the maker's instructions for the equipment in use.

With all types of DF it is usual to have an aerial switch with an 'identify' position. This enables the operator to listen for the beacons with the receiver connected to an omnidirectional or vertical aerial. This has the advantage that beacons are not hidden in the nulls of the loop aerial when listening blind.

The first step, then, is to tune to the frequency for the beacon group required and identify the signal. For the sake of the example (4.3) assume

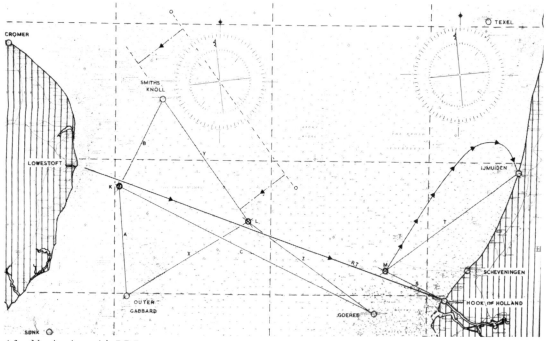

4.3   *Navigation with RDF*

that the frequency is 287.3 kHz and that the
beacon identified is Smiths Knoll. With this
information, assume that we have reached position
L, although at this stage its exact location will not
be known. Switch from Identify to the loop aerial
and rotate the loop into a null position; that is,
where the signal is at a minimum. It will be noticed
that when some types of DF receiver are switched
to the loop aerial the signal either disappears or
overloads the receiver. This is due to the automatic
gain control circuit being switched off in the loop
aerial position to sharpen the null. To overcome
this effect the RF gain control is then adjusted to
give a readable signal while swinging the loop back
and forth through the null; with care it will be
possible to take a reading to within plus or minus
1°. As explained earlier there are two possible null
positions, disposed 180° apart; for some purposes,
however, it is not important to identify a particular
null as being the true bearing. The initial laying off
of a radio position line is one of the time when the
null identity or sense is not important.

To take a reading from the loop it is necessary
to adjust the zero of the bearing scale to the boat's
head, which is usually indicated by a small lubber
line on the forward side of the scale with manual
loops; with cathode ray tube scales or goniometers

it will be at the top of the scale. As an alternative
the compass course can be set on the bearing scale
against the lubber line. With the first method
bearings are obtained relative to the ship's head
and in the second case relative to the course set
against the lubber line. With the first method it is
necessary to add the reading of the DF bearing
scale to the compass reading and drop any whole
360° from the answer in order to get the magnetic
bearing of the beacon. With the second method
the magnetic bearing is read directly off the scale.
To allow for the effects of yaw, pitch and roll it
will clearly be necessary to average several readings.

From position L the loop scale will read 150° or
330° magnetic after correction from the QE graph.
Refer to the chart and place the parallel rule to
this bearing on the magnetic compass rose as
shown by the dotted line 0–0. Now run the parallel
rule across the chart until it cuts the position of
the Smiths Knoll beacon and rule a faint line from
the beacon towards your estimated position: this
will establish line Y. When the Outer Gabbard and
Goeree beacons come up in the sequence the
position lines X and Z can be plotted in exactly
the same way.

The other fixes, K and M, are arrived at by the
same procedure. As Ijmuiden and the Hook are on

a different frequency the DF receiver will have to be tuned accordingly. The beacon at Cromer, although in the same group as Outer Gabbard, Smiths Knoll and Goeree, has not been used because due to the position of the line from Cromer there would be a possibility of coastal refraction. It will be seen from the plots on the chart that although we did not determine the sense of the beacons' signals, the position lines converge in the direction of the boat's position. It will now be clear that even if we had read the reciprocal bearings from the loop scale the lines of position would be in the same place and would still converge at the same point.

Another important facility provided by the direction finder is known as homing. This is achieved with greater ease with some sort of automatic DF as the boat can be steered by reading the DF bearing scale rather than the compass. (4.3) shows one hazard involved with this practice, due to the effects of drift. The best technique is to derive the course to follow from a fix and to steer by the compass; as land is approached the fixes are made more frequently with course adjustments to suit. By using the DF and compass together in this fashion drift rates may be quickly derived. With an automatic DF especially, there is a tendency to follow the pointer with the wheel. A moment's thought will make clear that it is perfectly possible to present the boat's head to the radio beacon from any bearing of the compass.

Imagine that when we reached fix M in our hypothetical voyage, we decided to head for Ijmuiden instead of our original destination. The boat's head is brought round until the DF indicates that the Ijmuiden beacon is dead ahead. The curved line to the north of line T shows the possible effect of following only the DF from fix M when influenced by tide and wind from the south. It will be noticed that the boat still reaches the destination, but does so via a long curved course roughly parabolic in character. Clearly, this is so because as the boat gets closer to the beacon the scale of the error decreases. It will be unwise to rely on this effect to get you home in practice, however, for if you imagine our example again with the wind and tide from the north, relying on only the DF in reduced visibility or at night would inevitably result in grounding just north of Scheveningen!

There are occasions when it is important to determine the sense of the radio wave from the beacon; for example, in fog or at night it may be necessary to establish even at reasonably close quarters whether you are to one side or the other of a beacon. Also, if searching for another vessel perhaps in distress, or when homing on a beacon, it is a comfort to know you are going toward the transmitter and not away from it. I have outlined earlier the method of checking the signal sense with a manual loop, and after some practice it is quite a simple operation. With automatic direction finders this operation is either automatic or may be checked by operating a small panel switch on the instrument.

Alternative Equipments

There are now a number of low cost automatic direction finders for small boats, many of which give good results; there are also several different principles of operation. All types give readings that are very much more stable than a magnetic compass, and due to this better readability sometimes assist the yachtsman to make the extensive and unintentional detour referred to.

Most direction finders, both manual and automatic, operate by sensing the null created when the signals induced in the aerial are at a minimum, or when they are equal and opposite and cancelled. This means that when the DF is aligned with the station it is not possible to hear its signal. When homing this can be a nuisance, as the station in a null cannot be heard. With some automatic equipments a switch is provided to allow the servo system to be deflected for checking and station identification.

One particular type of DF which could be described as semi-automatic overcomes this problem very well. The loop is rotated manually until the meter presentation is zeroed in the centre of its scale. The bearing can then be read off the cursor and the meter shows left and right errors continuously. This equipment (4.4) is manufacturered by Brookes & Gatehouse and has a very high angular sensitivity, which may be adjusted to suit conditions. The left/right meter may be equipped with a cockpit repeater. Signals from the loop and vertical sense aerial are

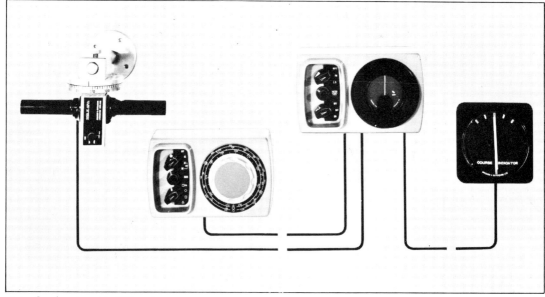

4.4 Semi-automatic DF equipment

combined to cause a displacement of the null point via an electronic switch which is employed to reverse the phase of the signals from the vertical aerial, at the rate of about 30 times per second. The null is thus displaced sequentially to the left and right of the horizontal axis of the DF aerial. The relative strengths of the signals at the two displaced positions are compared and after suitable processing are applied to the centre zero meter. Since the DF aerial is not operated near the null point the signal to noise ratio is higher than on many other types of DF and greater ranges are thus possible; also the station is audible all the time and thus several of the disadvantages of the null-seeking type are lost.

Brookes & Gatehouse also manufacture a small manual loop suitable for direct attachment to the Sestrel Moore steering compass. This is not a ferrite type, and by virtue of its direct compass attachment has a very high reading accuracy;

4.5 Koden KS-5H automatic RDF

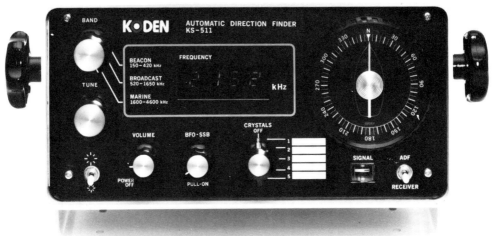

although a loss in sensitivity is encountered due to its small physical size it is nevertheless a significant contribution to small boat direction finding equipment design as it overcomes the problems of determining the accuracy of a movable ferrite compass/aerial unit.

The Koden KS 511, see (4.5) and (4.6), is a well thought out small automatic DF. Direction is determined without using a conventional goniometer, with its attendant problems of cost and frequency limitations due to mutual capacitance. The design uses a switching system which sequentially reverses the signal from the loops, and compares it with the sense aerial. A sample-and-hold circuit is used to store the information, which is displayed on a circular scale driven by a DC synchro which resolves the receiver output in angular form. The frequency of the receiver is displayed digitally, this being achieved by counting the local oscillator signal against a suitable offset. The frequency range covered is 150 kHz to 4·6 MHz and it will function on CW, MCW, AM and SSB signals. Among the servo-driven type of ADF the most spectacular performer I have seen is the Marconi Marine Lodestar II (2.5). One version of this equipment will switch itself on when activated by the radiotelephone auto-alarm signal, take the bearing

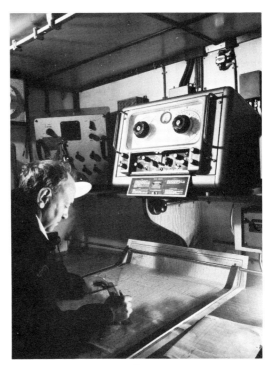

4.7   *Automatic DF equipment*

4.8   *Cathode ray tube DF display*

of the casualty or station, lock its bearing scale and close itself down. Even apart from this specialised application, I have yet to see equal performance from any manual or automatic direction finder. For very large yachts the expense of such an equipment would no doubt be justified.

A type of DF using a cathode ray tube display is shown at (4.8). This instrument is manufactured by Plath GMBH of Germany and typical responses are shown (4.9). The single line trace is that obtained from a single CW or MCW signal; the rectangular trace is that obtained when two such signals are received simultaneously on the same frequency.

4.6   *Aerial for Koden RDF*

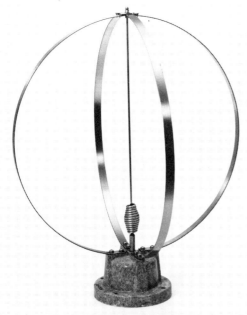

The trace that has the appearance of an isometrically projected rectangle is the result of three signals on the same frequency received simultaneously. In all cases the bearing of each station is parallel to one of the sides of the figure. Where pulsed transmissions are received in this way (e.g Loran signals) the three bearings show simultaneously as three crossed lines.

It is not unusual to achieve an accuracy of about plus or minus 1° on small boats after calibration, and this will give a high standard of position fixing. As most of the ingredients for this standard are associated with effort, I don't think the small boat owner should be happy with anything less. Some years ago I wrote an article for a yacht club magazine on the subject of DF calibration and later noted a very fair comment by a reader, who said that 'perhaps not everyone would wish to do this amount of work'. I confess the time involved is often quite considerable, but the rewards also, as confidence in the accuracy of the direction finder is a very comforting commodity. So many readings are taken during calibration that it provides an excellent exercise for those who have not yet had a lot of DF experience; it is also an excellent wit sharpener for those who have.

Portable types

Many small boats have difficulty in finding space for DF equipment, and for this and economic reasons there are a great number of portable types in use, i.e. those which come under groups (1) and (2) listed at the start of this chapter.

A number of manufacturers produce portable DF sets and it is something of a problem for the average yachtsman to sort out which one to buy.

Sensitivity and bandwidth are clearly linked so far as useful range is concerned. High sensitivity infers that overall amplification of the receiver is sufficient to make the smallest receivable signals audible in the headphones. Bandwidth affects the useable sensitivity. The term itself refers to the small group of frequencies around the carrier frequency to which the receiver is tuned. A narrow bandwidth will make the group smaller and discriminate against more noise thus making it easier to pick out a single frequency. For purely direction finding applications the bandwidth can be

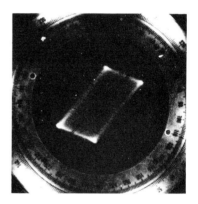

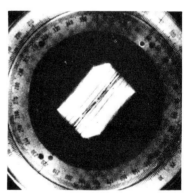

4.9 CRT
display traces

made extremely narrow as for example in the Aptel DF (4.11) where the bandwidth is only 170 Hz, resulting in near ultimate performance for the size.

When you purchase a new DF, check it on a known beacon on the edge of a nominal range. In these conditions the difference in the output between the loop maxima and minima will need to be at least 3 to 1 in order for you to get reasonable bearings. My own fixed 0.5 metre loop DF will do this at double the normal range of the beacon, and it does not have a narrow band filter.

Accurate tuning to the beacon frequency has always needed a certain amount of skill; however, the application of microelectronics has produced a form of tuning that is can be set rock steady by a calculator type keypad. The technique is called synthesis. The Aptel DDF 300 uses this principle, indicating frequency on a miniature light emitting diode *(led)* display. A 6-minute beacon sequence clock is also provided on this display.

There are some portable types that embody a compass, such as the seabeam, shown in 4.10. The first requirement is to provide a small pivoted base. The base can then be fastened in a fixed position and the compass corrected as described in chapter

4.11   Aptel digital DF

12. The DF aerial should of course be calibrated in exactly the same way as for the fixed installations described earlier. A very careful study should be made of the maker's specification for any portable equipment: one or two examples I have seen are no more than poor quality, but expensive, toys.

Hints on Use

With all types of DF, operation can be made considerably easier and comfortable by using a pair of noise-excluding headphones. Even on sailing boats there are always background noises which make listening to a loudspeaker very difficult. As there are now many good quality headphones available at very reasonable prices there can be no excuse for using the horrible ear-tweaking plastic stethoscope type which I am given to understand should be worn 'hanging down the back of your neck' to prevent magnetic interference with the portable compass. Advances in industrial ceramics have produced a material called lead zirconate titanate which has been very successfully applied to manufacturing completely non-magnetic head-phones. This type are often commonly referred to as 'crystal' headphones; many originate in Hong Kong, are well finished and are good value for money.

Having done a lot of work to make sure that the direction finder is dependable, there will be many

4.10 Seafarer Seabeam DF

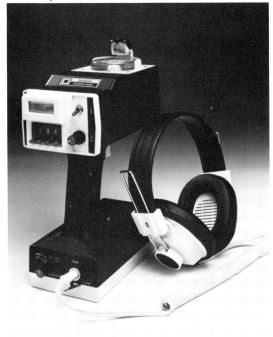

occasions in use when one station booms through above all the rest of the signals bumping about just above the background noise level. The signals that are easily found generally emanate from the Consol stations or from national broadcasting networks. A question arises as to the validity of bearings taken from these stations. Bearing in mind that Consol stations are intended for use by shipping of all descriptions and that conditions of minimal land refraction will have been taken into account when siting them, I feel that straight line bearings may often prove very useful. Refraction will in all cases be no worse than that encountered when using the station on Consol count.

So far as broadcast stations are concerned, the case is rather a different one as the stations are sited for best coverage of a particular land mass. When using broadcast stations for homing or direction finding it is essential to have experience of the station and the area for reliable work. However it must be said that a good strong signal from a broadcast station from which you can get a clear null will often suffice when nothing else can be found in the area. One point I would like to make in view of the odd stick of technological rhubarb that circulates from time to time on this subject: it is neither holy nor unholy to take and use bearings of radio signals emanating from stations other than marine beacons. If you can take a bearing which will improve the standard of the data you have to hand, take it and use it with common sense based on background knowledge of all the circumstances. When using these high power stations, on occasion the yachtsman will find himself able to take radio bearings over several hundred miles. In this situation, which will not occur normally with DF beacons, I would remind you to use the half-convergency tables (in the nautical almanacs) to convert the great circle bearings read from the DF scale to Mercator bearings to be laid off on the chart. The correction varies with latitude and the difference in longitude between observer and beacon; however in small boats at distances up to 100 miles this correction may be disregarded.

You can find out the radio beacon's exact frequency, transmission time and call sign by referring to *Reed's Almanac*, the Admiralty *List of Radio Signals* and other publications such as ROFAC charts.

Emergency DF Loop

It has been known for a deckhead DF loop to become faulty or to sustain damage during a voyage. A temporary DF loop can be improvised by inserting four large screws or hooks into an athwartships bulkhead with one at each corner of a square marked out with roughly 2 ft (60 cm) sides. Start at the half past six position and wind a piece of insulated wire round the square formed by the screws to make about ten turns. Finish at the bottom and tape or twist the start and finish together over their insulation to hold the wire on. The two ends can then be taken to the DF loop connection on the receiver and the required station tuned in. The boat is slowly swung until a null is found; the bearing is then read directly off the compass. It will be realised that no sense determination is available and that the system has not been calibrated—however it may be better than nothing when all is considered, as errors are generally at a minimum in the fore and aft direction.

He had bought a large map respresenting the sea,
Without the least vestige of land:
And the crew were much pleased when they found it to be
A map they could all understand.

The Hunting of the Snark
Lewis Carroll

VHF Direction Finders

The high cost of 2 MHz SSB equipment, and the allocation of frequencies with a view to localising as much traffic as possible, has led to a vast increase in the number of VHF radiotelephones fitted over the last decade. As a result, a demand has been created for a VHF direction finder, particularly from coastguard and lifeboat services. To the small boat operator the advantage of using the harbour or marina radio stations as a beacon has much to be said for it.

The principles on which VHF direction finders work are significantly different from the lower frequency counterpart. Very high frequencies produce a situation in which the wavelength is

4.12   Intech Mariner 360 RDF

comparable in size to the aerial array. Consider for a moment the widely used MF Bellini-Tosi loop aerial; although the signal from each loop varies sinusoidally with the angle of the signal, the same part of the wave excites both loops almost simultaneously because the wavelength is much bigger than the loop dimension. The signals from such an array are said to be 'space phased' as the same point on each wave period coincides in time but varies in amplitude in sympathy with the spacial position of the applied signal.

VHF direction finder aerials do not need to have inherently directional properties. As the wavelength is so short, simply using more than one aerial with a space between will suffice because the signal from the first aerial the signal encounters will have an output advanced in *time* compared with the second element; see (4.12).

Clearly by arranging 4 aerials, two abeam and two fore and aft, a 360 degree means of detection exists. A practical application of these principles is embodied in the Intech 360 DF and the SRD21 Homer. The former unit is a digital readout doppler direction finder, the latter is a homing device giving left and right indications rather than 360 degree readout which makes it less expensive. There is no magic at VHF which relieves the operator of responsible operating standards. The effect of drift on homing devices is shown in (4.3). Remember:

(1) take the bearing or centre the homer display
(2) take the steering compass reading
(3) steer by compass
(4) if after an interval of time the homer reading has moved *you are drifting*
(5) time elapsed between readings on the log, together with the difference between the compass and the homer reading, will tell you how much and in what direction you have drifted
(6) return to the homing course *after* you have checked that it will not involve you in crossing sands, rocks or, if you tend to do things in a big way, the Panama isthmus.

It has been said that VHF direction finders are more accurate than low frequency equipments. Take care! the virtual absence of night effect is one thing, but the effect of local reflections is something else and cannot be overstated. Calibration is absolutely essential and the aerial array must be mounted above all the other aerials and rigging on the boat. Just breaking up the rigging with strain insulators will not help with VHF. Calibration is best carried out at sea at least a mile off shore using a pelorus ring with an optical sight. Probably the best method is to lay at anchor and arrange for a second VHF equipped vessel to make a circle round you some half mile away. If you are doing your first calibration, have in mind that errors are due to the geometry of aerials and boat and that therefore the bearing must be noted relative to the ships head, not the compass. At VHF it is possible to find errors of as much as 90 degrees where the aerial site is poor. If used on vessels working in conjunction with helicopters or other large vessels, while in close proximity, the bearing will be seen to wander when relative movement takes place. Remember the effect on your television picture when aircraft fly over.

5 Echosounders

*. . . about midnight the shipmen deemed that they
drew near to some country; and sounded and
found it twenty fathoms: and when they had gone
a little further, they sounded again and found it
fifteen fathoms. Then fearing lest we should have
fallen upon rocks, they cast four anchors out of the
stern and wished for the day.*

Acts of the Apostles
Ch. 27 v. 27-79
Anno Domini 62

The hydrographic department of the Admiralty
was formed in 1795, when the English first began
seriously to survey the seas of the world. For this
purpose sounding required a better standard of
accuracy, for if a meaningful record was to be
established, the 'hand' with the lead line was a man
with responsibility: it was no longer sufficient to
know that there was a great enough depth of water
for the ship's safety.

Professor William Thomson, who later became
Lord Kelvin, gave his attention to the
measurement of depth, which at the time was a
laborious operation and sometimes required that
the ship be stopped. After his wife's death in 1870,
Professor Thomson purchased a large yacht of 126
tons named the *Lalla Rookh* and spent much of his
spare time cruising. His sounding device comprised
a sinker attached to an inverted tube which was
closed at one end and coated on the inside with
silver chromate. When this tube was lowered into
the water, the air within the tube was compressed
and the depth could be deduced from the height of
the water mark inside the tube, shown by the
remaining film of silver chromate. This method of
sounding was further improved by attaching the
tube to a thin piano wire which offered such a low
resistance to the water that measurements could be
made while the ship was in motion.

The problems arising from mechanical sounding
became evident very early and much research was
devoted to improving the techniques employed.

The sinking of the *Titanic* in 1912 gave stimulus
to the search for an improved method of sounding.
R. A. Fessenden, the American scientist, used a
moving coil transducer at a frequency of about 1
kHz in experiments taking place just before this

disaster, and had succeeded in detecting icebergs at
a distance of about 3km (2 nm). It was necessary at
this stage to devise a means of measuring time
intervals between pulse and echo, and initially this
was achieved with clockwork mechanisms operating
photographic paper recorders.

Just after the 1914–18 war, the Admiralty
produced the first British echosounder. In this
equipment a hammer struck a diaphragm, which
projected a 'packet' of energy to the seabed. The
echo from the seabed was picked up from the
water by a second diaphragm and passed to a
recorder on the bridge. In the 1920s echosounders
were in commercial production and the Port of
London Authority purchased one of the early
equipments for the survey ship *St Katherine* in
1924. Initially these worked at audible frequencies,
but in the natural course of things, having a basic
echosounder created a demand for a better one,
which brought about research on depth penetration
and discrimination. Ultimately the application of
the technique to the detection of submarines, and
later fish, produced the present level of technology.
During the 1920s the frequency of operation and
the pulse shape became better defined to improve
the discrimination, and also research into a better
form of transducer had begun. A noteworthy
contribution to the present high standard of
discrimination and penetration was made as far
back as 1930, with the development of the
magnetostriction transducer: the magnetostriction
principle had been discovered in 1842 by J P Joule,
who was an acquaintance of Lord Kelvin. The
recording echosounder came into being around
1933 and was designed by scientists at the
Admiralty Research Laboratories. Just as

important as Joules' work was the discovery in 1880 by Jacques and Pierre Curie that certain crystalline substances change in length when subject to an electric charge and are, moreover, capable of producing an electrical charge when subject to pressure. This is now called the 'piezo electrical effect' (piezo means pressure). This discovery particularly relates to small craft as almost every echosounder produced for this market in the last two decades has used a piezo electric transducer element.

During the course of research work the *Glen Kidson* made an experimental trip to Bergen in 1933. This was in a way historic because the recording equipment produced a continual record of the seabed on a scale of 70 fathoms to 5 in. on the recording paper. The recording paper was of the wet type and not the dry, surface coat burnout type we are now familiar with. Around 1935 Oscar Sund, using one of Hughes' MS3 echosounders (5.1) in the Norwegian research vessel *Johann Hjort*, began studying fish echoes and was able to positively identify cod and herring shoals. The wreck of the *Lusitania* was located with similar equipment and a photograph of the recorded trace is shown in (5.2). From this early work the potential was obvious, and the photographs reproduced here show that although by today's standards the equipment was very large, the results were very good.

Around many coasts and the British Isles really deep waters are not encountered, and as the bottom echo is always the easiest to see, the ultimate depth penetration of even small craft echosounders is rarely put to the test. The big commercial equipments are capable of considerable range: I believe the record for acoustically sounded depth is 10,540 metres, which was achieved by the Danish research vessel *Galathea* using a Kelvin Hughes MS21J echosounder off the Phillipine Islands. A recording of a sunken schooner shows a surprising amount of detail (5.3), (5.4) shows the wreck of the *Rawalpindi*—discovered the hard way by skipper Henry Ford, whose trawler *Kingston Sapphire* came fast on it and had to be hauled clear. The wreck is now lying in 168 fathoms. This business of 'coming fast' when trawling is a hair-raising experience. I have only seen it happen once and if I am unable to witness a similar event again I will not be disappointed. One moment the vessel

5.1   Early echo-sounding equipment

5.2   Trace of Lusitania *wreck*

5.3   Trace of sunken schooner

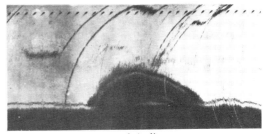

5.4   Wreck of the Rawalpindi

was peacefully towing its gear and seconds later she heeled violently and the heavy steel towing warps twirled up like grocery string. The skipper, who was on deck, shouted down the engine room ventilator 'Stop her', and when the vessel slacked off, the crew, and lastly me, emerged from behind the nearest solid objects. Photo (5.5) shows an interesting trace of echoes received from hippopotami in the water—which goes to show that you can never be quite sure what's underneath.

Virtually total reflection from the seabed occurs at about 10 kHz; below this penetration of the strata below the bottom begins to take place. As acoustic absorption and attenuation increases with frequency above this point, it will be understood that the lowest frequency which will give adequate discrimination for the job will be the best one to employ.

With present low cost equipments for small boats, the operating frequency is often in the region of 150 kHz, usually because of the availability of ceramic transducers of suitable physical dimensions that fall into this region. The performance of many small craft echosounders is regrettably mediocre, although it must be said that at the price some equipments are sold for, there is no question of much engineering being involved.

The business end of the echosounder is the transducer and this is usually mounted through the hull. Although there were many different types of

transducer in the past, in recent years they have settled down to two principal types. The earliest units employed a diaphragm and a hammer striker for transmitting, and a moving coil pickup and diaphragm arrangement—rather like a headphone—for receiving. Development progressed to the magnetostriction type, which relies for its effect on the characteristic of certain metals to constrict under the influence of a magnetic field. Two notable examples are nickel and permendum. Nickel gets shorter as the magnetic field strength increases and permendum gets longer. For use as transmitting elements this type of transducer is sometimes magnetically biased, because an unbiased bar of nickel will, when subject to an alternating magnetic flux, shorten its length on both the positive and negative peaks, thus producing mechanical vibrations that have two maxima and minima for every cycle of the applied pulse. It will thus produce mechanical vibrations at twice the frequency of the exciting wave. If a static magnetic bias is introduced to hold the nickel at approximately its midpoint on the strain curve, the mechanical maxima and minima will occur only in sympathy with the applied wave. This type has been extensively used for professional work, although in most areas it is being replaced by arrays of high power versions of the peizo-electric ceramic type. A small magnetostriction transducer manufactured by Kelvin Hughes for their MS39 sounder (5.6).

5.5 Traces of hippos

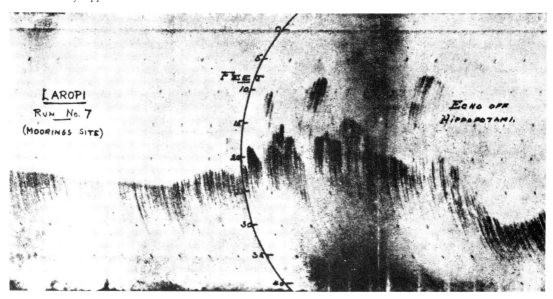

The electrostrictive principle is used extensively in small craft echosounders, as the transducers are very simple constructionally and economic to manufacture. The vast majority of commercially produced smaller units have a piezo-electric ceramic disc, sometimes barium titanate and more recently lead zirconate titanate, mounted in a metal or plastic skin fitting. The mechanical vibratory effect is created by the crystalline structure of the material distorting under the influence of an electric field. The reverse of this effect also holds good: if the material is subjected to mechanical pressure, electricity is generated, hence the name piezo-electricity—'pressure electricity'.

For practical purposes, from the circuit point of view the magnetostrictive type is electrically equivalent to an inductance with a parallel resistance representing the load, and the electrostrictive type is equivalent to a capacitor with a parallel resistor representing the load.

The ceramic (electrostrictive) transducer is the only one that will be described further as it is virtually the only device suitable for a relatively low cost unit, in a size and shape that is practicable for small boat engineering. An example of a well made unit is shown in (5.9).

Of the types using electrostrictive transducers, one or two notable examples exist which have been developed over a long period, such as the Ferrograph range. The Offshore 500 (5.7) was used to produce the recordings shown later in this chapter. Then there is the ubiquitous 'Seafarer' (5.7a). There are probably more flashing light sounders on the market than any other type. The reason for the popularity of this type no doubt stems from the fact that it can be built down to a price in quantity, due to the simplicity of the design. The light producing device in the present day echosounder is a gallium arsenide phosphide diode. These devices have much better linearity than the neon flasher and are considerably more reliable. An example of the digital type is produced by Datamarine of America, shown together with its transducer and repeater units (5.8). This company has a range of products having digital readout. Of the meter presentation echosounders available, the Brookes & Gatehouse system, has a separate amplifier available for extended depth performance, together with several options such as repeaters and gravity switch for dual-transducer installations

5.6   Magneto striction transducer

(5.9). The Elac Miniscope is a very good example of a cathode ray tube presentation equipment; it is manufacturered in West Germany (5.10). It is available as a self contained echosounder working at 50 kHz, or as an indicator only, for use with a recorder. It is fitted with a scale expander which enables the operator to examine more closely any predetermined strata of water by expanding it to fill the whole screen.

5.7 Paper recording echo sounder

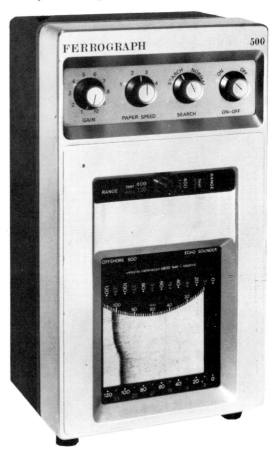

5.7a Seafarer echosounder

5.8   Digital display and repeater, transducer

Below, I have set out the various classes that the equipment can be grouped into and have commented generally and irrespective of make on the performance of the particular types. If you are considering the purchase of an echosounder, the following summary of types will be of interest.

Out of the vast number of small craft echo-sounders presently manufactured, the many different types may be grouped according to the manner in which the information is displayed:

Flasher indicator
Meter presentation
Cathode ray tube display
CRT display and memory: black and white or colour
Paper recording
Digital
Computing digital

All have proved to have various advantages and disadvantages.

By far the most prevalent form in very small craft is the flasher type. It suffers from two disadvantages.

The flash is difficult to see in daylight without a large hood which restricts the angle of view. Some types have an angled viewing window caused by a raised centre in the dial. This introduces parallax and makes reading at an angle very difficult.

Moving coil meter displays were introduced because of the problems associated with other types, but have proved to be generally worse for other reasons. Advantages are that it is easy to read and easy to compensate for the depth of keel below transducer.

Disadvantages are:

Ambiguous when fitted on craft where engine noise or water turbulence is a problem, as the meter reads low.
Any echo failing to return allows the display to move towards maximum depth. Thus the boat could be resting on the bottom and the equipment would give an indication of infinite depth.
Only capable of indicating depth. Midwater echoes do not show unless stronger than the bottom echo.

The paper recording type is proved to have by far the best all round performance:

It is always readable, irrespective of ambient light.
Fairly linear (by comparison); large echoes show dense black, small echoes show light grey.
Continuous recording makes navigation easier, as apart from the reference to ground previously covered being available, the record displayed makes it possible to form a mental forward prediction.
Permanent record available.

Disadvantages are the cost of the paper, and at present the higher relative cost of manufacture. With digital types, I foresee problems that have been associated with meter types in the past:

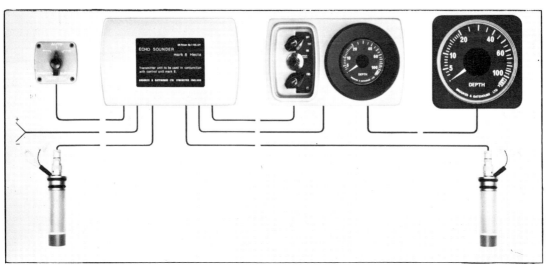

5.9   Dual display system

The display will be just as difficult to read as the neon in bright sunlight.

Some types can indicate maximum depth when on or close to the bottom.

Counting short when subject to vibration or noisy conditions, e.g. in high speed craft. In general more expensive than paper recorders and not as good.

Computing types (digital) are designed to provide information for navigation by sounding both downwards and forwards. While the theory associated with such electronic computing is by no means overwhelming, the practicalities of applying the electronics to the total environment are more of a problem. These equipments suffer from all the disadvantages of the digital type and are much more expensive.

Cathode ray tube display types are in general quite complex, but in my view come close to the paper recording type for results. In fact for some applications such as fish finding or location of underwater objects, the performance can be more flexible. Disadvantages are:

Expensive

5.10   Cathode ray tube display with scale expander

5.10a   Memory type CRT display

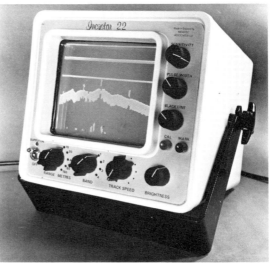

Hard to see in bright sunlight without a viewing hood.
No permanent record.
For search purposes, needs constant monitoring.

The most recent CRT display sounders give a very similar standard of performance to the paper recorder type. In the Incastec equipment shown here (5-10a), echoes are written into a digital store and displayed continuously, new information appearing on the right hand side of the screen, with past events being discarded from the left hand edge. Colour versions of this type of equipment are also on the market, the background being normally blue. The intensity of the echo controls the hue of the trace producing an attractive display.

Comparison

All small craft echosounders operate on the principle of a short pulse of energy being transmitted from the transducer fitted in the bottom of the boat. A small proportion of this energy will be reflected by any object it strikes. This reflected energy is received by the transmitting transducer in lower cost equipments and by a special receiving transducer in better quality types. The transducer reconverts the received energy to an electrical signal which is then greatly amplified and processed to create a readable display.

The transmitter is an oscillator designed to send a pulse of electrical energy (typically 150 kHz) to the transducer. Dependent on the depth and resolution required, this pulse has to be given a certain identity by making it last for a discrete interval of time. The amplitude is also adjusted in some designs to the optimum for the range in use.

The transducer is a means of converting this pulse of electrical energy into a pulse of pressure waves in the water which behave in sympathy with the oscillator. Although the outgoing pulse from the oscillator may produce a peak to peak amplitude of typically 300 V across the transducer the amplitude of the echo will be very small. The echo in very shallow water will be capable of producing several millivolts at the receiver input, but as the echo strength falls off at a rate proportional to the inverse fourth power law relative to depth, a much more typical echo return

will be a few tens of microvolts (1 microvolt = 0.000001 volts). The receiver must therefore, have a high sensitivity. It must also, in order to produce a clear display, have the ability to preserve the original characteristics of the outgoing pulse. While the foregoing is representative of all echosounders, the means of displaying the information received differs from type to type.

The flasher type has a small light emitting diode attached to a rotating arm, which flashes at zero as a pulse is emitted downwards and again when the echo is received. As the arm is rotating at a constant speed, it is possible to measure the time taken for the pulse to reach the seabed and return to the boat by scaling the distance between the two flashes on the dial.

The meter type has an electronic switch which is shut when the pulse goes out and opens when the echo returns. It will be clear that the longer the echo takes to return, the higher the meter reading will be, and of course conversely. If the signal fails to return, either because the bottom is too close or too deep, the meter will move to its maximum, which may be misleading.

The paper recorder has a stylus which sweeps over the width of the paper. At the edge of the paper corresponding to zero depth the pulse is sent out. As the stylus travels at a constant speed, the time between transmitted pulse and echo can be measured. The shape of the path across the recording paper followed by the stylus varies considerably with different designs. The Ferrograph, for example, describes a segment of a circle; the Koden has a clever mechanical device to resolve an elipsoid and describes one of the long sides of the elipse on the paper; the Kelvin Hughes MS39 has a belt to carry the stylus and gives a straight presentation. Although from any point of view a straight vertical trace must be the least ambiguous, it can be said that no serious difficulty is experienced in the interpretation of a curved recording trace, as is well illustrated in the last section of this chapter.

In the digital type, an electronic 'clock' makes pulses spaced in time by the period taken for ultrasonic energy to travel the smallest distance the equipment must resolve, i.e. typically 1 ft. When the pulse is sent out this 'clock' pulse is connected to the display circuit. When an echo is received, it is disconnected again. The indicator thus displays the total of 'clock' pulses before the echo was received. As each pulse is sent out the display is automatically zeroed. This process takes place at a rate proportional to the depth range required.

Digital readout computing types work on the same principle as digital types except that two transducers are used. One of these faces forward at a predetermined angle. The two sets of information are processed in an electronic computing unit and activate display devices and alarms according to the mode of operation.

Operation

With all echosounders, if every time a pulse was emitted an echo was received and this echo signal just became attenuated proportionally with distance, everything would be fine. However, this is far from the case; distortions, pulse to pulse differences and noise from water turbulance make the received echo rather imprecise. Controls are provided to ease this situation and probably the one of main importance is the gain control. The setting of this control will vary considerably as several factors influence the overall gain required for any given set of conditions. In normal circumstances the greater the depth the higher the gain setting will be. Where the aim is to detect underwater objects, many of which have poor reflecting qualities, the gain will have to be increased.

Under these conditions, reflections will appear as the result of particles in suspension, or air bubbles and other small objects that in general increase the background noise level. If the gain control is further increased under the same conditions, a re-echo will appear at twice the true depth. This is the result of the pulse travelling to the bottom and being reflected to the surface where it is reflected to the bottom again; the second reflection from the bottom is indicated as well as the original. Where the seabed is very hard, this may recur many times.

The echo may disappear under some conditions. For instance, when a power boat goes astern the screw tends to throw air under the hull. This layer of air will prevent the pulse of ultrasonic energy getting to the seabed. A similar effect can be

noticed when passing through the wake of another ship. Both of these effects may be more or less pronounced, and in most cases a general increase in the background noise level will result.

At high gain settings echoes may appear from any change of state within the water, i.e. warm or cold strata, as at power station outfalls and tidal rivers where temperature and salinity changes are pronounced. In the absence of any clear boundary, as may occur even at the seabed in the case of marine vegetation or freshly stirred up mud, the transition from liquid to solid is gradual and thus the transmitted power will be absorbed.

Variations due to salinity, density and temperature affect the accuracy of readings by a small amount. Assuming the pulse travels at a constant speed, depths will appear shallow in very warm, very salty water and deep in very cold fresh water. The difference will rarely exceed 6–7%, although when working in extreme conditions great care should be taken to check performance.

Installation

While the manufacturer's recommendations must be adhered to, there is an amount of work common to all installations. The display unit, which usually contains all the circuitry in small craft echosounders, should be mounted where it is clearly visible to the helmsman. Be careful to avoid placing it in a position where it can upset the compass, as many display units (and repeaters) embody some sort of magnetic material. If the equipment is other than a paper recorder or meter type avoid placing it in positions of high ambient light, and with all types avoid locations exposed to the weather. The electrical wiring to the boat's distribution board should be selected having regard to the current drain of the particular type installed and the length of the cable run; also the echo-sounder should have its own separate sub-circuit with an overload trip or fuse.

Ultrasonic Transducers
Much has been said in recent years about internal fittings for transducers. Boat owners naturally find the idea of not drilling holes in the bottom of the hull attractive. It must be said that, if for your

purpose you achieve results that satisfy you, there is a lot to be said for it. However, the idea is not new and was dropped in the 1930's because it is lossy in terms of transmitted power; the hull is inclined to 'ring' after each pulse which reduces discrimination, and the signal-to-noise ratio is degraded by the greater tendency of the transducer to shock-excite when subject to mechanical noise.

It is by no means uncommon today to find more than one ultrasonic transducer mounted in the hull; echosounder, doppler log and sonar all have similar types of lead zirconate titanate elements for converting the electrical signals from the instrument into pressure waves beneath the vessel, and vice versa. Where this situation exists it will be found that some interference occurs between transducers, even if the frequency of operation is widely different; this will take a form that depends on the type of display used by the affected equipment. For example, a sonar will produce a pattern of regular lines on a chart-recording echosounder, the intensity of which will vary with the orientation of the sonar transducer. As the unwanted coupling takes place in the water by interaction of the soundwaves under the boat, including those parts of the energy radiated by the sidelobes, the only method that can be employed to reduce this to a minimum is to select the site for individual transducers to give the greatest possible mutual spacing.

The transducer cables should be treated with respect as they are generally quite thin 75 ohm coaxial cable. When fitting these units it is a good idea to slip thick PVC tubing over the cables where they run through the bilge space; it can be pushed down over the stem of the transducer where it emerges from the internal doubling pad and fastened with a screw clip. Transducer cables should of course be supported on wiring battens up to the indicator position in the wheelhouse.

A number of manufacturers supply such items as 'transom mounts' or 'portable mounts'. These are probably sufficient when in shallow water or stationary but, in order to achieve the full capabilities of the instrument, it is necessary to mount the transducer properly and see that it is streamlined under the water.

The transducer must be mounted through the hull for best results, and should be in a position having minimum turbulence. The bottom surface of the transducer should be horizontal when the boat is trimmed normally and under way. In general always mount the transducer clear and forward of A-brackets, struts, propellers and rudders, or any other projection or skin fitting that may produce a perturbance in the flow of water over the face of the transducer. It should be remembered that the transducer is a means of converting mechanical pressure into electrical signals, and therefore it will help to attain the best results if it is mounted in an area of the hull as free as possible of mechanical vibrations from machinery, etc.

It is recommended that the transducer be fitted somewhere within the middle third of the vessel's waterline. If the transducer is fitted too close to a deep keel some screening may take place when the vessel is heeled. The main beam from the transducer is usually constrained within ±20° and a figure of about ±10° is typical for small craft types, so that it will be necessary to find a position that gives a total clear angle of 30° to 40° for satisfactory results. Where it is necessary to mount the transducer well to one side to get an acceptable site, care should be taken to ensure that the working surface will not be subjected to excessive aeration when the vessel is heeled. If the transducer is mounted close to the keel a spurious reflection may be obtained by virtue of the minor transmission lobes, which sometimes shows itself as a broadening of the zero—sometimes a bad case will produce a series of random echoes close to the transmission mark.

When a suitable site has been chosen the hull planking or shell should be drilled to the size of the transducer stem, a doubling pad used inside the hull, and sealing compound applied as necessary around the hole. The nuts should then be run down to the block in order to hold the transducer and make a waterproof joint; care should be taken to avoid excessive strain on the nuts. Outside the hull a wooden fairing block should be fastened, bearing in mind that it is just as important to streamline behind the transducer as in front; (5.11) indicates the arrangement of a typical small boat transducer. For very fast craft it is much better to completely recess the transducer in the hull. Do not make the transducer a tight fit in the fairing blocks as there is always a tendency for wooden blocks to expand after launching, thus either

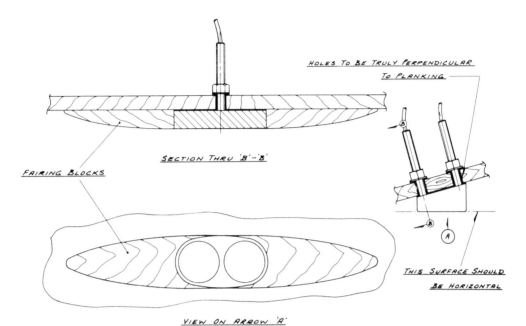

HOLES TO BE TRULY PERPENDICULAR
TO PLANKING

SECTION THRU 'B'-'B'

FAIRING BLOCKS

THIS SURFACE SHOULD
BE HORIZONTAL

VIEW ON ARROW 'A'

5.11   *Transducer mounting*

trapping the head very tightly or pulling it off the transducer stem. Care taken with this point will enable replacement to be carried out easily and quickly when the occasion arises. When launching, a good wash with a weak detergent in water will ensure good wetting. Do not paint the active surface of transducers as paint absorbs part of the ultrasonic energy.

Interpretation

My own belief is that the best value for money can be found in a paper recording echosounder, as it produces by far the most concise information for the navigator. The effects of the controls are very pronounced and may be clearly seen in the accompanying photographs of chart recordings. Some of the effects shown are due to the effects of the operating frequency and to other features of the instrument design parameters. The results speak for themselves and are excellent for all small craft purposes.

Effect of gain adjustment on recording
In all small craft echosounders the operating frequency is held constant and is determined by the design requirements; also most equipments have a fixed transmitter power output. The Ferrograph 500, on which the following traces were taken, works at 143 kHz nominally, and the power output is fixed. It follows that any control over the strength of the echo received and similarly the strength of the smallest signal to mark the paper must be carried out by varying the amplification of the received signal. This manual adjustment is effected by the use of the gain control.

Comparatively little gain is required when the instrument is to be used purely as a depth recorder showing only the contour of the seabed. The bottom echo signal is very pronounced and requires little amplification to make a clear mark on the paper with a low level of background noise.

When searching for fish, the reflected pulses are very much weaker, and depend upon the size, type and quantity in the shoal; consequently a much higher gain setting will be required. Photo (5.12) shows the effect of a gradual increase in the gain setting as the boat travelled over some distance. The lowest setting starts at the right hand side of the photograph with a single clear bottom echo. As the gain increases a second echo appears at twice the depth due to the pulses of energy being reflected from the bottom to the surface and back again to the bottom, where it is again reflected up to the transducer. This can happen many times

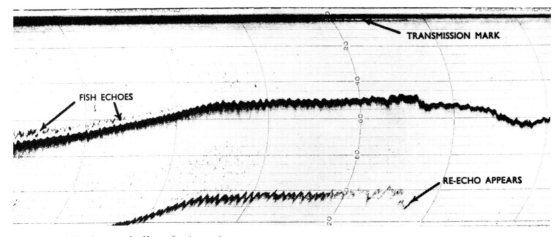

TRANSMISSION MARK

FISH ECHOES

RE-ECHO APPEARS

5.12–5 Fish echoes and effect of gain setting

with a hard bottom, as shown in (5.15) where the third re-echo can be seen.

As the gain setting is advanced further the bottom echo mark tends to become broader, the re-echo stronger, and the zero transmission mark will tend to increase in width. As the maximum gain setting is approached, background noise from suspended particles, bubbles, etc. will begin to appear. At gain settings of this order fish echoes become readily apparent, as can be seen toward the left of (5.12), where shoals just off the bottom are indicated. The photographs (5.13, 5.14) show large numbers of fish near the bottom and in mid-water.

An important aspect of echosounding is the ability of the display to differentiate between hard and soft bottoms. This is clearly not possible with meter presentation. In the interpretation of this sort of information from recorder echosounder charts there are certain rules which apply, although there is no substitute for experience under local conditions, which enables a much finer degree of interpretation. The actual contour of the seabed is a valuable guide, as a pronounced irregularity of the bottom echo at higher paper speeds is very rarely characteristic of a soft bottom. Usually the appearance of multiple echoes is a feature of hard ground, as mentioned earlier; however, it must be remembered that at the higher gain settings even a soft bottom can give a re-echo. It is in these circumstances that experience with the sounder in the particular depths of water being worked will show how these phenomena vary with the gain control setting. The effect of hard and soft patches in the bottom is brought out very clearly (5.14) by the Ferrograph echosounder on which these recordings were made. With all echosounders there

5.13

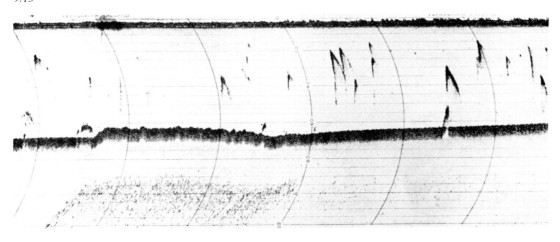

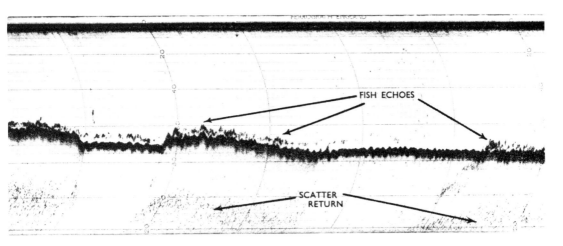

5.14

is a certain amount of scattered radiation which varies in its characteristics, depending to a large extent on the design of the instrument and its transducer. It appears as a speckled background after and below the first bottom reflection. In (5.14) it can be seen to have disappeared from the two softer areas due to absorption. Clear fish echoes can be seen over the hard ground and some are also visible in the trench.

Looking at (5.15), where several clear re-echoes are apparent, it should be noted that depth differences will always be magnified by a factor of 2 on the first re-echo and by 3 on the next. This will be clearly realised by comparing the height of the peaks and troughs of the various echoes in the photograph.

In order to provide for different instrument parameters required in different depths of water,

the equipment usually embodies a range switch. With the Ferrograph instrument, in order to provide a high and constant level of discrimination on all ranges, the writing speed of the recorder is held constant and the transmitter pulse is sent out at a specific time to suit the range, before the stylus commences its travel across the paper. (5.16) shows the effect as the boat goes into gradually deepening water: the second echo is seen to pass off the edge of the recording paper and as the bottom echo reaches the edge of the paper the range is changed. The ranges are made to overlap to avoid the necessity of continually changing range to keep the bottom under surveillance when cruising in water varying in depth around the maximum scale indication. A range of paper speeds is provided to give a wide variation in definition of the bottom contour.

5.15

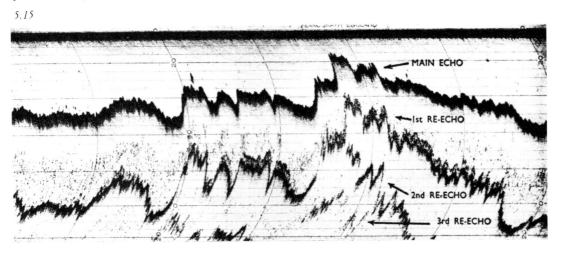

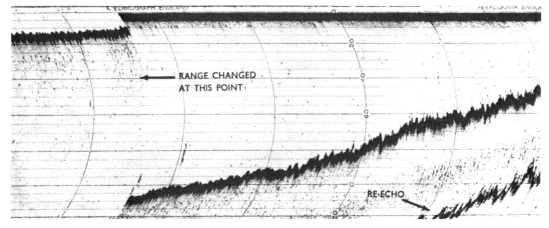

5.16   *Effect of range shifts*

In equipments where the stylus describes an arc across the paper some distortion is introduced into the display. This has the effect of steepening the trailing edge of a mound or the leading edge of a trough. This is most noticeable where the contour of the seabed varies rapidly.

The aspect ratio of the display will vary with the paper speed and the speed of the vessel. This affects the appearance of the display considerably and must be kept in mind. A typical comparison of horizontal scale would be where 0.1 m on the chart equals 370 m over the seabed (4 in. = 1200 ft).

Reference has been made to the disappearance of

the echo under certain conditions. Some of these conditions apply equally to all echosounders; however each instrument has characteristics that make these effects more or less pronounced. For example, whereas with commercial echosounders having a high power and operating at a low frequency it is unlikely that even a very dense shoal of fish would obscure the bottom echo, with equipments designed for inshore work and smaller boats the bottom can sometimes be obscured by fish. It may occasionally be necessary to decide whether there is indeed a shoal of fish or a pronounced ridge on the bottom. This can usually

5.17   *Effects of sea conditions and turbulence*

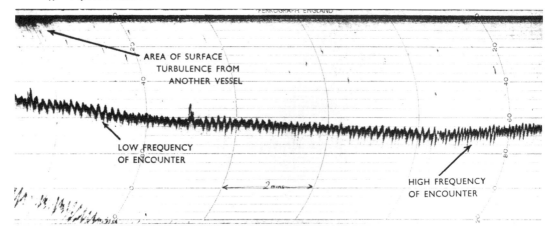

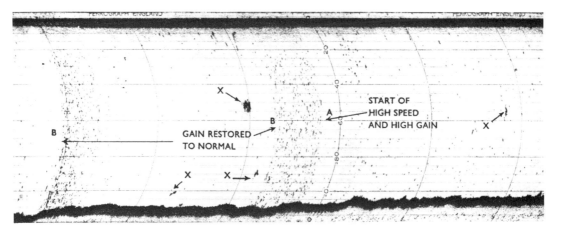

5.18   *Effects of speed on noise*

be established from the appearance of the edge of the 'ridge'. As the fish thin out towards the edge of the shoal some energy penetrates, and echoes from the fish and the bottom will appear at their true depths; the fish shoal appears as a 'ridge' suspended over a hole.

Sea conditions will affect the performance of the equipment. In small craft each wave will either lift it or produce a roll which will impress itself on the bottom contour to some degree (5.17). During the period of this recording the boat's heading was altered so that the rate of wave encounter reduced

from about 16 per minute to about 8 per minute. The general effect of swell is far more pronounced on vessels that roll heavily, particularly where the transducer has been mounted well away from the centreline. Even when the sea is very calm the apparent depth will vary in sympathy with the motion of the boat. Provided its beam is not masked, the transducer should be fitted as close as possible to the keel to minimise this effect.

Background noise has been referred to in this chapter and is illustrated in (5.17) and (5.18). The area to the top left of (5.17) shows the effect of

5.19   *Side lobe echoes*

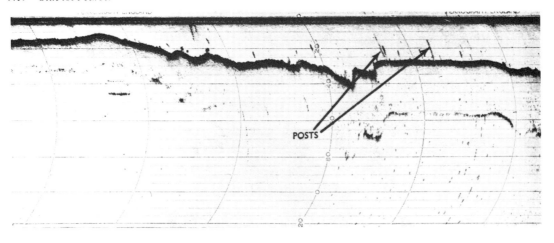

noise and turbulence caused by the movements of another vessel. Noise may vary with sea conditions due to the amount of suspended material present. The passage of the sounding vessel through the water, its propellers and machinery also create noise, the effects of which are usually only visible at the higher gain settings. in (5.18) the boat's speed increased to a maximum at A, where the onset of noise can be seen. At B the gain was restored to normal, and as can be seen the noise disappeared and strong mid-water echoes are evident. It is clearly advantageous to reduce speed when the highest definition and gain are required, as for example when searching for underwater objects.

There is of course a great deal of difference between the purely acoustical noise referred to above and electrical interference from other electrical equipment on the vessel. Electrical interference marks are generally coarse and more random than acoustical noise marks, although a regular pattern may appear if the repetition rate of the interference coincides with a multiple of the echosounder stylus speed. Where the source of interference can be traced to a particular piece of equipment on the boat, minimising this at the source can be attempted, as detailed in chapter 3.

From time to time odd marks will appear and it is difficult to decide whether they are echoes from an underwater object or whether they are due to single interference pulses caused by operating switches, etc. on other electrical equipment on the vessel. If on examination the recording shows that the mark has been repeated on two or more successive sweeps of the stylus, it can be taken as an echo from an underwater object. It is extremely unlikely that two or three single interference pulses will occur with precisely the same time interval between them. Such marks appear in (5.18) and are marked XX. It can be clearly seen that the chart has been marked on more than one traverse of the stylus. (5.19) shows an example of one of the unusual reflections that will be seen occasionally. The echoes from the posts occur because a small proportion of the acoustical energy from the transducer is radiated in the form of sidelobes around the main beam. When running parallel to a piled quay, spurious echoes may be received which may even have the appearance of bottom echoes; however, high gain settings are normally required

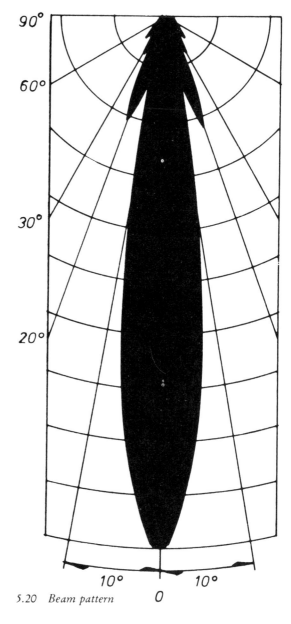

5.20 Beam pattern

before these effects show themselves (5.20) shows the beam pattern of a typical halfwave electrostrictive transducer as used by many small craft echosounders.

Selection of Suitable Equipment

Experience with echosounders has shown that it is well worth buying an instrument of reasonable quality as the considerable number of low grade echosounders on the market fail in many respects to provide the reliable performance that is essential.

Good in terms of general usefulness, and certainly high in popularity due to the price range, come the echosounders with flashing light displays. This type of presentation does enable the imperfections in the returned signal to be presented in a reasonably unambiguous fashion. For example, electrical interference or acute vibration can be identified separately from the echo response, as spurious signals of this nature generally appear as a series of regularly spaced flashes that rotate in either direction round the dial; thus the echo signal can be identified as a stationary mark. It is claimed that the nature of the seabed can be determined by the appearance of the echo flash. However, I feel it is highly unlikely that reliable conclusions could be drawn. For example if, as is claimed, mud produces a broad flash how am I, in unfamiliar circumstances, going to distinguish this from a smooth sloping sandy bottom which diffuses energy rather than absorbs it and gives a similar display? The answer is, of course, that it is not possible to know with any certainty without going to the same standard of equipment used for commercial craft, which embody special bottom discriminating circuits.

An advantage shared with the paper recorder, flasher type and CRT presentation is the ability to reproduce mid-water echoes. With all other types (meter, digital) of display, only one depth at a time can be indicated on the readout; also, due to the method of extracting information from the received signal for the display, interference or re-echoes can confuse the pulsing circuitry and can cause it to read high or low even in similar circumstances.

When you set out to buy an echosounder, ask for a working demonstration and carry out the following simple tests in the shop. With the instrument operating, turn to the greatest depth range and set the gain control to maximum. If the unit is a flasher type, make sure under these conditions that there are no regularly spaced faint flashes that would indicate motor noise. Point the transducer at a hard surface, such as the floor or

walls, at a distance of about 3 ft; as soon as a clear indication of depth is obtained move the transducer carefully away from the echoing surface taking care to keep it aligned so that a steady reading is obtained. The ultimate depth performance can be roughly assessed for 150 kHz types by the distance off at which the equipment ceases to give a steady reading, as follows: 6 ft = 40 fathoms, 8 ft = 60/70 fathoms, 10 ft = 80/100 fathoms. When one considers that in coastal waters around much of the British Isles it is difficult to find anything like 60 fathoms, probably the maximum sounding depth capability is not the most important aspect to consider.

Select the shallowest range on the instrument, hold the transducer about 24 in from a hard surface and note the reading, now slowly bring the transducer face closer to the echoing surface until a distance of about 6 in. remains. At this point move the transduer radially back and forth to optimise the reflection conditions and check the following points. With the meter or counter type a steady reading of minimum depth of about 2 ft is obtained and held. With a CRT, flasher or paper recording type a series of rebound echoes should be visible. Make sure that they do not fade out just after the transmit mark, which will indicate a design having poor receiver recovery or a poorly damped transducer. With the gain control and transducer adjusted to produce one clear echo at roughly 5 ft on the scale, make sure the scale is clear of spurious marks, the transmit pulse and the echo being the only indications visible, or that the meter or counter reading is steady.

If your intended choice survives these simple checks it will certainly give satisfactory depth readings on your boat. However we have left out one or two considerations which are everything in terms of price and installed performance. It is possible for example to buy a small craft flasher type echosounder at a low price; however the worthwhile things that separate the lower cost unit from performance are such things as a metal case to screen the electronics, a front dial that does not flop in when you look at it, RF filtering of the supply leads, a supply input circuit that will handle −10% to +20% on a nominal system voltage, good quality connectors, a balanced twin coaxial transducer lead, a screened transducer input transformer, a rugged transducer housing from which the head will not 'pop off', and so on ad infinitum.

It has become popular to quote the echosounder output in terms of watts, but it is unwise to take these figures at face value as some watts appear bigger than others. Consider the folowing approximate equivalents: 100 watts peak dc input power to the output stage = 40 watts peak output power to the transducer = 28 watts rms = 12 watts acoustic power in the water. It would be much better for the customer and the industry if the sound source level were quoted in dB's re 1 micropascal at 1 metre, so that we could compare like with like. In the absence of this, stick to the practical test described in this chapter.

6 Sonar and underwater gear

Errors like straws on the surface flow
He who would search for pearls must dive below.

Dryden

The use of sonar in small boats is only just beginning to emerge as a practical and useful proposition. The bulk and expense of conventional sonars had previously restricted the application of this equipment to large fishing vessels. While microwave radar looks around at objects above the surface and may be considered a high priority navigational requirement for many reasons, the small boat sonar is capable of similar functions in the region below the surface of the water, which is obviously just as potentionally dangerous. Sonar is a very short range instrument by comparison, operating over a range which is exactly where the microwave radar is unable to work. It is also hard to think of anything that one is likely to encounter on the surface that does not have its origins or part of its volume beneath the surface. The two equipments are of course vastly different, but comparison is possible to some extent because of the similarity in the pulse and display techniques of the latest small craft units.

The English ASDIC was probably the forerunner of the SONAR breed, the two names being made up from the name of the wartime administrations; in the case of the former Anti-Submarine Development Investigation Committee, and SOunding NAvigation and Ranging in the case of the latter. The original asdics used wet paper and a mechanical stylus for the display device, as did the early echosounders, and although this system was very far from perfect it became a standard display technique on fishing asdics used since the war.

Historically, sonar is closely linked to the early years of echosounder design, as many of the techniques are similar. The principal difference is

that the sonar transducer is usually retractable, rotatable and tiltable. In 'state of the art' sonars even this statement needs qualification, in that methods of slewing the beam from a fixed transducer have been developed.

It is curious that, although operational sonar was some 20 years ahead of radar, few people know about or have seen a working sonar, whereas most people have quite a clear impression of what radar is and what it can do. The early paper recording types needed more experience to operate as the transducer was often hand steered, and the display indicated range and time as the conventional chart recording echosounder does. Although sonar was developed to a useable level by 1918, its wartime advantage was highlighted during the Battle of the Atlantic at the beginning of World War II. Paul Langevin, the French physicist, carried out considerable studies of the piezo electric effects of quartz. He was in close contact with Professor R W Boyle, a Canadian leading the British team which included Lord Rutherford (then Sir Ernest). It was Langevin's quartz element between two steel plates which was to provide the forerunner of today's high power sandwich transducer. For use in early British anti-submarine sonar, the quartz was cut into small slabs and mounted in a mosaic pattern to define the beamwidth required. At the time Britain became involved in World War II, our customary lack of preparedness (of playing bowls on Plymouth Hoe) was showing again, and it fell to the tombstone makers of Lambeth, Farmer and Brindley, to cut the quartz to size.

Another interesting parallel between radar and sonar is that some of the earliest operational experiments were carried out within a few miles of each other on the east coast of England; radar at Orfordness and sonar at the Admiralty Research Station at Parkeston Quay, Harwich. Wider application of sonar seems inevitable, particularly as smaller equipments become available. There are various established forms of sonar that all use pulse echo principles, but differ in the way the information is displayed or in the type of soundome or transducer used. The equipment described here will find application in commercial and pleasure fishing, small scale surveys, diving, locating wrecks, and other related work.

Sound in Water

Performance is related to the behaviour of sound in water and, as this is a subject on its own, I will leave the reader with just a few points affecting design to consider when selecting equipment. Taking the speed of sound in water as 1500 metres per second, it is fairly easy to figure out that, at a range of 750 metres, the time taken for the sonar pulse to get to the target and for the echo to return will be exactly one second. By comparison, a radar pulse would travel a total distance of 300,000,000 metres in 1.0 seconds. The practical effect of this is that, although we are able to see objects (in some cases on a radar type presentation), the whole process is dramatically slowed down. If one pulse is emitted every two seconds for every two degrees of rotation, it will obviously take 6 minutes to complete a search through 360 degrees. Sector scanning is used to shorten the time between successive responses and, although high speed scanning systems exist, they are complex and expensive. Even in such cases high speed is a relative term and it is still slow compared with radar; however, it is a problem the operator acquires a skill to surmount.

Operating Frequency, Beamwidth, Resolution

The frequency of operation affects the penetration of sound through water. Taking this factor in isolation, one would say that the lowest frequency must be the best one to choose; but we then encounter practical problems like physical size and resolution.

The beamwidth problem starts with what can be tolerated as a maximum size for a through-hull fitting, that will find general acceptance in the small boat market. Certainly for pleasure craft, a

75 mm(3 in.) skin fitting valve and pipe are the largest likely to be tolerated because of size and cost. For fishing or survey work, a larger diameter would no doubt be acceptable, but would cost more. Beamwidth is the angle between two points, one either side of the main beam, where the transmitted power has dropped to half the maximum value. Whatever this figure is, it does not mean that the bearing accuracy is limited to this figure. Due to the shape of the beam, the apparent resolution on a single target can be improved by use of the gain control so that the response just shows. Moreover, as small craft are inherently unstable there is even an advantage to be had in avoiding a very narrow beamwidth, in that targets will not be lost so easily due to the movement of the boat.

The beamwidth is determined by the number of half wave-lengths of the applied wave that can be divided into the diameter of the transducer element; the bigger the diameter, the narrower the beam. In a practical sonar, the transducer is usually gimballed in a steerable mount and this takes up space; taking 75 mm (3 in.) as the skin fitting size, we are clearly being pressed toward a high frequency.

Range resolution is also affected by frequency, as something like 10 cycles of the output wave are **required to produce a reasonable pulse shape. For** the sake of example, at a frequency of 10 kHz, 10 cycles would take 1 mS to emit, and the length of this pulse in water is about 1.5 metres. This means that about 2 metres spacing in range is required between objects that are to show as a separate

6.1   Wesmar small sonar, Type SS90 B

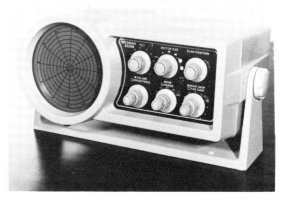

6.2   Wesmar sonar Type SS 160

mark. If we move up in frequency by a factor of 10, all the other figures can be adjusted to give a range resolution of 0.2 metres.

Typical Equipment

Wesmar (USA) have manufactured sonars for some years now, and their smallest unit is the type SS90B shown in (6.1). This has a maximum range of 240 metres, an operating frequency of 266 kHz, power output of 200 watts peak, and the soundome will pass through a 75 mm skin fitting. For larger craft and fishermen, the SS160 (6.2) offers 160 kHz operation, 6.5 degree beamwidth, 600 watt peak output power which gives a range of about 500 metres.

A mini side-scan sonar is also produced (6.3). This equipment emits a fan shaped beam, narrow horizontally and of about 35 degrees arc in the vertical plane. The effect of this is to illuminate objects in the water and on the bottom so that they show in relief. Surprisingly detailed pictures can be obtained, and it brings a useful survey technique down to small boat size. So that the transducers are not affected by the aerated water in the wake, they are mounted in a fish which is

6.3   Wesmar mini side-scan sonar

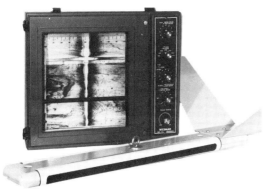

towed 60 metres (200 ft) behind. This is a very lightweight unit and, due to the use of a towable transducer, is completely portable; power requirements are 12 v 36 w; range about 500 metres.

In much the same way as with conventional echosounders, when the sound wave strikes the object, some of its energy is reflected back like an echo. This reflected energy, when it strikes the transducer, creates an electrical signal, and after suitable processing the signal brightens the rotating trace on a cathode ray tube. At the instant the pulse leaves the transducer, the trace on the CRT is initiated, and the spot travels radially to the outer edge of the screen in a direction determined by the orientation of the transducer. At some point in the course of its travel an echo returns and this affects the trace as described above. The range and bearing of any reflecting object are thus clearly indicated by the display. Since the transducer and trace are continuously rotated, a complete picture of the underwater area surrounding the ship is built up. The soundome is raised and lowered within a special housing fitted to the bottom of the boat and can operate manually or automatically when the equipment is turned on. This arrangement gives the maximum protection for the underwater unit.

The performance of the soundome may be greatly enhanced by stabilising the internal transducer elements during pitch and roll motions. Such stabilisation, although in the past associated only with very expensive equipment, has been brought to a high level of development and is embodied in the unit described in this chapter. The second great advantage of this system is that the vessel's trim does not have any significant effect on the accuracy of the presentation. As trim is a very significant factor in all small craft, this point is most important.

The electrical functions that take place during operation are as follows. The power supply converts energy from the vessel's mains, which may be nominally 12, 24 or 32 V, to a suitable form for the circuitry. This may be at various levels for different requirements, such as CRT HT at about 12 kV DC down to 6 V AC for the heater supply. Some input stabilisation will be necessary as the boat's supply will vary considerably due to factors discussed earlier. A range of—10% to +20% is normally allowed for, and it will be clear that a power supply of some complexity is necessary. At the appropriate level, power is applied to the various parts of the circuit.

In the trigger pulse generator a pulse is created at discrete intervals and applied to the transmitter and timebase simultaneously. The transmitter gives a burst of oscillation and causes the transducer within the soundome to emit pressure waves which are substantially constrained within a pencil beam. The interval between the pulses, which is defined by the trigger unit and the duration of the transmitted pulse, is automatically optimised for each sounding range provided by the instrument, with a tandem switching facility on the range switch. During the transmission period the receiver input is protected from the high energy outgoing pulse by a special duplexing circuit. There is, however, some leakage, which causes a bright patch to appear in the centre of the screen. This is accented by a small part of the transmitted energy making parts of the soundome structure and the ship's structure 'ring'. Effects of this type are normally minimised at the design stage by damping, although ultimately some overriding influence may be caused by installation conditions.

At the instance the timebase receives the trigger pulse it commences the scanning period, and initiates the 'bright up' circuit. The scanning circuit causes current to flow through the scan coils around the CRT neck. This current is arranged to increase linearly with time for a period suitable for the sounding range selected. The bright up circuit switches the CRT circuit into a condition which electrically creates a pedestal voltage on which any echo may be superimposed. At the end of the scanning period the current in the scan coil is switched off together with the bright up pulse. This is the 'rest' condition and the circuit is now quiescent until the next trigger pulse. The bright up circuit is used as out-of-range echoes could show in the flyback period, which would be ambiguous, and also the background illumination would increase, giving reduced picture contrast.

Immediately after the transmitter pulse the receiver recovers and any echo appearing within the scanning period will be amplified and applied to the CRT brightness circuit via the video amplifier. The amplification of the receiver is very great

indeed and in fact is considerably in excess of the usable range. This is done to achieve a situation where the overall performance is limited by water noise and other factors outside the equipment. Care must, as always, be taken during installation to avoid the introduction of electrical noise. The high sensitivity of the receiver will be severely limited if good installation practice is not followed. Insofar as electrical interference is concerned, chapter 3 outlines the necessary work to quiet any offending equipment. It should, however, be noted that sonars use the lower frequencies, and noises from rotational machinery increase towards the lower end of the spectrum, i.e. 15–200 kHz. The interference limiting specifications have been framed with this in mind. I should, add that if each equipment on the vessel has been properly installed and if its terminal noise is not in excess of that given in BS 1597, little trouble will generally be experienced.

The bearing transmitter sends the angular position of the transducer head to the display in a form that allows the bearing receiver powering the scan coil to remain coincident in orientation.

Operation

Environmental conditions affect the range and general performance of sonar equipment in a manner similar in many respects to the symptoms encountered with other marine electronic equipment under adverse conditions. Heavy rolling, choppy seas or extreme temperature inversion (where surface water is at a substantially different temperature from lower stata or bottom water) cause distortions which are sufficient to reduce the maximum range at which useful results can be obtained. Under stormy conditions wave motion may interfere with the range and clarity of signals near the surface. However, with experience an operator learns to make effective use of sonar even in heavy weather. The following diagrams and notes show some of the practical aspects of operation. Basic rules are:

Practice.
Take great care with setting all controls, brightness and sensitivity controls in particular, as maladjustment will impair results.

If you wish to check the receiver sensitivity train the transducer on the wake.

If troubled by wake noise tilt the transducer down as far as possible.

Maximum horizontal range is achieved with transducer angles between 0° and 10°. If the water is particularly choppy, you may need to tilt down to get under the air bubbles.

As a target is approached it becomes more difficult to hold in the beam and it must be followed closely with the tilt control.

Water conditions will effect performance on a day-to-day basis and therefore it is a good plan to check performance before each trip against known pilings, breakwaters, the wake, etc.

For maximum range in shallow water, always look towards deeper water.

To achieve maximum flexibility of performance, the transducer can be set to project the beam at any desired angle. If the sensitivity control is set at too high a level, the responses can make the display ambiguous due to energy from the transducer sidelobes producing echoes. I should make clear that when in shallow water, say 30 ft or less, even with the transducer beam parallel to the surface, there is a small amount of energy from bottom returns which will produce a circle on the display. The radius of the circle will be equivalent to the depth.

Typical manual controls accessible on the display unit of small craft sonars are as follows.

The brightness control is adjusted in much the same way as on a radar display. It is set so that the trace is at the threshold of visibility; if it is too far advanced a high level of background illumination will destroy the contrast and obscure weak echoes.

Volume control of the speaker output is set to suit the operator and the ambient noise level, and does not create adjustment problems. The sensitivity control enables the amplification of the echo signals to be adjusted to suit conditions. For instance, if working at short range with clear targets such as pontoons, piles of jetties, the display can be improved by a reduction in the sensitivity. In practice it is adjusted in conjunction with the brightness control to produce the optimum contrast between water noise and echoes.

Noise due to random returns from the surface, seabed and hull may be reduced by the use of the anti-clutter control. Two forms are in use: one type is the swept gain variety, which works very much like the radar sea clutter control; i.e. the receiver gain increases with range thus reducing small short-term returns. The correct method of setting this control is to adjust the level of clutter to the point where it is only just visible; it is then possible for any echo in the clutter area to add in brightness to this level of visibility. The second type of anti-clutter circuit is a differentiating arrangement by which only the leading edges of echoes are displayed. This may entail some loss of weaker signals and may need an increase in the setting of the sensitivity control.

The transducer assembly may be tilted in the vertical axis of the beam between +10° and—90° from the horizontal. The transducer tilt control enables the function to be conveniently handled at the display.

Range: various points of the circuitry need adjustments to their respective time or voltage constants in order to effectively handle differing radial parameters. For example, on the Wesmar SS 150 unit the ranges are 100, 200, 400, 800, 1600 ft. The pulse width and pulse repetition frequency are optimised as necessary by tandem wafers on this selector. Note that the ranges have been arranged to increase or decrease by a constant factor of 2, to reduce operational ambiguities when changing range.

Due to the propagation constants of sound in water a complete plan presentation could take an unacceptably long time to build up on the longer ranges. In order to reduce this possible inconvenience the transducer has a control system which allows the search pattern of the soundome unit to be pre-selected. By adjusting this scan control the transducer can be made to search any desired sector or rotate continuously. When the transducer scan is set to the sector scan mode the size of the sector can be set by adjusting the scan size control.

The following series of pictures gives some indication of the standard of information from CRT presentation sonars. (6.4) shows a shoal of fish directly ahead of the vessel; (6.5) shows the shoal slightly to port and closer; (6.6) shows screen full of fish echoes; (6.7) shows the start of setting a seine net (lower right). (6.8) shows netting continued; (6.9) shows fish, net and echoes from

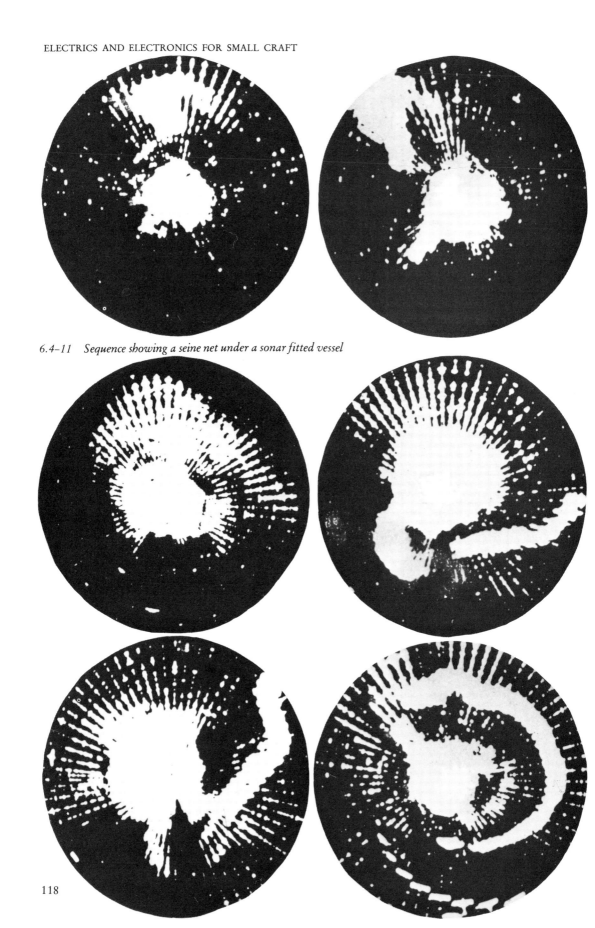

6.4–11   *Sequence showing a seine net under a sonar fitted vessel*

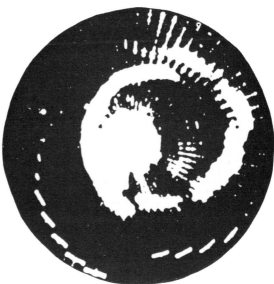

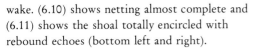

wake. (6.10) shows netting almost complete and (6.11) shows the shoal totally encircled with rebound echoes (bottom left and right).

Installation

Care is always necessary when installing any marine equipment and sonar is no exception. There are certain additional disciplines concerning the soundome, but the work involved is by no means beyond the scope of the average small boatyard.

Display units resemble radar displays and can be mounted in any position convenient to the operator. This can be either the deckhead or bulkhead, and if there is room, on a horizontal surface. Bear in mind that as with radar displays there is a safe distance from the compass to be observed (typically 1 metre/3 ft). Apart from the effect of the display unit on the ship's compass, other magnetic objects may interfere with the display and care should be taken to avoid a site where stray fields from an autopilot motor, pump or power transformer can cause unwanted beam modulation. In general 2-3 ft will be sufficient to avoid such effects. Interpretation is less ambiguous if the display can be oriented so that when the operator is standing in a forward facing position the display screen is horizontal, or vertical and facing aft. When the display is mounted behind the operator's position so that it faces forward and the operator faces aft, the echoes shown at the top right-hand side of the display will be in fact from

objects off the starboard bow and not off the port after quarter.

The Soundome

The ideals of sonar operation cannot weigh very heavily in the design of yachts and other small craft, for obvious reasons. As usual a compromise is reached, and therefore the performance will to some extent be limited by the installation. Probably this will mean that the sonar will be placed where it least interferes with the rest of the equipment. This being so, the things to be taken into account are akin to those associated with echosounders. The usual sources of acoustic noise are propellers, bow wave, wake, mechanical vibration from machinery, etc. Electrical noise should be dealt with as detailed in chapter 3.

The various methods of hull construction make hard and fast rules impossible; however the soundome (6.12) must have, when lowered, a clear all-round view under the keel; also it must not be positioned too close to the propellers. In general it should be placed as far forward as possible without being exposed to the bow wave, water inlets or outlets, echosounder transducers, log impellers, or air entrained in the water. The tube housing the dome should be faired in to reduce perturbance around the dome to a minimum.

It is generally better to make the tube long enough to extend well above the waterline, to facilitate removal of the soundome without slipping the boat. If it is not possible to arrange

6.12   *Soundome*

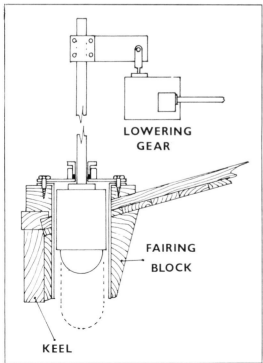

6.13   *Soundome housing*

LOWERING
GEAR

FAIRING
BLOCK

KEEL

for either a seacock or an extended tube, the unit may be fitted as shown in (6.13). This method has the disadvantage that it will be necessary to slip the boat, or use a diver, every time service to the soundome is required.

Applied Sonar

Underwater technology has leapt ahead in the last decade, and in the UK this has been stimulated by the growth of the offshore oil industry. Not all the electronic devices available are developed purely for industrial application however, and an increasing number find their way into work undertaken in small craft. It is also significant that the number and use of small craft for commercial concerns in surveys, salvage and treasure hunting has increased. Sonar can be valuable aid in this area, and a number of low cost facilities are now available; see (6.14), (6.15).

Position Fixing Equipment
At Lowestoft the local MAFF laboratory has an electronics section which, among other things, is pioneering work in the miniaturisation of electronics for biological studies on fish. A package about half the size of the average writing pen can be tagged to a fish and, at a range of several hundred metres, it is possible to derive range, bearing from the research vessel, speed at which the fish is swimming, orientation of the fish with respect to magnetic north and heart beat in real time. This will give some idea of what is possible. For small craft applications, such as the underwater beacon system shown in (6.16) a device can be positioned on the sea or river bed by means of a weight and a flotation collar to hold it roughly vertical. A diver can then pinpoint the beacon from a distance of up to about 300 metres, using a form of underwater direction finder.

These particular examples are low cost devices that anyone can use without sophisticated shipborne equipment, and they find application in any form of underwater marking from power lines to wrecks. The beacon belongs to the family of acoustic markers called 'pingers', as its function is to emit pulses of ultrasonic energy, at a typical rate of 2 per sec from the time it is turned on until the time it is recovered.

6.14   *Divex sonar acoustic transponder*

At a higher level of technology, the transponding marker beacon offers more complex functions. These devices lie dormant until interrogated by a sonar, thus greatly conserving battery life. They can also be programmed to emit an identifying code so that around a wreck, for example, one could have a series of markers each emitting a coded reply to every interrogation, so that accurate identification of any part of the wreck could be made. The same system could be applied to free-swimming divers, as the transponders are light and can be worn without discomfort. The increasing number of sub-aqua clubs and organised archeological studies could clearly benefit from the use of such equipment.

6.15   *Divex submersible sonar*

Communications Equipment

Underwater communications equipment is also available and, although most divers work with a lifeline (which often embodies a communications cable), free-swimming divers can use wireless equipment that employs an ultrasonic carrier. The environment is particularly hard on underwater electronic equipment, as the effects of pressure at depth are considerable. The carrier frequency and the form of modulation varies with the duty the equipment has to perform. The underwater world is full of noise, and sound travels for long distances. The quality of communication is affected by a number of factors which includes diver stress, microphone, mask or helmet, earphone, line losses, connectors, and seawater loss. It is easy to understand therefore that you must aim for quality in the whole system rather than any particular part, as the results will only be as good as the poorest element in the system.

Because of the difficult circumstances a diver works under, any speech produced will be distorted to some extent even as it is voiced. The

6.16   *Divex underwater beacon*

psychological effects of immersion, pressure, temperature, limited vision, and the physical limitations of speaking within a mask or helmet, often with a small back pressure, tend to produce an unnatural and poorly articulated form of speech. Because of the very low volume of gas into which the diver speaks, there is a complete absence of the enhancement given to the human voice by reverbration of sound within the confines of a normal room; furthermore the volume of the mask cavity must clearly be kept at a minimum to avoid a large build-up of carbon dioxide. This is at odds with the requirement for a large volume in front of the mouth to allow both the high and low frequency components of speech to be produced.

A full face mask with the microphone mounted in the oro-nasal unit is advised when communications are to be used, and equipment manufacturers usually supply a complete package of microphone, earpiece and acoustic transceiver, which normally fastens to the air bottles with a webbing strap. The surface equipment usually takes the form of a control unit for the tender, to which is connected a hydrophone normally immersed to a

depth of about 2 metres and roughly pointed in the direction of the working divers. Directional characteristics are embodied in this unit, to minimise distortion caused by multiple path reception caused by reflection of the ultrasonic signal from surface, bottom or objects. Installation problems with electronic diving aids are comparatively few, as most are designed as portable equipments and operate from dry or rechargeable cells.

Metal Detectors

Much underwater activity is associated with search and location and, although sonic aids such as those already described are at present providing most of the services required, an underwater metal detector such as the Littlemore 700 (6.17) can prove very useful. The principle of operation is based on analysis of eddy currents created in the search object, following a high power magnetic pulse which is transmitted from the search coil. It will work on ferrous or non-ferrous metals, and the following is an indication of useful ranges:

6.17   *Littlemore underwater metal detector*

6.18   Small boat towable magnetometer

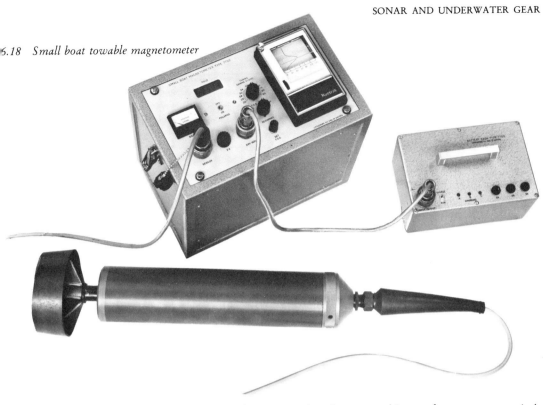

1 25 mm (1 in.) copper coin	= 50 cm (20 in.)
20 25 mm (1 in.) copper coin	= 55 cm (25 in.)
Brass plate 100 mm sq 1.5 mm thick	= 90 cm (35 in.)
Large iron cannon	= 3 metres (10 ft.)
Steel gas pipe 23 cm dia 12.0 mm wall	= 2.5 metres (8 ft.)

This equipment uses a single coil 46 cm in diameter and can be used to a depth of 200 metres or so. Indication of detection is by the meter scale or a bone conductor worn by the diver. It is powered by internal rechargeable batteries and can be adjusted to neutral buoyancy by filling the handle.

Magnetometers

For those involved with commercial work, a small boat version of the highly sensitive proton precession magnetometer is now available. A typical underwater application would be location of pipelines, wrecks and cables, or indeed any ferrous object. The high sensitivity demands that it is towed some 50 metres from the survey vessel. The readout is presented in two forms, as a numerical value of the total field in nT (nano-Tesla) and on a paper recorder, so that changes along a track can be easily logged. The principle of operation is based on the hydrogen proton being a spinning mass and exhibiting north and south magnetic poles. When subject to a heavy superimposed field the protons align their axis parallel with the field. If the superimposed field is then switched off, the proton cannot snap back to alignment with the earth's field due to gyroscopic effects, and must therefore precess. As the strength of the field determines the frequency of precession, it is clear that by measuring the frequency we will be able to derive the strength of the field. In a practical realisation of these principles, such as the Littlemore 7702 (6.18) a proton sample is enclosed within a coil used both to polarize and sense the particle precession. Typically the coil is polarized every 2 seconds, and the precession frequency measured between each polarization. The equipment requires a power supply of about 36 watts which can be supplied from a rechargeable battery pack. In operation the equipment is towed in a prescribed search pattern, and disturbances in the field intensity can be seen on the chart recorder.

7 Automatic Pilots

What pilot so expert but needs must wreck,
Imbarked with such a steersmate at the helm.

John Milton

Automatic pilot principles were probably first applied by Hiram Maxim about the year 1890, for stabilising a flying machine. This very early equipment was surprisingly sophisticated and used a gyroscope driven by compressed air as the sensing unit. Although very effective systems have been available since the 1920s for both aircraft and commercial shipping, the history of small craft automatic pilots in this country starts around the end of the 1939–45 war.

A wide range of automatic steering equipment is now available, microelectronics having played their part in the evolution of sophisticated signal processing circuitry used in the more advanced designs; even the smallest boats are well provided for by the Autohelm which has been developed mechanically and electronically so that the power required is minimal; indeed, for the 'round the world' yachtsman the vulnerable mechanical self steering gear can be replaced by a solar-powered tiller pilot.

Few owners consider such a device to be less than a necessity once they have had experience of what it can do. Standing at the helm for hours on end, and the concentration required to hold even a mediocre course in a small boat, have little esoteric appeal. Even the simplest automatic pilot is a considerable aid to navigation and provides small craft with an economic means of holding course automatically and for carrying out steering manoeuvres under power control. The helmsman is relieved of the physical exertion required to hold the boat on course and this makes him a better watchkeeper; also a considerably more precise course is steered under automatic control than a human helmsman is capable of, thus improving the standard of navigation, which in turn reduces fuel consumption and overall passage time, in many cases by as much as 20%.

A typical automatic pilot of traditional design will consist of a number of units which, although their form will vary slightly will follow this basic pattern:

> The error sensing device
> A device to monitor the rudder angle
> A control unit where the various signals are co-ordinated
> A motor to turn the helm
> A remote control unit or dodger.

The diagrams (7.1, 7.2) show the electrical and mechanical relationships between the various units and the boat.

Various makes of automatic pilot have their arrays of knobs to twiddle, all rejoicing in different names. The following is a short description of what they do (7.3).

Sensitivity Weather	Controls the course error allowed before the steering motor makes a correction. An adequate range is about ±1° to ± 5°.
Ratio Rudder Response	Controls the amplitude of rudder movement for a given course error and allows manual adjustment for conditions of loading and speed. Very often, as well as a front panel control a pre-set adjustment will enable the correct range of control to be set to suit the vessel.

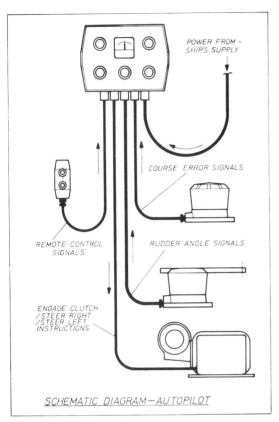

7.1 *Autopilot system*

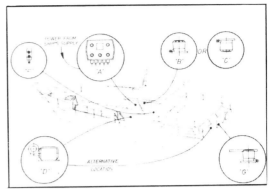

7.2 *Siting autopilot components*

7.3 *Controls*

Trim	Electrically offsets the balance
Standing helm	point of the autopilot, thus
Bias	allowing a predetermined
Weather helm	amount of rudder to be applied.

This compensates for things such as one engine out of action, or in sailing craft allows for the weather helm more often than not applied.

Counter rudder A control which is not really suitable for small craft autopilots. In the case of a typical fast twin screw outdrive configuration it would be a total disaster. The effect of the control is to make the rudder go past its balance point momentarily and then return after a predetermined period. If you imagine a boat responding to a course correction, as the boat

approaches the required heading opposite rudder is applied for a short period in order to check the tendency to continue the swing. However, these conditions do not obtain in small craft, which are in general grossly overpowered and thus will respond instantly to the smallest helm movement. (See later section on setting up autopilots.)

Principles

It is difficult to describe automatic steering systems without resorting to the word 'servo'. Servo systems may sometimes be very complex, but are basically an arrangement of contrivances whereby one component of the system controls or slaves the other. Although the theory and practical

125

application of servo mechanisms is somewhat outside the scope of this manual, for the sake of clarity I will outline the basis of the two forms of servo system, i.e. open loop and closed loop, for the purpose of describing a marine automatic pilot. An open loop system may be compared to a petrol engine and its throttle control. Where the load is constant the engine speed will vary in step with the control setting, i.e. the engine speed is the slave of the control. However, if we now consider what happens when the load on the engine is increased, it will be clear that some manual control is necessary in order to restore the engine speed to its original level. If, by some mechanism such as a governor, we are able to sample the engine speed and translate this information via a suitable linkage into throttle movements, it could be arranged for a manual throttle control to set the required range of speed and to advance or retard this mean setting to suit the engine load conditions. This would in fact constitute a closed loop servo system. To sum up then, an open loop system is a device in which the output varies as a function of the input, and a closed loop system is a mechanism which allows a sample of the output to be fed back to the system input for the purpose of stability. The system output then varies as a function of both the input and the output conditions.

Against this background we have to consider replacing the human helmsman with an electromechanical device, at least in the sense that we will relieve him of the second-to-second mental computation and physical manipulation of steering and leave him able only to make a decision on which direction he wishes his boat to travel. To enable a satisfactory mechanised solution to be arrived at we must examine the human helmsman and his efforts in detail. The complete servo mechanism, i.e. input, output, and effect of output, are all sensed or enacted by the human frame. The direction and deviation from direction input is taken by the eyes from the compass. The rudder angle is assimilated from an indicator or via the hands from the position of the wheel or tiller. The output is from the hands to the helm, and the effect of the output is again gathered by the eyes from the compass. Unconsciously the helmsman solves several simultaneous equations (including those of you who claim to be no good at maths) and applies the solution to the boat's helm. This in

fact happens as an impression in the mind whereby the helmsman senses an error in sign, acceleration and magnitude and continuously applies a proportionate correction to reduce the error. One other piece of information is available to a human helmsman that cannot be used in a low cost automatic pilot: the human frame has information on pitch and roll to apply to the computation, derived from the balancing mechanism within the human ear. In very small and fast boats this has meant that in weather where there are enough random accelerations to upset the compass sense unit, the automatic pilot would not work effectively.

In a practical small craft autopilot, to replace the human helmsman we must have a means of extracting a signal from the earth's magnetic vector giving both sign and magnitude or rate of change of any course error, and secondly a signal from the boat's rudder giving the sign and angle of rudder applied, or the rate at which helm is applied. These two elements are sensory and may be likened to human sensory perception. The two signals need to be compared and the difference used to control a means of electromotive force, which may be an electric motor or electric valves controlling a hydraulic system. The application of the motive system must be arranged in a manner that will reduce the error in the same way as the human helmsman.

Autopilots need to be attached to various parts of a boat's anatomy and their performance can be made or marred by the installation work to a far greater extent than many other items of equipment. This, in my view, is because each boat varies considerably in its characteristics; even, on occasion, boats out of the same mould. In these varying conditions of behaviour, which it will be understood form part of the servo loop, it is difficult for a manufacturer to do more than produce an equipment with a wide range of adjustment.

Error sensing devices

Magnetic compass types
The means of relating the boats heading to the earth's magnetic field must be the first link in the control chain. Most equipments are based on specialised versions of the magnetic compass.

produce a 360 degree read-out but simply to indicate errors left or right of a datum position, it is possible to produce a low cost version. It functions by using a core of material sensitive to magnetic fields (high permeability), on which is superimposed a known alternating field. The earth's field influences the point at which each cycle of the alternating field takes the core into saturation; by sensing these points and comparing them with the origin of the AC field, a signal emerges which is proportional to the orientation. The unit is suspended in a single gimbal over the north/south line to remove the effects of dip.

Mechanical feedback

This is effected by rotating the whole compass assembly by a flexible cable drive from the steering motor. The signals from the compass cause the motor to run in the appropriate direction and to stop when alignment is reached. This has two

7.4   Pinta sense unit

Indeed, much ingenuity has been applied by many people over the years to extracting course information from a conventional compass without disturbing its function; (7.4) shows the Pinta sense unit. Most employ a photo detector and light source on opposite sides of the compass card which has been slotted, grated, shaded, polarised or otherwise treated to vary the light falling on one or more photo detectors in proportion to its mechanical position. Another type uses printed coils on the compass card to couple differentially with fixed coils in the compass bowl. Fluxgate magnetometers are also used, and more recently Hall plates. Irrespective of the method, the aim is to convert the mechanical position of the compass card into a proportional electrical signal.

Earth's field sensors

The mechanical compass, although excellent in many ways for its original purpose, has shortcomings such as pivot friction, liquid swirl, and oscillatory movement. During World War II a device called a fluxgate appeared; in essence a sensitive magnetometer, in its simplest form it gave a signal proportional to the cosine of the angle of the imposed field. It was designed because of the effects of aircraft motion on conventional compasses. As an autopilot sensor does not have to

7.5   Electrical feedback sensor

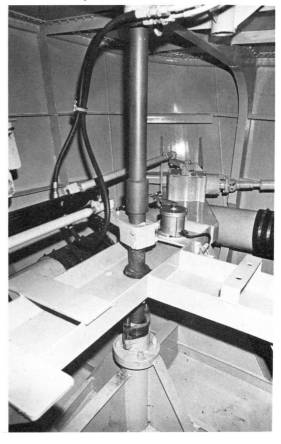

consequences: the compass body effectively follows the movement of the card, and the motor shaft rotation is proportional to the amount of turn made by the boat. It is therefore only necessary to provide a suitable drive from the steering motor to the boat's steering gear via a clutch to provide proportional control to the vessel's rudder. Variants of this kind of arrangement have become very popular and are used in many auto-pilots. One attractive feature is that it enables the drive to be engaged from any wheel position by an electric clutch, without the need for a course setting device. (7.4) shows a sense unit of this type; the flexible drive connection can be seen bottom centre.

The mechanical feedback type is set up by steering on the required course by hand, and when the steering motor stops its follow-up a clutch is engaged, whereafter the helm will be automatically applied in a direction to reduce the error. To change course with this type of autopilot the clutch must be disengaged and the vessel moved onto the new course by hand steering; the clutch is

then re-engaged after the steering motor has stopped on the new course.

Electrical feedback types

Pilots using this principle have a sensor attached to the steering motor or the rudder which gives an electrical output proportional to the rudder position; see (7.5). Exactly how this is done varies considerably, but in the simplest designs a mechanical potentiometer is used. To avoid wear present in such devices a photo-electric unit giving a similar analogue output has been used. In digital control systems an optical encoder giving binary numbers proportional to the rudder position does the same job. Whatever the means of deriving the feedback signal, it is compared with the error signal from the course detector, any difference emerges as a command to the steering motor to rotate left to right, reducing the error. The advantage of this type of system is that the course can be preset and is visible on the sense unit; changes in course are made by simply adjusting the sensor without the

7.6   Pinta electric motor

need to de-clutch the drive. If fully proportional remote power steering (as distinct from dodger buttons) is required, clearly an electrical signal giving rudder position is essential anyway. So that steering conditions can be varied to suit the installation, the relative proportion of the sensor and rudder signals can be varied by the front panel control.

Rate systems

One or two manufacturers now offer small auto-pilots with rate control. Historically this field has been restricted to large vessels, as a rate gyroscope sensor made the equipment expensive. In low cost equipment the compass signal is processed to derive the rate of swing; the signal is then used to adjust the rate of helm application to reduce the error. The system has no requirements for a trim control and weather helm is automatically applied.

No feedback of a mechanical nature is applied and therefore the system does not hunt due to overshoot no matter how sensitive the error detection is made. The Benmar Course Setter 21 is one example of this type.

Steering motors

The prime mover employed to power the helm is in many cases an electric motor (7.6) of the compound, shunt, or permanent magnet variety for low cost units. In more expensive equipment power is provided by a small hydraulic unit controlled by spool valves (7.7). It is often in the power unit that the cause of the familiar system instability called 'hunt' arises. Before discussing this point further I must clarify the term 'hunt', which seems to mean all sorts of things to different people. When the first small craft automatic pilots appeared on the market, there was a unit of

7.7   Solenoid hydraulic power block

obscure manufacture which was in fact an open loop type. When the sense unit indicated an error, the steering motor responded by turning left or right according to the sign of the error. Obviously this action caused the vessel to hunt violently back and forth across the required course. This particular unit quickly sank into oblivion. However, its seagoing antics became famous, and when other and later equipments using closed loop systems appeared, the boating public wanted to know if the new units suffered from the same defects. In anticipation, the sales brigade prepared literature extolling the virtues of 'non-hunting' autopilots. That breed on non-hunting types were the real forerunners of the small boat systems available today. Most of these present day non-hunting types exhibit a tendency towards a vastly different type of hunt under certain conditions. It is this particular hunt which can be relevant to the

power unit design, and in order to over come it we must understand the reasons for its appearance.

When an error occurs the motor will create a torque on the steering wheel which will accelerate itself and all the components of the steering system; subsequently, energy the motor draws from the supply is stored as kinetic energy in the rotor and these components. The system is moved due to this energy toward a point where the rudder angle feedback signal is proportional to the error, which causes the motor to be switched off. At this point the energy stored in the motor and steering system components begins to release itself and carries the system past the point where the rudder feedback is equal to the error signal. The motor then reverses itself due to the feedback signal and the same process happens in the opposite direction, thus causing an oscillatory movement about the proportional balance position. Clearly one method

7.8   Rams acting directly on rudder

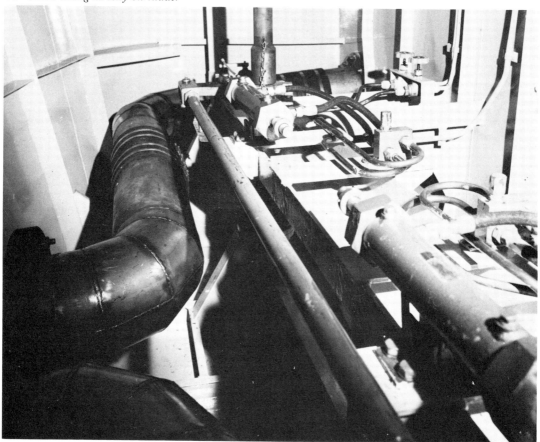

of improving this situation is to apply some sort of brake to convert the surplus energy to heat, at the same instant the balance condition is reached. In fact this is exactly what is employed on many commercial equipments. The motor armature is short circuited immediately after disconnection from the supply, thus creating a braking condition by armature reaction. In order to enhance this effect the compound type of winding is often used with the parallel field permanently connected, which consumes about 5% of the motor full load current for the whole of the time the unit is on duty.

This works to some extent and many present equipments employ this method of reducing the problem, although the method is limited for the following reasons. As the brake is not applied until the balance point is reached there must always be a delay which will cause some degree of overshoot, no matter how small. While this is not critical with early boat designs that need a fair amount of helm for steering, say 1° of rudder for 2° of error, with modern boat designs the steering is very light and the rudder generally has a balance area so that more typical steering ratios are in the order of 5° of error for 1° of rudder. It will be seen from this that the angle the rudder moves through for automatic steering purposes is a very small part of the total rudder angle capability, and clearly the smallest overshoot becomes significant. There is also very little point in applying precious battery power to a system merely to waste it in heating up a brake. Lastly, with a braking arrangement, as the system sensitivity is increased, i.e. wider ratio, the residual overshoot would always be in excess of the level that would sustain a hunting action.

In equipment of more recent design the motor is powered from a source where the mark to space ratio of the motor current is proportional to the system balance. Thus when the balance point is being approached the motor slows down in anticipation. At the point of balance the speed of movement in the system is low and therefore very little inertia exists. The natural damping of the steering mechanism is enough to produce a stable balance condition when the motor stops. The problems associated with stopping the helm exactly at the balance point can be considerably reduced with hydraulic systems where spool valves control rams acting directly on the rudder (7.8).

Solid state switching for motor control is now generally used to obviate the electromechanical relays that have caused unreliability since autopilots began, due to pitted contacts or sticking.

Remote controls

If remote control is important to you there are a few points to consider at the outset. For example, if you require fully proportional control you will have to purchase one of the types embodying a rudder angle transmitter, as a rudder reference signal is imperative. In operation the signal from this type of remote control is switched into circuit in place of the error detector signal; simultaneously, the ratio is set to unity so that the rudder follows exactly the hand control settings. Alternatively, where the ability to make instantaneous changes is all that is required, a simpler system generically called a 'dodger' is adequate. With this arrangement, left and right push buttons are provided to effect the temporary course offset required without disengaging the autopilot, and the preset course is resumed when the button is released.

Installation

When siting the units, care must be taken to establish the magnetic safe distances from the boat's compass and the sensing unit. In order to avoid the possibility of interaction between the compass and autopilot sense unit, they should be spaced about 3 ft apart. Ultimately sitings must depend to a great extent on the construction of the vessel and the convenience of the owner. Remember that all parts of the equipment will need protection from freshwater seepage, salt water, spray, bilges, diesel oil, petrol and gas installations. Unless you are very able and have light engineering facilities available, so far as the mechanics of automatic pilots are concerned, I suggest that the work be placed in the hands of a competent boatyard. Most autopilots are sold by agents who will usually employ electronics engineers to carry out the installation. Only very exceptionally are they good shipwrights as well, and therefore the services of a yard will help to secure a sound fitting.

Associated with installation work is the task of suppressing the radio interference due to either the relays or the brushgear in the steering motor. Before placing an order for a unit you should check with the makers that the terminal noise of the equipment conforms to the requirements of BS 1597 and is not at a level likely to cause problems. The equipment casework must be properly connected to the boat's bonding system, and if the batteries are grounded (which is bad practice) the bonding lead to the casework should have a 1 μF paper capacitor in series in order to prevent the instrument case from becoming live. I have dealt more extensively with radio interference problems in chapter 3. All cables should be run using the recommendations in chapter 1 as a guide.

Safe magnetic distances

The following table gives a guide to the order of space required between the sense unit and other magnetic objects in the wheelhouse or cockpit and about the boat's structure. Distances given also apply to the spacing between all autopilot units and the boat's compass. Minimum distances should be observed carefully and whenever possible greater spacing should be provided. Minimum distances are:

Electric motor unit	130 cm	4 ft
Control unit	100 cm	3 ft
Rudder angle transmitter	60 cm	2 ft
Remote control	60 cm	2 ft
Sense unit	100 cm	3 ft

After fitting an automatic pilot it is normal practice to readjust the boat's compass.

Remember also that in some instances one unit will be combined with another, i.e. the control unit can be made integral with the motor unit; also the rudder angle signal is sometimes derived from the motor shaft position and is thus mounted within the motor unit. This latter system is not available for boats with hydraulic steering as there will be a degree of slip.

The control unit in a new vessel will look very much nicer if console mounted with the rest of the instrumentation, although in craft where this would involve a lot of alteration a gimbal mount will allow a great variety of mounting positions. Many manufacturers supply such brackets as

standard. The control unit, whether attached to the motor or not , will need to be in a position adjacent to the helm and engine controls. If this position is in an open cockpit, mount the unit through the bulkhead or under the coaming and provide a weather flap. This position will allow the watchkeeper to check the heading and have controls to hand. Consult the minimum safe distance table before positioning the unit. Some units incorporate lights and others a meter which enables the balance point to be established; these should be visible from the position chosen for the course sensor. In units such as the Kelvin Hughes, Neco and Decca this is no problem as the course selector is on the control panel (7.3).

Course sensing unit

For units with a remote sensing compass the following comments apply to the sensing head and not the course selector. If necessary a mounting pad should be used so that the unit is level when the boat is in normal trim. The lubber line marks should be parallel to the fore and aft line. The Neco remote compass is shown in (7.9).

Positioning this unit is a very important part of installation. A site must be chosen which is as near the centreline of the ship as possible, and clear of disturbing magnetic fields caused by such things as steel stanchions, other electronic equipment, compasses, canopy frames, etc. A preliminary magnetic check should be made on the position chosen for the sense unit, using a small pocket compass and a wooden rule or straightedge. First place the rule fore and aft with its centre at the

7.9 Remote sensing compass

proposed location and move the pocket compass back and forth along the rule for 30 cm (1 ft) on either side of the intended position. The needle must show no appreciable change in field direction over this distance, say no more than 2°–3°. Repeat this test with the rule athwartships and again with the rule placed vertically. If all checks show little or no change in field directions, the site can be expected to give good results. When this test is carried out care should be taken to see that the boat is in normal seagoing trim, with all tools, deck gear, anchors, dinghy, etc. in their proper stowages. In difficult installations or cases of doubt the advice of a compass adjuster should be sought.

With an autopilot the correction procedure for the sensing unit is carried out by moving the ship's head to balance the lights or meter when the pilot is switched to the standby position. It may be calibrated against a compass that has already been corrected, or it may be treated as a separate entity and calibrated without reference to any other device. For example, if calibrating by conventional methods, a pelorus ring and sight is set up and sighted N/S; the course selector on the boat is then turned until the control unit of the automatic pilot indicates balance. Move the sighting ring 180° and turn the ship until balance is again obtained. If a difference between the sight reading and the sense unit results, note the amount and apply a correction magnet to halve this error. Repeat this process until the results are acceptable. Proceed then with E/W correction.

Although certain companies have categorically stated that it is impossible to correct a magnetometer type sense unit, the fact is that it responds to the earth's magnetic vector in exactly the same way as a compass with the exception that it does not move in so doing. It will thus be apparent to the simplest of minds that it will respond to correction in the same way as a compass adjusted by standard techniques and magnets.

In steel-hulled vessels it will be advantageous to take a relative vertical field measurement with a declinometer. In these cases the boat should be turned about on its moorings for three to four hours before adjustment begins. The declinometer should be set up ashore at some known undisturbed area. The weight should be set to balance the indicator to zero with the needle along the N/S line. The instrument may then be set up on the boat again along the N/S line, in the position the error sensor is to occupy, and the vertical component due to the boat's own stray fields measured and compensated before swinging takes place.

In practice it will not be necessary in the majority of cases to carry out any correction of the error sensor provided the simple field direction survey described earlier is carried out before siting, results quite adequate for normal use will be obtained. A calibration chart (12.12) can be found in chapter 12. When one is forced to use a poor site for overriding reasons such as space, or in case of problems with a steel hull, the sensor may be fully corrected and calibrated. This should be undertaken by a compass adjuster in difficult cases. For those who feel competent to make a reasonable adjustment, I suggest that the procedure laid down in chapter 12 be applied.

Rudder angle transmitter or feedback unit
As explained earlier, the feedback unit is a signal reference taken from the boat's rudder (7.5). The

7.10 Rudder angle feedback unit

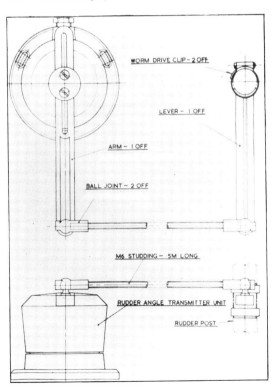

purpose of the unit is to produce an electrical signal indicating the sign and proportion of the rudder angle. Obviously the best place to extract such a signal is at the rudder itself. It may in some cases be integral with the electric motor until, but this arrangement cannot be used on all vessels.

The unit works in the tiller flat and should be secured on a suitable bracket or pad, which may be fabricated to suit the exact conditions of the site (7.10). The mounting bracket should have slotted holes to facilitate final adjustment of the linkage. An excellent linkage can be made by using heavy gauge brass rod fitted with ball and socket elbow joints as used for the throttle linkages of autos. Care should be taken to avoid play or backlash in the linkage as this will produce continuous hunting about the balance position, with attendant poor steering, extra battery drain and unnecessary wear of all moving parts.

Where a feedback signal is derived at the motor unit from an integral potentiometer, the appropriate gear ratio for the number of turns hard over to hard over of the helm should be set up to the maker's instructions. On some of the smaller units the feedback to motor shaft turns ratio is fixed, and in that case the feedback ratio is associated with helm speed. This compromise reduces flexibility but may be acceptable in many cases.

The drive unit
The means of creating power to turn the rudder may be either direct electric or electrically controlled hydraulic. The most common form for small craft is a direct chain drive to the wheel from an electric motor unit. The reason for the popularity of direct electric drives is twofold: they are relatively simple to install and considerably lower in cost, by at least half as a general rule.

When selecting your automatic pilot the type and size of drive unit available is probably the limiting factor in your choice; it will therefore be necessary to check the torque required to turn the wheel under actual running conditions so that this can be compared with the specification of the equipment that interest you.

It will be understood that with conventional rudders the greater the amount of rudder applied the higher the torque requirement becomes. If the automatic pilot is to be used for hand remote

controlled steering, i.e. where the rudders must be capable of electrical drive from hard over port to hard over starboard, then the torque measurement must be based on the rudder fully applied condition. If the equipment will be used for automatic steering only, the torque required can be measured at the 15° of helm position. The only time that the boat is likely to achieve anything like 15° of rudder when steering on autopilot (once the equipment has been properly set up) is when changing course by something like 90°. In modern boat designs much has been done to minimise the torque on the wheel and also the torque differential between rudder amidships and rudder fully applied conditions. Many motor craft are designed to embody outdrives which operate as active rudders with a virtually constant steering torque requirement, and in sailing craft balancing the rudder area fore and aft of the rudder stock has resulted in a similar improvement. There will clearly be a considerable difference between motor and sailing boats under running conditions as there is invariably a degree of weather helm applied under sail and the torque measurement has to be taken under typical cruising conditions.

The torque required and the speed at which the wheel will be rotated dictates the size of the steering motor. The procedure is to count the number of turns the wheel makes from hard over to hard over. The weight required to turn the helm should then be checked by means of a spring balance attached at a known distance from the hub of the wheel. Measure along one of the spokes and mark off a distance from the centre of say 10 in. or 0.2 metres; take the vessel to sea in normal trim, and when safe to do so apply about 25° of rudder. Attach the spring balance at the mark on the wheel and pull the balance so as to increase the mount of helm applied, then take the reading. For the sake of illustration, assume the balance gave a reading of 10 lbs or 5 kg. If this weight is multiplied by the distance of the mark on the wheel from the hub, i.e. 10 × 10 or 0.2 × 5, the torque required to move the wheel is arrived at, i.e. 100 in. lbs or 1 metre kilopond (mkp). If the wheel requires 3 turns to move the rudder from hard over to hard over and it is to achieve this traverse in 15 seconds, which is a typical figure for a small boat, it must be made to turn at 12 r.p.m. Thus we have the key data to establish the size of the drive unit required: it must be capable of producing a torque of 100 in. lbs or 1 mkp at 12 r.p.m.

Strictly speaking, we should now make an allowance to cover frictional losses in the chain drive, etc. However, as we have measured the torque with almost full rudder applied and it is unlikely that even under hand remote control conditions this situation would occur frequently, we can usually dispense with this consideration.

The speed of the output shaft on the autopilot drive unit varies considerably from one manufacturer to another, and when assessing the suitability of any particular unit for your application it is essential to translate the torque figure given for it into figures that relate to the speed at which the boat's wheel will rotate. For example, if the equipment that interests you is designed to have an output speed of 36 r.p.m. it will need a 3:1 sprocket ratio between the motor shaft and the wheel on the system described above, with three turns hard over to hard over. This means that the torque will be just over 33 inch pounds or 0.33 mkp at 36 r.p.m. in this particular case.

The main requirements associated with fitting any unit to drive the helm are that it should be kept as clear of the compass as possible and be mounted substantially, with suitable weather protection. The sketches show examples of typical arrangements (7.11, 7.12). The countershaft layout would be required where the ratio between the drive unit motor and the boat's wheel is very wide. The use of a countershaft arrangement should be avoided if possible as the extra chain and sprocket makes the steering system heavier to move under manual control.

An increasing number of craft are fitted with either a rod and pinion or hand hydraulic steering linkage. In the former type frictional losses are at a minimum, and if the drive unit is arranged to operate the wheel at speeds very much in excess of 15 sec. hard over to hard over, there could be a tendency towards a hunting condition with some autopilots due to inertia in the components of the steering system. This will not always be the case, however, particularly when the glands on the rudder stocks are tight, as the associated mechanical losses there damp the system. Two simple remedies can be tried for this condition: the first involves changing the sprocket ratio on the wheel drive to slow down the speed at which the system is driven, thus reducing inertia; the second method is to reduce the sensitivity of the system to probably in the region ±2°. This latter suggestion is not suitable for light fast boats, and care must be taken in such cases to make sure that the design of the equipment you obtain has parameters that will allow satisfactory operation.

7.11 Drive unit installation

7.12 Drive unit with countershaft

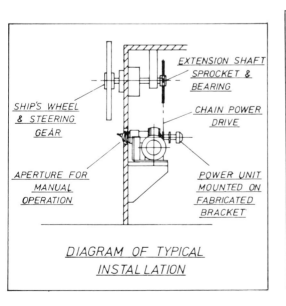

DIAGRAM OF TYPICAL INSTALLATION

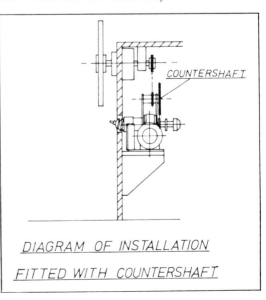

DIAGRAM OF INSTALLATION FITTED WITH COUNTERSHAFT

Where hand hydraulic steering is fitted, a small hydraulic pump and a lock valve will enable the system to be driven without connection to the wheel via sprockets and chains. These systems are in general more expensive than a simple electric motor; however, if your boat already has a hydraulic system, it is certainly a most elegant way to connect the automatic pilot to the rudder.

Hydraulics are often encountered in the more expensive yachts for various applications apart from steering, such as stabiliser fins, winches, etc., and for the sake of clarity the four diagrams show types of systems layouts for steering that are by no means uncommon and may have to be considered in some cases (7.13, 7.14, 7.15, 7.16).

There is more work in fitting a hydraulic drive unit than a simple electric motor, and it should not be undertaken unless you are reasonably competent to carry out a certain amount of mechanical work. I thoroughly recommend sticking to the maker's prescribed kit of parts if you do undertake the job personally, as all manner of nuts, pressure pipes, unions, etc. are sometimes difficult to obtain locally. Another point to remember is that the hydraulic oil recommended by the makers of the equipment must be used as the seals found in each unit may decompose in the wrong fluid. After running the pipework and before connection to the equipment, it is extremely important to inspect the pipes carefully for swarf or foreign matter. This will surely cause spool valves to stick at some awkward moment unless removed with a pullthrough or by blowing out with high pressure air.

Adjustment

Because all boats have different siting requirements, the makers of automatic pilots design the equipment to be as flexible as possible by providing various reversible connections. For example, the heading sensor may be mounted on the deckhead or table top, the motor sprocket could be facing forward or aft, the limit switches and feedback potentiometer likewise. This means that when the equipment is first turned on it is odds on that something will be the wrong way round for that particular boat. With the steering motor turning the wrong way the boat tries to steer a hairy, swingy reciprocal; with the feedback

potentiometer reversed it will apply full rudder in a direction depending on the error, making tight circles. If the limit switches are also on the wrong side in combination with the above, it is very probable that the steering gear will jam hard over one way. When the wrong limit switch opens it is impossible to drive the helm back to midships electrically, so you feverishly try to disengage the clutch and descend into the tiller flat, armed usually with a large bar and a big hammer.

The way to avoid the foregoing highly traumatic experiences is to systematically check these details one by one, with no engines running and the vessel alongside.

1. Make sure that the boat is not sitting on the bottom and that it is safe to move the rudder
2. Check the polarity and availability of the electrical supply and switch the equipment to standby.
3. Check that the system balances, by rotating the sense unit while observing the call lights or error meter.
4. Be sure when the sense unit is rotated to a higher reading, 090° 180° for example, that starboard helm is indicated.
5. Set the sense unit to call for starboard helm.
6. Momentarily switch to Duty and note the direction of wheel movement. If starboard helm is not being applied, reverse the motor rotation as directed by the maker's handbook.
7. Set the Ratio control to minimum rudder, and the Sensitivity to maximum.
8. Balance the sense unit and then increase its scale reading by 10°. Switch to Duty on and off for a few seconds to inch the helm over. If the feedback potentiometer is in the correct sense, something less than 10° of rudder will be applied and the motor will stop at this balance point. If incorrect it will continue to drive the helm over while switched to Duty and the connections must be reversed.
9. Switch to the dodger or Remote control and check that when pressing the starboard button or moving the knob to starboard that the wheel rotates to starboard. Reverse the remote control connections if the sense is incorrect.

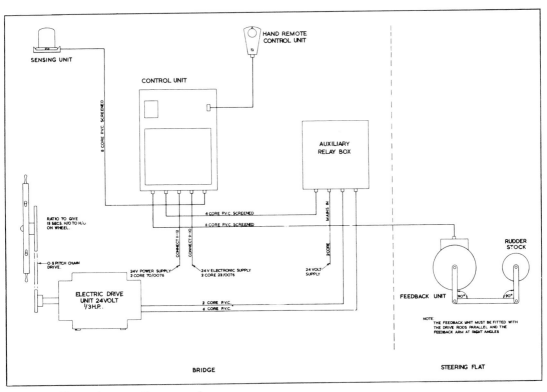

7.13–16   *Alternative autopilot system layouts*

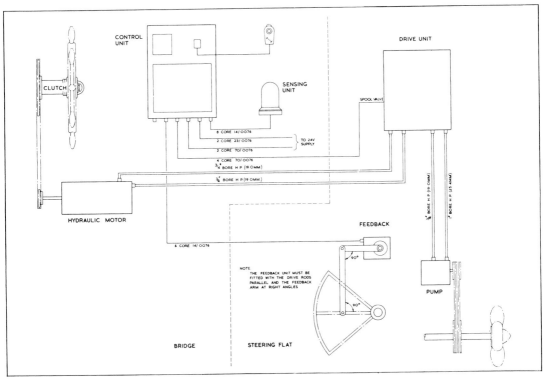

7.14

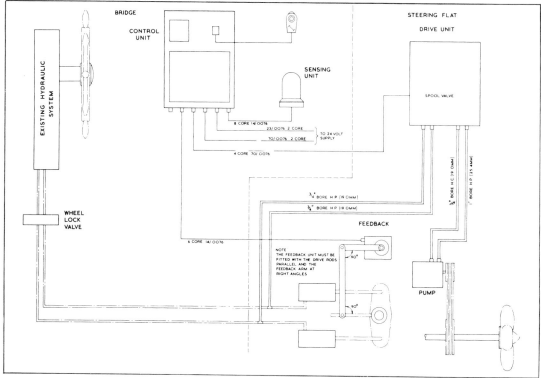

7.15

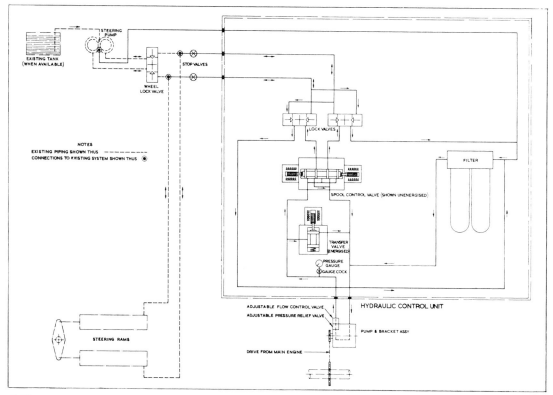

7.16

10. Great care must be exercised to avoid driving the helm hard over should a limit switch prove to be either faulty or connections reversed. If adjustable limit switches are provided these should be provisionally set at 25–30°. Use the remote control or dodger to apply about 30° of helm and check that the limit switch is operating.

11. Balance the sense unit and switch to Duty. Check that when the sense unit is rotated, the rudder follows up in proportion to the error, in both port and starboard directions.

12. Prepare for sea trials.

Having achieved a state where the automatic pilot functions basically in the correct sense in all respects, we must now take the vessel to sea for various adjustments to be made to the signal ratios so that it will steer the boat correctly and with a minimum of helm movement.

The term 'ratio' when applied to the signal system refers to the quantitative error element set against the quantitative correction element. Thus if a course error of 5° develops and a correction of 5° of rudder is applied, the ratio is 1:1. If for the same error the applied rudder angle is 10°, the system has a ratio of 1:2. Conversely, if the error is 10° and the applied rudder 5° the ratio is 2:1. The adjustment to vary this is brought out for the user and is usually labelled 'Rudder' or 'Ratio'.

Taking one extreme, a short 20 ft smooth-bottomed boat with outdrives or outboard engines will need only the smallest touch of helm before it is swinging heavily. Its period in azimuth is thus very much a function of the speed with which helm is applied. Therefore, for automatic steering in this case helm must be applied and taken off quickly, and only a very small amount of rudder may be applied for any given error; for a 5° error, probably only 1° of rudder should be applied. Outdrives and outboards are in fact 'active' rudders and do produce very high rates of swing.

If we take the case of a 30 ft craft with a lot of windage, small twin rudders well aft of the screws, and a top speed of 6–7 knots, it is highly probable that to steer it successfully by hand one would need to be something of an athlete. I had the embarrassment on one occasion of trying to persuade a boat of this type through a swing bridge

channel in the propeller wash of a coaster. In the end with helm hard over and one engine full ahead, and the other full astern, the wind blew us through sideways. To fit automatic steering gear on any boat like this will always be fraught with problems and one excellent starting point would be to improve the normal steering characteristics, perhaps by enlarging the rudder or adding a balance area. When fitting the steering motor the sprocket ratio should be arranged to turn the helm quite fast and a large proportion of helm is required—possibly 2° of rudder for every degree of error. Fortunately, few small craft of recent design handle in this way.

The signal ratios in the autopilot control loop are all-important in the setting up procedure after installation. While it is easy to define the ratio capability of any automatic pilot, it is something of a nightmare to assess the ratio requirement of any particular vessel. For this reason I will attempt to shed some light on how to check autopilot system performance.

The behaviour under normal hand steering is a first guide to what is required, and much is to be gained by observing what happens to the boat after a discrete alteration of course. A change of course made by applying roughly 20° of rudder for about ten seconds and then returning the rudder to amidships is a rough method of applying a step function signal to test the vessel's response. The effect is that the boat will weave backwards and forwards across its new course until it slowly settles down. This weaving will occur with a period equal to the vessel's natural period in azimuth. In a well designed vessel the oscillatory movement about the boat's mean course will be quickly damped without further use of the boat's rudder. If it is found that a considerable number of cyclic helm movements are necessary in order to damp the swinging, then it will be highly desirable to effect an improvement in the boat's steering system.

Sea trials

For tests to be performed to satisfaction it will be necessary to take the craft to sea so that plenty of room is available for a few spectacular manoeuvres. A calm day is also necessary so that one can get a clear idea of what the system is doing.

In order to apply the step function signal

7.17   Nautech Autohelm for tiller

referred to above to an automatic pilot, a small permanent magnet may be momentarily placed close to the sense unit. With sense units having a graduated scale for course setting, the reading may be altered by 20° and the performance of the vessel noted as the new course is taken up. The electronic signal ratio system may then be set up as detailed below for optimum performance.

Having put to sea, switch the autopilot to Standby and balance the sense unit to the maker's instructions. Set the Sensitivity or Weather control to maximum (usually Weather controls are at their most sensitive when turned fully anticlockwise) and the Ratio or Rudder control to minimum (again usually anticlockwise). Switch to Duty, and if a manual clutch is fitted it should now be engaged. The boat will probably lurch a bit at this point as it is always difficult to set the sense unit to precisely the course you were steering by hand. With plenty of sea room you should now be able to adjust the sensitivity and rudder controls so that the boat steers with a minimum of helm movement. From the moment of switching to Duty, with the controls set as above the boat will do one or a combination of two things:

Steer reasonably well but have a short fast 'hunt' on the steering wheel.
Understeer by applying insufficient rudder to correct the error, and wander off course.

Turn down the Weather/Sensitivity control slowly (usually clockwise) to reduce the hunting and then advance the Ratio control until the system oversteers. This condition can be recognised easily as the boat will steer back and forth over its mean course at a rate determined largely by the speed of the boat's wheel. The Ratio control should be readjusted to produce the stable steering conditions obtainable between the under- and over-steering positions.

It will be clear that these controls will need a certain amount of adjustment from time to time with different conditions of lading and weather, and a little experience and a few experiments at sea will provide the best guide in each individual boat.

While at sea, after setting up the equipment for optimum performance carry out the following simple check to establish the likely presence of heeling error. Steer a course along the N/S line, and see if the effect of heeling to port makes the autopilot apply starboard helm. If this is excessive recheck the sensor for vertical errors.

7.18   Nautech Autohelm for wheel

Tiller Pilots

Something of a revolution has occurred in small autopilots; high quality products like the Nautech series can be fitted by the owner with a minimum of trouble, and they give excellent performance. By acting directly on the tiller a minimum of power is consumed, as there is no steering cable or linkage to waste power. The Nautech 2000 pilot has a unique method of establishing system balance without a feedback potentiometer, thus eliminating wear and hunt due to overshoot. Installation is particularly simple as can be seen in (7.17) for tiller and (7.18) for wheel. Though the functional states apply as much to the tiller pilot as to any other, the difference worth a mention is the method of measuring the tiller torque, so that you can select a product with sufficient power.

Measure from the centreline of the pintles along the tiller and mark at a convenient distance, say 2 ft or 60 cm (0.6 m). With the vessel at sea under cruising conditions apply about 25° of rudder and by attaching a spring balance to the tiller at the mark, pull in a direction to increase the amount of rudder applied and note the reading on the spring balance. This reading, which for example might be 70 lbs or 32 kg, is then multiplied by the distance on the tiller. The rudder torque in this example would be 140 ft lbs or 19 mkp.

The above method of measurement is of course not used for sailing craft. In this case the vessel is sailed as close to the wind as possible, and then brought to a stable cruising heading, which typically may be about 20° further off the wind.

Under these conditions an amount of weather helm will be carried, and a reading should be made of the weight necessary to increase this weather helm.

8 Radar

If we have cleared the expectant reef
Let no man look for his relief
Only the darkness hides the shape
Of further peril to escape.

Rudyard Kipling

The origins of microwave radar as we know it appeared as recently as the 1940s. This seems very surprising, as in 1886 Hertz, experimenting with Maxwell's theories, had demonstrated the similarity between radio and light waves, proving that radio waves could be reflected by metallic and dielectric bodies. In 1904 a German engineer by the name of Christian Hülsmeyer obtained British patent No. 13170, entitled 'Hertzian-wave projecting and receiving apparatus adapted to indicate or give warning of the presence of a metallic body, such as ship or a train, in the line of projection of such waves' (8.1, 8.2).

In 1922, Marconi said in a speech to the Institute of Electrical Engineers, 'It seems to me that it should be possible to design apparatus by means of which a ship could radiate or project a divergent beam of these rays in any desired direction, which rays, if coming across a metallic object such as another steamer or ship, would be reflected back to a receiver screened from the local transmitter on the sending ship, and thereby immediately reveal the presence and bearing of the ship in fog or thick weather.'

However it took the imminence of World War II to stimulate sufficient money and effort to produce a successful radar system. The British 25 MHz chain home stations were fully operational and on duty by 1938 and had a range of about 90 miles at that time. In 1939 the 200 MHz aircraft interception radar AI was developed and used for locating ships and submarines. It should be noted that these radars all worked at VHF frequencies: it was not until Randell and Boot working at Birmingham University produced a suitable magnetron in 1940 that microwave radar became a reality. The first magnetrons had an output power of about 1 kW at a wavelength of about 10 cm. At this wavelength a highly directional aerial of practical proportions was possible, and the power produced was about two orders of magnitude greater than anything available at that time.

Coming right up to date, I feel that the continuing advance of solid state technology will shortly produce a replacement for the magnetron for radar purposes, as improved low-noise receiver devices make the transmitter power required even lower.

There are now many small craft radars on the market, manufactured in this country, Japan and the United States. In general, marine radars can be quite complex systems, and embody a considerable number of components. One of the early and commonest problems with small boat radars was how to provide for a consumption of approximately 400 W. Also, the appalling supply regulation normally encountered on small craft, due to float charged battery systems, gave rise to unreliability. The latest small craft equipments have an excellent level of performance and are extremely useful, although the facilities offered must be curtailed due to cost. This improvement has in general been possible due to the advance in component technology in the last decade.

To get to closer grips with the practical operation, let us examine the elements of a typical small boat radar. Energy is sent out from the radar aerial in a given direction and part of this transmitted energy will be reflected by certain objects, i.e. hills, thunderstorms, ships, coastlines, etc. As a result of this reflection some of the energy may be received by the radar aerial for

Nº 13,170   A.D. 1904

Date of Application, 10th June, 1901—Accepted, 22nd Sept., 1904

COMPLETE SPECIFICATION.

"Hertzian-wave Projecting and Receiving Apparatus Adapted to Indicate or Give Warning of the Presence of a Metallic Body, such as a Ship or a Train, in the Line of Projection of such Waves".—

I, CHRISTIAN HÜLSMEYER of 3 Grabenstrasse, Düsseldorf, Germany, Engineer do hereby declare the nature of this invention and in what manner the same is to be performed to be particularly described and ascertained in and by the following statement:

5   This invention consists, broadly, of improved apparatus for projecting electric waves in any desired direction combined with improved apparatus for receiving said waves when reflected back from any metallic body, such as a ship or a train, said receiving apparatus being adapted to put into action an audible or a visible signal and thus give warning of the presence of such metallic body 10 in the line of projection of the waves.

My invention is based upon the property of electric waves of being reflected back towards their source on meeting a metallic body, and will be readily understood by imagining a transmitting and a receiving station such as indi-

8.1-2   Patent specification for early radar

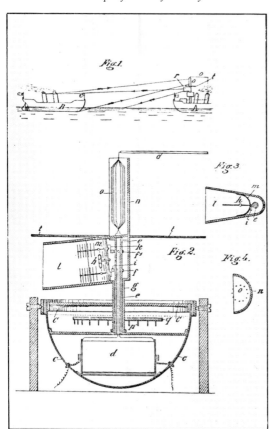

8.2

processing into visual information. The part played by the target, i.e. the reflecting object, is crucial. In some instances the reflecting properties of the object are so poor that little or nothing is received. On the other hand the reflective properties may be so good as to produce a response from even the minor sidelobes of the aerial system. It will thus be seen that some understanding of what happens to the radar signal will be necessary in order for the navigator/operator to extract and use safely the information from the system.

The following explanation of the operation of radar applies specifically to small craft equipment. In broad outline, any particular equipment will contain the following basic units: aerials, transmitter, receiver, display unit, and a means of transmitting the aerial position in azimuth to the display unit.

Aerials

Depending on the particular compromise the radar equipment designer accepts, sometimes two aerials are used, one for transmitting and the other for receiving. The object of this is to isolate the outgoing high energy pulse from the delicate mixer stage of the receiver. The alternative is to use a special switch (called a TR cell) and only one aerial. This method has been more extensively used, although it may be possible to use the former scheme more economically for small craft. The advantages of the former are that cost and losses are lower; the disadvantages are that it is still possible to damage the mixer crystal by operating the radar when the aerial is 'looking' straight at the harbour wall, or from other people's equipment operated at close quarters. The second system has higher losses and cost, but with a modern TR cell the chance of damage to the mixer is considerably reduced. In some cases, even when the radar is switched off (i.e. the TR cell not primed) the TR cell will protect the mixer from energy received from other radars.

Disregarding the eventual use of phased arrays on a commercial basis, which is at least a decade away, whatever form of aerial is used must rotate in order for it to gather the necessary information. Its precise bearing must also be transmitted electrically or mechanically to the display. In order to rotate the aerial we must have some form of motor. If the aerial unit is of the open type, as most commercial equipments are, the power required to rotate the aerial array in any sort of wind will be very considerable, and the construction will have to be very substantial. Most manufacturers try to conform to the SOLAS specification, which lays down suggested minimum performance standards. If, on the other hand, the aerial is housed within a radome, the construction can be much lighter and there will be no windage on the rotating parts. One of the original arguments against this configuration was that it was necessary to work outside in the weather when tuning or servicing the equipment. As later versions of small craft equipment become available, the argument vanished as all manufacturers were 'in the same boat'; however, the fact remains. Most small craft radars in the future will have radomes covering the aerials, for the following reasons:

Higher rotating speeds are attainable without excessive increase in power.
Lighter construction
Dramatically lower aerial turning power is required

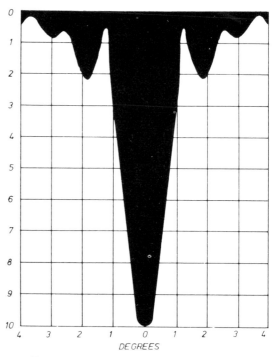

8.3 *Beam pattern*

The aerial system also defines beam widths, both horizontal and vertical; the physical size and construction profoundly effects the radiation pattern or polar diagram. This is illustrated in (8.3) which clearly shows the parts of the energy distribution which can give responses capable of making the display ambiguous. Basically, the bigger the aerial is, the better. However, take a look at the literature on the one you intend to purchase; ideally you want one with the narrowest possible horizontal beam angle and the lowest side-lobe level. Don't forget that the size of the radome is not the size of the aerial. Beamwidth should be measured at the 3 db or half power points and this is important when comparing equipment specifications.

There is a popular misconception that slotted waveguide aerials have a better sidelobe performance than other types; this is particularly untrue of small centre-fed designs; indeed, without a polariser the performance *is* poor. In bigger radars, where the scanner is not housed in a radome, its advantages are lower weight and windage, and absence of responses on the back of the aerial due to spillage over the reflector, as in the orange peel type which it superceded. Pillbox and cheese can perform just as well if carefully designed, and they have other qualities that make them attractive for small boats.

Polarization

The designer's selection of a particular plane of polarization does not seriously affect performance; however the marine racon beacons installed in recent years are designed with horizontal polarization. If you want to use these, you must have a radar with compatible polarization. Because of roll and pitch scattering effects, a horizontally polarized racon will often respond at close range to a vertically polarised radar, however, at distances of over half a mile, a reply is unlikely. With transponding beacons, the signal received is proportional to the inverse square of the distance, whereas an echo from a passive reflector suffers inverse fourth power attenuation. If you have compatible equipment, you would expect to see racon responses as soon as the beacon is over the radar horizon. Circular polarization has been used with success to penetrate rain. In this system the electrical field is made to rotate about the direction of propagation; however such schemes are more complex and expensive and are therefore outside consideration for small craft.

Components

Transmitter
As the name implies, this part of the equipment does the 'sending'. It consists of a trigger, or clock, or PRF (pulse repetition frequency) generator—all words for the same device, which generates an electronic signal at a low level at fairly precise time intervals. The interval between each signal can be varied by the operator, normally in conjunction with the range switch, so that the highest possible PRF for the range in use is achieved. It will be understood that, statistically, the higher the number of 'hits' secured while the aerial is 'looking' at any particular target, the greater the probability of getting a usable echo signal. The timed 'pips' from the PRF generator are fed to the modulator. This unit in present day techniques consists of a means of storing energy in the intervals between pulses and quickly discharging

this stored energy by a means of a solid state thyristor into the magnetron. The latter is a power oscillator capable of producing very short pulses of high power radio energy (generally less than one millionth of a second) at a very high frequency. Magnetrons for small craft operate within X band on a frequency of 9410 MHz approx., at a pulse power of about 3 kW typically.

Pulse rate
The number of pulses emitted per second is usually 2000 pps for ranges up to one mile and 1000 for longer ranges. The precise rate is not critical and, in order to conserve power it is not made as high as is theoretically possible.

Pulse length
The pulse length will determine the minimum range and the minimum resolution and this can be taken theoretically as just over half the distance covered in the pulse length (0.1 μ sec. = 16.4 yd). This order of definition will rarely be achieved other than in specialised river radars, due to the practicalities of the system. At the other extreme, the longer the pulse length the greater the statistical chance of obtaining a usable echo. See (8.4, 8.5).

Receiver
This unit accepts from the aerial the minute electronic impulses returned from the target. It is

8.4 'Short' pulse separates close objects

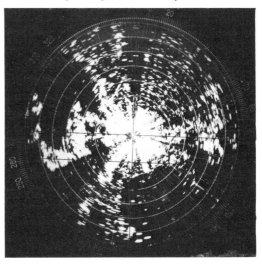

8.5 'Long' pulse merges close echoes

in fact an amplifier with special characteristics. It must have a low inherent noise, a very high gain, and adequate bandwidth to successfully reproduce the transmitted pulse. The receiver may have means by which the gain is varied in step with range, called swept gain or sea clutter. The echoes may also be better defined when shorter ranges are employed by differentiation, sometimes called rain clutter.

Display
The small craft display unit is quite a simple package as radars go. It consists typically of a cathode ray tube with a long-persistence screen, rotating equipment to turn the scan coil about the tube neck, a timebase, range marker generator and a video amplifier.

Apart from scanning, the cathode ray tube operates similarly to that in a domestic TV set, in that it is used to display the collected information visually. Because the rate of rotation of the radar aerial is fixed at a speed determined by other considerations, the screen has a phosphor that continues to glow after the spot has moved on. This allows succeeding echoes to integrate and produce an acceptably steady display. The method of scanning is different from television in that the spot moves radially from the centre to the edge of the tube. The timebase is the part of the circuitry that causes this to happen.

A lock pulse from the transmitter causes the timebase to commence the sweep from the centre to the edge of the screen, and the rate at which the spot moves radially is determined by the timebase constants pre-selected by the range switch. The range marker also receives the lock pulse and this initiates a train of pulses of precise spacing. These are fed to the brightness circuit to produce range rings.

The timebase also generates a square shaped pulse to brighten the spot while it is scanning, and to extinguish it while it flies back to the centre between scans. The video amplifier mixes the echo signal with the bright up pulse and the range marker signal. It also increases the intensity of the composite signal in order to operate the CRT.

The aerial and the scan coil must rotate in step in order that the radial trace on the tube points in the same direction as the main beam from the aerial. This is usually accomplished by synchronous or stepping motors driving both aerial and scan coil from a common power source, in lower priced equipments; and by means of servo motors or synchros in more expensive types.

To clarify the terms used in the foregoing description of radar equipment in operation, it will help to refer to the glossary that appears at the end of the book.

Interpretation

So far as operation is concerned, even for small and simple radars the subject is extensive. I assembled a pictorial guide in this chapter which I hope will be of assistance to all users of radar.

From the small craft point of view, it is often difficult to recognise the number of bits of misleading information that can be presented alongside the vast number of genuine echoes. Radar, like television, has to present three-dimensional information in two dimensions. In the case of radar the means of gathering information introduces various distortions, and also the scale of reduction is infinitely greater. The operator must, therefore, acquire the skill which will enable him to discriminate the self-evident and essential detail and, as operating ability improves, add to this the further information which may be obtained by taking into account various external influences that

146

affect radar performance. The effects referred to are mainly inherent in radar energy transmissions and thus disturb all makes similarly, although obviously the more expensive sets have control refinements which enable the operator to minimise any undesirable effect.

Small craft radars display information based on ship's head up relative motion. With this type of display the craft carrying the radar is positioned at the centre of the picture with the ship's head always pointing to the top of the display. Echoes are shown in their correct dispositions to port and starboard. Relative bearings of echo paints are taken from the bearing scale around the edge of the display. If the boat alters course the heading line on the display remains stationary and the whole radar picture rotates by the amount the boat's heading has changed. The position of the boat does not alter on the display and all movement on the display will be relative to the boat. A stationary target will thus appear to move on the reciprocal of the boat's course and speed.

To extract the closest line of approach, speed and course of targets with a relative motion radar, it is necessary to produce plots on a specially prepared plotting chart. As in small craft generally there is not the time, space or equipment to handle plotting effectively, I feel that the best recommendation I could make for the operator in these circumstances is to have the display readily viewable from the steering position and to follow as closely as possible the radar picture at all times. The manoeuvrability of small boats will make up for the anticipation necessary with big ships, provided one is careful in close quarter situations.

In order that any object may be detected, it is obvious that it must be in a position that will allow it to be illuminated by the beam of radar energy emitted from the aerial. For small craft the aerial height is always so low that the minimum range is defined by the radar performance itself. It will seldom be possible to effect an aerial height in excess of 3 metres (10 ft) and thus the maximum range will be limited by the apparent height of the target. This, due to the earth's curvature, severely restricts the maximum range. A guide is given in (8.6) which is an earth curvature nomograph relating aerial height above waterline to range and target height. Possibly an area of maximum range interest is that distance at which land can be detected. This depends profoundly on the local topography. In areas where the coastline is very low, high inland features will become distinguishable for many miles before the true coastline builds up (8.7).

Apart from considerations of height in relation to the earth's curvature, the detectability of any object will depend on the reflective properties exhibited by the object. These properties are affected by the nature of the material, its shape and its reflecting area. Usually the larger the object the greater the range at which it will be detected. However, if one of two objects of the same size at the same range exhibits better reflecting properties, it will be shown before the other. Even this rule is bent in the case of an excellent reflector positioned obliquely. This tends to deflect energy in exactly the same way a light is deflected by a mirror. Strong echoes will therefore be received from abruptly rising cliffs, whereas from low-lying

8.6   *Aerial height, range and target height*

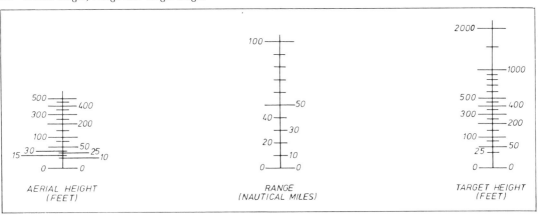

AERIAL HEIGHT
(FEET)

RANGE
(NAUTICAL MILES)

TARGET HEIGHT
(FEET)

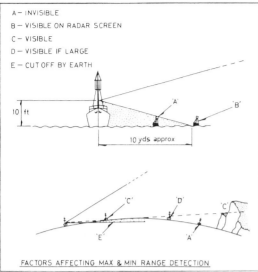

A – INVISIBLE
B – VISIBLE ON RADAR SCREEN
C – VISIBLE
D – VISIBLE IF LARGE
E – CUT OFF BY EARTH

10 ft

10 yds approx

FACTORS AFFECTING MAX & MIN RANGE DETECTION

8.7   Factors affecting detection range

beaches or gentle slopes or hills the returns are much weaker.

When the radar beam 'sees' a high, reflecting surface such as cliffs or large buildings close at hand, a sharp echo with a blank area behind it is painted on the display. The radar beam passing over low flat areas will paint the display with echoes from every small reflecting surface in its path for several miles. Another factor is that a high coastline will be above the line of sight and will paint echoes on the display long before reflections are obtained from a low coastline. This can be seen by comparing (8.8) and (8.9). At long range (8.9) the cliffs and harbour at Dover are clearly defined, but the low coastline of Dungeness Bay (8.8) is not painting the display. The position of Dungeness Point is indicated by the broad response of the racon beacon installed there. With the distance reduced (8.8) the low flat coastline of Dingeness Bay becomes clearlydefined. Because of the nature of the low coastline, echo paints are obtained from several miles inland. While one side of Dungenesss Point is clearly defined, only a few reflections are obtained from the side which the radar beam cannot see.

Close inshore, echoes of individual objects show on the display and the interpretation of a radar picture becomes more difficult. Furthermore, a radar picture at low water may look very different from one obtained at high water, due to the reflections from mud banks and channels uncovered by the tide.

Even to the person untrained in interpreting radar displays, the radar picture (8.10) shows a striking similarity to the chart of the area (8.11). At B2 on the chart the entrance to a creek is clearly shown. The radar picture, which was taken at low water, shows a confused outline because of reflections from exposed mud banks; and there are sharply defined echo paints of the promenade and the built-up area on the rising ground behind the pier (C2). Very few reflections from inland targets are obtained here except from multi-storey buildings, which rise above the general skyline and appear clearly defined on the display. In area D2 the land is fairly flat and reflections are obtained

8.8–9   Effect of target height and range

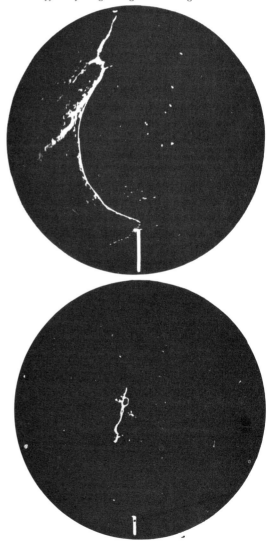

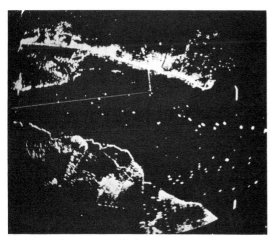

8.10 *Radar picture of Thames estuary*

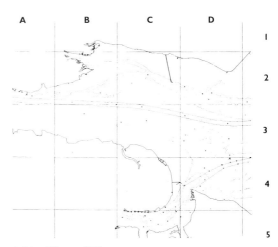

8.11 *Chart of Thames estuary*

from much further inland. These produce echo paints on the display in which street patterns can be seen, but this must not be regarded as a bird's eye view looking down on the area. The jetty at the extreme left of the picture in area A2 is quite prominent, but the small inlet adjacent to the jetty appears only as a break in the outline of the river bank. Of the two inlets on the other side of the river, one appears as a break in the outline whereas the other is clearly defined. Because the land on this side of the river rises very gradually to a range of hills several miles inland, targets in this area are clearly defined, especially the line of electricity pylons in area D5.

The channel in the area D4 is clearly defined by the line of buoys. These are fitted with radar reflectors and produce echo paints of the same magnitude as those of ships in the channel. Also of interest is the large jetty at the edge of the channel (C4); oil tanks at its shore end give the impression of a sharply defined coastline. The rest of the Medway estuary in this area looks featureless on the radar picture because the low-lying mud flats will only produce a minimum of small reflections at this range.

Reflections from objects on land

At short ranges, broad structures such as bridges, jetties, warehouses and dock installations usually produce well defined echo paints, often bearing a marked resemblance to the object itself. Objects such as round towers, chimneys, gasometers, lighthouses, etc. generally produce poor echo paints because their curved reflecting surfaces

scatter the reflected energy over a wide area. To distinguish these objects it is often necessary to reduce the gain control setting and to use the Diff switch to make them stand out on the display.

A direct comparison may be made between a short range radar picture and an Ordnance Survey map of the area (8.12, 8.13). The radar picture was obtained on board a vessel in the River Thames whose heading line shows it to be proceeding SE down river towards the Dartford Tunnel. The radar picture and map are to the same scale.

Very little of the built-up area of Purfleet shows on the display as at short range the height of the buildings along the river bank effectively masks the buildings behind them from the radar beam. Along the river banks, piers and jetties produce well defined echo paints on the display. On the Aveley Marshes the rifle range butts are clearly shown, but the absence of echo paints in the area behind the butts shows this area to be masked from the radar beam. The railway is clearly defined by reflections from the overhead gantries that carry the power lines. Between the railway and the adjacent road the path of a line of pylons can be followed. Behind Purfleet the lines of the roads are lost, but the line of the pylons is still shown because their height permits them to be seen by the radar beam over the general skyline of the town. Only the general outline of the village of Aveley can be seen on the radar picture.

On the Erith side of the river the entrance and course of the River Darent are shown in detail, and every detail over the flat marshland is painted on the display. The complete outline of the factory

149

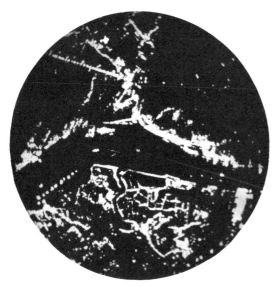

8.12   *Radar picture of Thames at Purfleet*

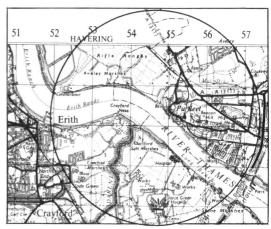

8.13   *Map of Thames at Purfleet*

buildings at the bottom right corner of the radar
picture is painted in detail together with the line of
pylons running to it. In contrast only very poor
echo paints are obtained from the navigational
marks along the river bank.

On the river a typical echo paint is obtained
from the vessel off Crayford Ness; the aspect of
the vessel is clearly shown by reflections along its
length. The echo paints midway between the 'own
ship' position and this vessel are probably from
waves caused by the wash of the two ships passing
each other. The row of echo paints on the river in
Erith Roads shows the position of barges moored
near the cement loading pier.

Recognition of targets

It is vitually impossible to detect the aspect of any
particular target; for example a seagull at a quarter
mile may look just the same as a 5000 ton ship at 6
miles. Possibly the ship would have a trail in the
afterglow in the screen phosphor that would enable a
guess to be made, but this in itself is hazardous.
The course of any target may be plotted, but
instantaneous changes of course must be allowed
for.

As a ship underway with radar will in all
probability have a moving relationship to its
targets, intermittent painting of targets will occur
due to its geometry, in particular at long range.
The salient points of coastline may show up and
disappear again even though the range is closing.

On closer targets effects are generally confined
to echo strength relative to sea return. When the
surface is very calm it is possible to pick up
driftwood or even a single seagull. Some buoys,
though, have a shape which is highly diffusive and
on their own are very difficult targets. The
important ones, however, are fitted with reflectors
of the corner type, which does much to improve
matters.

Sea return (clutter)

The undulating surface of the surrounding water
produces an enormous number of small echoes
covering a small area in the middle of the display,
which tends to obscure surface objects close to the
boat. The amount of reflection is greater as the
wave height increases, and as the aspect of the
reflecting surface is greater to windward, the effect
of sea return may be biased in this direction.
Generally the area affected is limited to 2 miles and
it can be reduced to an acceptable level by the
Swept Gain control.

Spurious echoes

These false responses are produced by multiple
reflections of the radar pulse. Energy is deflected
by one object and strikes another. From this
second object a signal returns along the same path.
These echoes always appear on the bearing of the
first reflection but at a range equal to the total
distance covered by the pulse. To clarify this point,

those of us who have observed our beloveds putting up their hair will have noticed that they have evolved a cunning technique to investigate the backs of their heads. This is brought about by standing with back to the bathroom mirror and looking into a small hand mirror held before the face. Thus the results of three hours in the hairdressers on a bearing of 180° is clearly visible on a bearing of 030° or 330° at will, the range in each case being the total length of the optical path.

It will be evident that in narrow or congested waterways, these images may be quite stable and confusing. A reduction of gain may help to clarify the screen, but in general this sort of situation is more difficult to remedy than sea clutter. At sea, however, these effects are rarely seen except when due to a known offender on the superstructure, such as the dinghy (8.14).

The effects of sidelobes are in general easily recognisable (8.15). The sidelobes are usually at level of less than 5% compared to the main beam, and because of this are only likely to become evident where echoes appear from good reflecting surfaces at short range, such as from cranes, pylons, power station towers, etc. These echoes are occasionally very strong and produce an arc or even a complete circle on the display. It should, however, be stressed that modern aerials of the larger type usually have a high level of sidelobe suppression, which will prevent these effects from appearing other than exceptionally.

To suppress this sort of response a considerable reduction in gain would be required. It may be better in some cases to adjust sea clutter and gain so as not to unduly decrease longer range sensitivity.

Discrimination

The ability of the instrument to discriminate between two objects closely spaced in azimuth is defined by the horizontal beamwidth of the aerial system, which is fixed to a large extent by its size. Referring to (8.16) it will be understood that if the leading edge of the beam illuminates a second object before the trailing edge of the first object, then only one echo will appear, the two objects being merged into a composite arc on the screen. Most small craft radars are able to produce a horizontal beamwidth of between 2.5° and 3.5° and this is entirely satisfactory for their purposes.

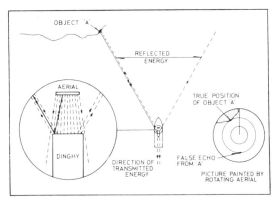

8.14   False echoes

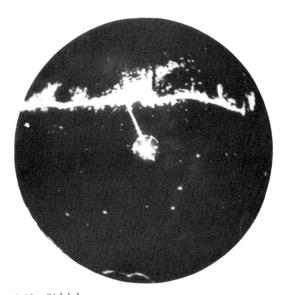

8.15   Sidelobes

In the more expensive types with 6 ft scanners a beamwidth of 1.2° is obtained, with attendant greater crispness in the radar picture. The ultimate discrimination in this respect depends on the range of the objects. Obviously the closer the ship gets to the objects, the greater the angle between them. It should be mentally registered that any echo might be a composite of two reflections and may at any moment move off in two directions! The range discrimination, i.e. the ability of the radar to distinguish between two closely spaced objects on the same bearing, is determined by the length of the pulse of radar energy transmitted. A typical short range discrimination is about 6 m, which corresponds to a pulse length of just over 0.1 μsec. The pulse length also determines the minimum range at which an object can be detected.

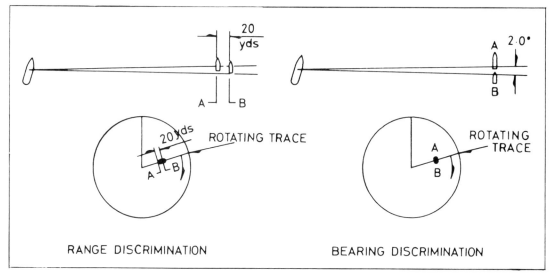

RANGE DISCRIMINATION   BEARING DISCRIMINATION

8.16   Discrimination

Atmospheric effects

The weather will affect the performance obtained from the instrument. The smallest effects are caused by mist, light rain or dry snow. Rain scatters the radar energy and indeed the presence of rain squalls can be readily detected by observing the screen. Some reduction of range in these circumstances is unavoidable. The attenuation experienced depends largely on the intensity of the rainfall, also the depth of the storm area that the pulse has to penetrate. On the display rain appears as areas of speckled haze, and echoes in the affected parts will be obscured. A reduction in gain or adjustment of the clutter controls will usually enable the operator to discriminate between rain targets.

Hail and snow produce effects similar to rain clutter. Damp snow has a great effect than dry snow, which sometimes hardly effects the display at all.

A slight reduction in maximum range may be expected in foggy conditions; however, the effect is not serious as can be seen from the picture of shipping fog-bound off Southend during the five-day fog in January, 1964 (8.17).

Wind, of course, will raise a swell which will increase sea clutter, and it then becomes more difficult to distinguish between sea clutter and small targets such as buoys and small boats. In rough water two more effects combine to make matters worse from the small craft aspect. The first is that small objects like buoys will paint intermittently as they disappear behind waves from time to time, and the small craft itself will be so unstable by comparison with its bigger sisters that it will also drop below or level with the crests of waves in the vicinity. Added to this, the aerial on this unstable platform is not always pointing in the optimum direction to receive any reflected energy.

Although line of sight conditions are normally understood for radar wave propagation, this understanding only holds good when temperature and humidity are uniform over the distance between radar aerial and target. As this rarely happens in practice, as temperature and humidity vary with altitude, the radar beam is refracted downwards (8.18). On many occasions the increase in range resulting from this effect is not discernable. On occasions it will produce spectacular increases in range by ducting the signal round the earth's curvature (8.19).

Ice

The detection of ice echoes is of great importance to craft in cold climates. Although this may not apply to many yachts, the effects are interesting as they have a bearing on interpretation generally.

Smooth flat ice reflects most of the radar energy away at its angle of incidence and provides little return. Consequently the corresponding area on the display will be free of echoes. It is sometimes

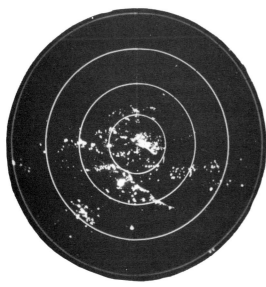

8.17   Fog

an advantage to set the controls to obtain sea clutter up to the edge of the ice. Patches of water in a smooth ice field are often revealed by clutter return if there is sufficient wind to ruffle the water. Strong multiple echoes are usually obtained from pack ice, producing a display pattern not unlike sea clutter. The piled up ice marking a ship's passage can often be seen (8.20).

Provided they are not of a shape to scatter the radar energy, ice walls will usually give strong echoes. Icebergs are usually not detected at long range because of the scattering of reflected energy from the smooth sides of the berg. Also the cold air surrounding the berg produces conditions which cause the radar beam to bend upwards, thus reducing detectability. Detection of growlers by

radar is very uncertain owing to their shape and small size above the water; echoes are often impossible to distinguish from sea clutter.

Interference

The effect of other radar equipments in the same band being operated in the vicinity will sometimes be encountered. This appears on the display as radial flecks (8.21). It may disturb observation but does not affect operation; also it is usually temporary and not often experienced. On more expensive radars it can be removed by a de-fruiter, (8.22).

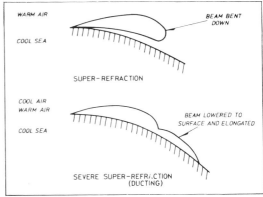

8.20   Ice

Radar Beacons

An increasing number of radar beacons are appearing around the coastlines of the world. There are various types in use, e.g. racon and ramark. The signal displayed may be a continuous

8.18   Sub-refraction

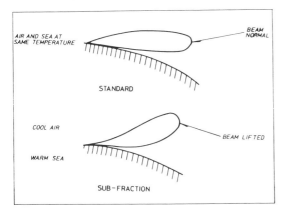

8.19   Super-refraction (ducting)

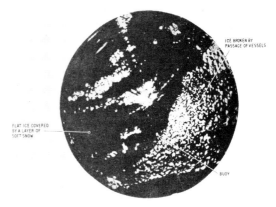

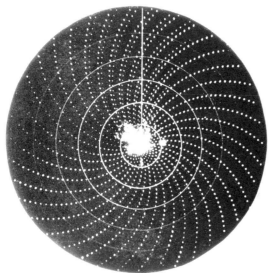

8.21   Radar interference before de-fruiting

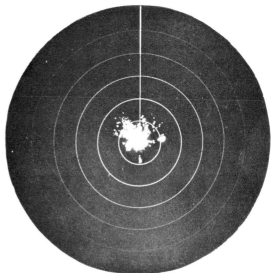

8.22   Radar interference after de-fruiting

line from the beacon to the ship, or a series of dots or dashes, or both. The radar beacon may be considered as a reflector that will produce an electronically generated answer. This has considerable advantages in terms of range performance. Where a radar equipment responds to the echo of its own transmitted signal, this is attenuated with range by an inverse fourth power law. If, as with a radar beacon, a new signal is originated in reply, it has only to travel in one direction and the signal will only be attenuated by the inverse square law with distance and thus the beacon can be interrogated at a considerably increased range. The ultimate range is the point at which the beacon appears above the radar horizon. The beacon will be a fixed installation and can therefore have a substantial transmitter with which to send a reply. Further, by coding, the beacon can be made to identify itself. There are various types of beacon, however, and some require special equipment to enable the ship's radar to receive the reply.

The racon is a special radar transceiver with a fixed aerial capable of receiving and transmitting signals over a wide arc, or if necessary 360° in azimuth. If range permits its reply will commence almost on top of the echo from the structure housing the racon. The reply to the radar interrogating pulse is delayed by the racon system for a short period and correction to the range must be made for this. The displayed range will be greater than the true range and must be subtracted. A typical beacon signal is shown in (8.8) where the coded reply gives both bearing and range, which is measured up to the edge of the reply pulse nearer the centre of the screen (less the correction figure). The beam-width of the radar aerial defines the angular width of the racon reply received, and the racon's bearing from the radar aerial is measured through the middle of the arc. There are various odd effects that are worth mentioning here. The racon will be interrogated by pulses reflected off nearby objects as well as by the direct radar beam. Also, the sidelobes of the aerial beam will trigger the racon at closer ranges and this means that unlike an echo the racon will reply at full power. This results in its arc width being increased considerably. Responses from the beacon can also be triggered by reflection from objects or structures on the vessel carrying the interrogating radar (8.14).

Operation

To achieve proficiency with an inherently visual presentation such as radar, a certain amount of experience will be necessary. I am sure the following collection of photographs and diagrams on the adjustment of controls will be invaluable to the small craft operator.

The radar controls for adjusting the presentation and alignment of the picture are termed

Brilliance
Gain or Sensitivity
LO Tuning
Sea Clutter or Swept Gain
Differentiation or Rain Clutter
Horizontal Shift
Vertical Shift.

The adjustment of these will determine the operational efficiency of the equipment. In order to make clear the purpose of each I will describe their functions in turn, and how to optimise the display.

The brilliance control is adjusted so that the rotating trace is at the threshold of visibility. Under these conditions only the echo pulses will brighten the trace (8.23). If the brilliance control is insufficiently advanced (8.24) the energy from weak echoes will not reach the visibility threshold and these signals will be lost. If the brilliance is advanced too far (8.25) the screen will become unnecessarily bright and reduce the contrast between the echo and background; again this will obscure weak echoes.

The correct setting for the brilliance control will be found by setting the following controls to minimum: Brilliance, Gain, Sea Clutter, Diff (off). As the brilliance setting will need adjustment when switching to different ranges, select the required range at this point and advance the brilliance control until the rotating trace is just visible; the control should then be adjusted to just extinguish the trace. The gain control should now be adjusted.

The gain control enables the 'magnification' of the echo signals to be adjusted to suit conditions such as entering harbour, where low gain can be used with a consequent increase in clarity; or on maximum sensitivity when searching for buoys or other small objects or long range echoes. The optimum setting is shown in (8.26). If the gain is set too high the background noise will produce 'grass' without any further increase in usable gain and may also obscure weak echoes (8.27). If set too low the effect is that small echoes insufficiently brighten the screen with consequent loss of range (8.28). The gain control should therefore be adjusted so that the blank areas of the screen have a faintly speckled appearance. LO tuning should then be adjusted.

The LO tuning control tunes the klystron, Gunn effect device, or oscillator-multipler used as a local oscillator and enables the receiver to operate on the same frequency as the transmitter.

Obviously this has to be optimised in order for the echoes to receive the maximum amplification. The control is adjusted by slowly moving it through the whole of its travel to find the position where a long range echo appears at maximum intensity. Local oscillators of all type have coarse and fine adjustments. The LO tuning control on the display will occasionally be found to give optimum results at one extreme of its travel. When this occurs the advice of a radar technician should be sought, as the adjustment of the coarse control is usually beyond the scope of the user.

Sometimes it will be found that under very cold conditions when first switching on, the LO tuning control will need setting as above; however, as soon as the radar has been on long enough to reach a stable temperature, the control setting will be within the normal range of operation. This is not an effect that needs to unduly concern the owner—it does not happen on all makes of equipment and generally only lasts for a few minutes after switching on. Photo (8.29) shows the appearance of the picture with the LO off tune, and (8.30) the same picture with the LO control optimised. The sea clutter or swept gain control should now be adjusted.

At close range, small radar echoes are received from the surface of the sea (8.31). In the centre of the display, especially in rough weather, it is difficult to identify small echoes from buoys, boats etc. The unwanted sea echoes only occur at short range and as the amplitude of these signals is in general lower than the return for wanted targets, the gain of the receiver is reduced for a period just after the transmitted pulse. The sea clutter control enables the operator to vary the extent of the reduction in gain and also the length of time for the receiver to return to normal. This method of clarifying small close echoes is assisted by the echo signal from an object being relatively constant in position, and therefore several successive echoes will integrate in the screen persistence, whereas the sea return is somewhat specular and diffuse and the likelihood of any sea echo appearing in the same place for any two successive scans is remote.

This control must obviously be adjusted to suit sea and weather conditions. It may also be used

8.23–28   *Effects of controls*

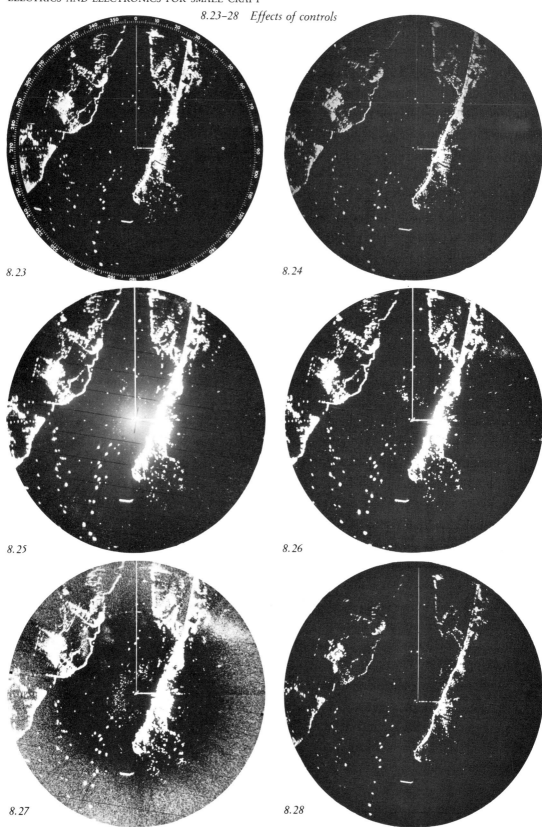

8.23

8.24

8.25

8.26

8.27

8.28

with advantage to reduce the apparent over-brightness at the centre of the screen when using high gain settings to obtain long range echoes. A typical picture of correct adjustment is shown at (8.32), and overadjustment in (8.33). To clarify the general concept of swept gain, (8.34) shows the area of the picture effected by the circuitry and also the tapered recovery.

Rain and rain clouds and to an extent hail and snow can mask areas of the screen. This effect is called rain clutter and can generally be seen at the longer ranges; it will, however, cause problems if the vessel is in the rain area. The differentiation or rain clutter control introduces an effect which discriminates between rain echoes and wanted target responses by displaying only the leading edge of the echo signals. This may produce some loss of

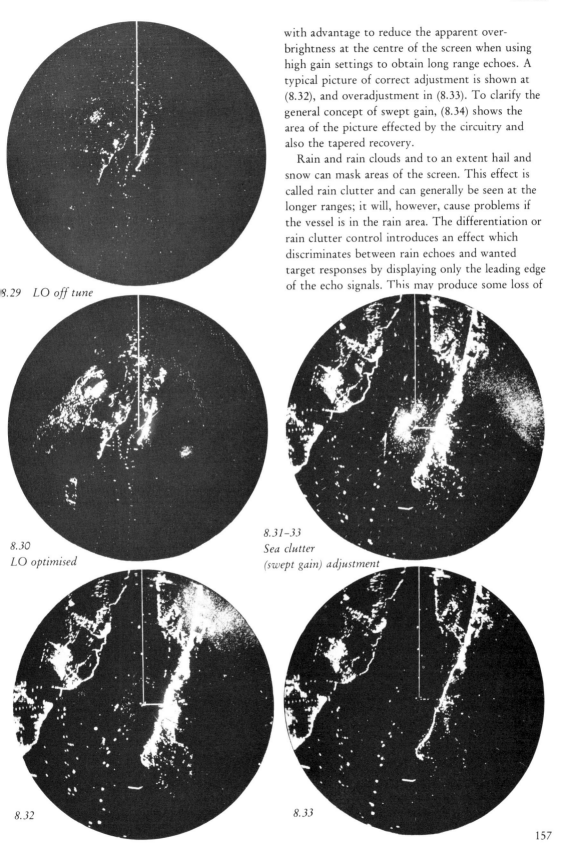

8.29   LO off tune

8.30
LO optimised

8.31–33
Sea clutter
(swept gain) adjustment

8.32

8.33

weaker echoes which can sometimes be partially offset by an increase in the gain control setting. The picture will be improved on short ranges where the presentation is congested. (8.35) shows a display with extensive rain clutter; (8.36) shows the same picture with the differentiation control advanced and the gain control slightly increased.

The centring controls, sometimes called X and Y Shift, are provided to enable the radar picture to be moved along its horizontal and vertical axes to a limited extent. These controls are necessary because magnetic influences both inside and outside the display unit combine to displace the electron beam within the cathode ray tube. (8.37) shows an off-centred picture; it will be obvious that correct bearing will not be obtained from a

misaligned picture of this sort. Also, the heading flash will sometimes appear displaced when a left or right displacement exists (relative motion). (8.38) shows a properly centred picture.

The following pictures illustrate how to use the controls to clear the picture. (8.39) shows a typical radar picture with numerous ambiguous responses present. (8.40) shows these cleared by adjusting the clutter control and reducing the gain control setting. Rain clutter will be seen on the top left of the display and this was not reduced by differentiation as it was not in a critical area. The picture shown in (8.40) was taken first and the controls were incorrectly set. It will be seen that the two ships just below the centre of the picture have moved further to the left in (8.39) and their

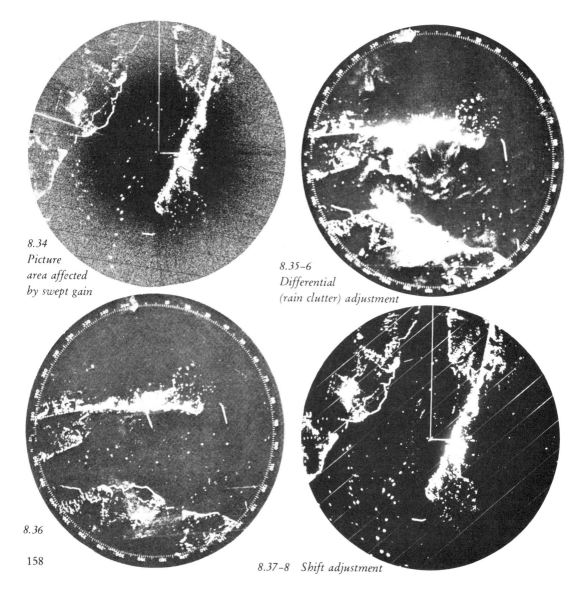

8.34
Picture
area affected
by swept gain

8.35–6
Differential
(rain clutter) adjustment

8.36

8.37–8 Shift adjustment

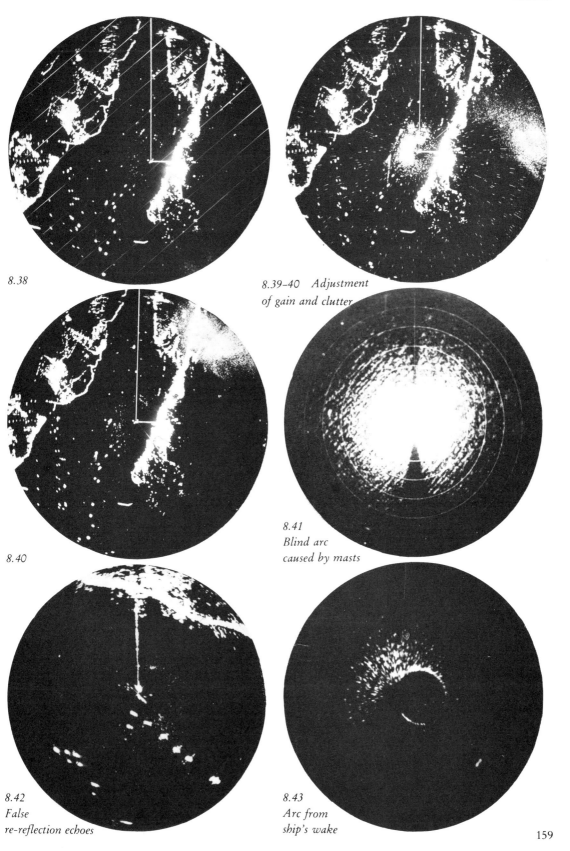

8.38

*8.39–40 Adjustment
of gain and clutter*

8.40

*8.41
Blind arc
caused by masts*

*8.42
False
re-reflection echoes*

*8.43
Arc from
ship's wake*

wakes are now showing. The white radial flecks are radar interference. The rain clutter has also thinned out and moved away in a north easterly direction.

Interesting effects

Where some part of the signal path to the aerial is interrupted by masts or some other part of the superstructure, an arc of reduced sensitivity is created. If the obstruction is large in azimuth a blind arc will be formed. The effect of this can be seen in (8.41) where blind sectors fore and aft, due to masts, are clearly shown by the absence of sea clutter within the arc. The other feature in this picture is that it is possible to detect the wind direction from the regular formation of the swell.

(8.42) shows a line of destroyers to the east of Southend pier; the return signals were sufficiently strong to reflect backwards and forwards between the hulls of the ship carrying the radar at the pier and the first destroyer in the line. This has produced two further echoes at multiples of the range, which are false information. Echoes that appear in these circumstances may be recognised by the fact that they appear on the same bearing and move radially at twice the speed of the true echo, at exact multiples of the range.

The effect created by the wake of a ship turning in a tight circle is shown in (8.43).

Effect of range switch

When changing to a different range, the effect is for the spot on the CRT to travel faster as the range period is reduced, i.e. on the 5 mile range the spot travels from the centre to the edge of the

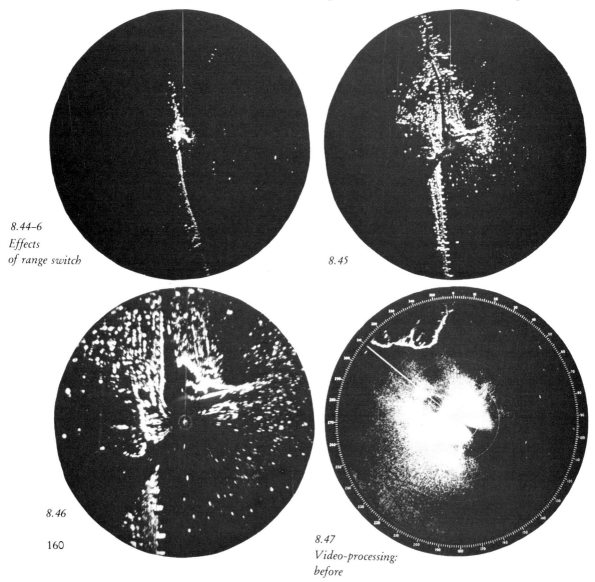

8.44–6
*Effects
of range switch*

8.45

8.46

160

8.47
*Video-processing:
before*

8.48   Video-processing: after

screen in approximately 60 micro seconds, whereas on the 0·5 mile range the time drops to only 6 microseconds. This affects the apparent brightness of the picture, making it necessary to reset the brightness and gain controls for optimum performance. The change in appearance of the screen can be seen in (8.44) 6nm, (80.45) 1½nm, (8.46) ½ nm, the heading markers shown point north and the sea is on the right of the picture, which is from Great Yarmouth coastguards lookout, clearly showing shipping in the river Yare and at sea.

Video processing

The principle application of microelectronics to radar techniques has been that of processing the raw radar responses before displaying them on the screen, all without appreciable delay. This is called video processing, and it is a powerful means of conditioning the signal to attenuate clutter, noise and interference, and accentuate the required echoes. The circuits operate by dividing the range in use into a large number of time slots; each slot is usually smaller than one spot diameter on the CRT. On each scan, a series of time slots are produced and the echo information in each slot is stored. Successive series of slots have their respective information compared, and any response that does not appear in the same slot on successive scans is dumped. Those responses that do appear in the same slot on successive scans are additive, thus improving the signal to background ratio.

Commercial processors such as the Decca Clearscan are much more complex than this, however, it is the kind of technique which will appear increasingly due to the nature of the electronics industry; (8.47) shows the remarkable effect of the device before, and (8.48) after.

Radiation Hazards With Microwave Equipment

Microwave energy is likely to be encountered on small boats at levels which can be harmful if care is not taken. The likely sources of such radiation are of course radar equipment and microwave ovens. There can be no doubt that the best level of radiation for any human to be exposed to is zero. Much has been done recently to tighten up regulations and specifications covering leakage of energy that might be harmful. Although the data available on human radiation cases is too small for practical analysis, a safe level of 10mW/cm^2 had been accepted by most authorities. There are now signs that this level will be reduced to 1 mW/cm^2 in the near future.

The biological effects of microwave radiation are largely thermal and its effect is more pronounced on those parts of the body tissue that do not contain blood vessels. Heat caused by radiation is only able to disperse by conduction to surrounding vascular tissue. This is particularly true for parts of the eyes, gall bladder and urinary tract, for example. When the radar is operating do not work within three feet of the aerial unit, and make a point of not looking directly into the scanner. If you have a microwave oven, if it is ever stressed or damaged in any way make a point of having it checked for leakage by a specialist. Suitable equipment for measuring radiation in both the radar and cooking bands is manufactured by Magnetic AB of Sweden. This equipment reads directly in milliwatts per square centimetre (mW/cm^2) and can be used by unskilled personnel.

Radar Reflectors

Many small craft owners take the precaution of having a radar reflector to enhance the reflectivity of their boats. Marconi Marine produce a collapsible octahedral corner reflector, Type 1532B, designed to increase the radar range of objects having poor radar reflecting properties, such as small wooden vessels, ships' lifeboats of wood or fibreglass construction, or buoys, and thus provide an effective target to ensure early recognition by vessels fitted with radar (8.49).

It is of simple construction, inexpensive, easy to install or dismantle, requires no electrical power and can be stowed in a very small space when not in use. The whole assembly comprises three aluminium plates, each measuring 0.35 m (14 in.) square. The plates are slotted and the corners truncated, with shoulders to provide positive location when assembled. The provision of pressed tongue clips ensures the automatic retention of the plates at right angles to each other in the assembled position. The unit can be assembled in less than thirty seconds. Two dog clips are provided with each assembly; these serve the dual purpose of retaining the three plates together in the stowing position or providing simple attachment to a halyard by means of the elongated holes in the main plate, when the reflector is hoisted in the rigging.

The effectiveness of such reflectors is based on the principle that, providing three metal sheets of

high conductivity are retained at 90° angles to each other, incident radar energy is reflected back along the incident path from the corner reflector formed by the three plates. The assembly forms eight such corner reflectors to cover all angles of incidence, both horizontally and vertically. The resulting radar cross section, or reflecting area, is approximately equal from all angles of view and is much greater than that of any buoy or small vessel.

Ranges

The radar range depends mainly on the height of the reflector above the sea, the peak power of the radar equipment, the length of the radar pulse and the existing weather conditions. The following observed results indicate typical ranges in moderate weather conditions.

Reflector height	Scanner height	Peak power	Pulse length	Range
2.5 m (8 ft)	4 m (12 ft)	50 kW	1 usec.	3 n.m.
4 m (12 ft)	12 m (40 ft)	20 kW	1 usec.	4 n.m.
4 m (12 ft)	25 m (75 ft)	50 kW	1 usec.	6 n.m.

8.49   Octahedral radar reflector

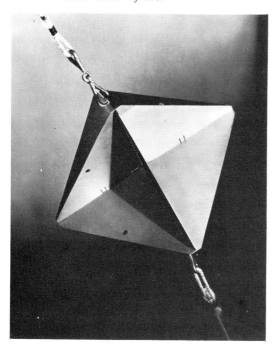

The above figures are representative of the sort of radar fitted to commercial shipping, as of course the yachtsman's main interest is in being seen. It will be noted that these ranges would normally ensure pickup outside of the sea clutter area.

Recently I have noticed the appearance of a number of weird looking reflectors which, on closer inspection, seem to have been produced by people with more imagination than test facilities, so I recommend that you do not allow yourself to be separated from too much money without being very sure. (8.49) shows how the corner type should be mounted, i.e. one corner cell upwards; if you hang it aloft you will probably need more than one halyard to hold it in this best radar aspect position. As an alternative, there are now available completely spherical lens type reflectors (8.50), it is important not to confuse this type with a similar looking product, which is simply a corner reflector in a spherical case. To understand how the lens type works, remember the last time you looked over the side at the anchor chain: you may have noticed that it appeared to bend away at the point appearance of the information displayed, particularly in small craft, because of the difficulty of maintaining a straight course. The operator has to try to pick out additional movement within a moving picture. If singlehanded, the use of an autopilot greatly improves the radar picture, as a much better course is held. There can be few easier ways of wandering off course than looking into the radar while holding the wheel. When changing course to avoid other vessels, make large changes (60 to 90 degrees at least), so that even with the distorting effect of relative motion your action will still be clearly seen.

If another vessel is going to make close quarters, it will only show on the radar screen as a line of constant bearing. If there is just one suspect echo it is possible to bisect it with the bearing marker; if it stays on the bearing marker, some avoiding action is required. It is important to remember that the other vessel's speed as well as your own affects the apparent course on your ship's radar.

Taking radar bearings

Many publications place great emphasis on the accurate measurement of the bearing of any particular target; but resolution is often confused with accuracy, because the value of the reading is downgraded by such things as the centring of the PPI, setting accuracy of the heading marker, parallax and interpolation errors, the finite angular resolution of the scanner, and the instability inherent in all small craft. Even in moderate weather, finite heading accuracy is a big problem where accurate measurement is concerned. Where this is important you will have to average several readings on a temporary heading where wind and sea allow the best stability. Taking everything into account, plus or minus 5° is an acceptable error. The means of indicating the bearing may vary from an electronic bearing marker to a simple graticule; the former will generally appear as a dotted line superimposed electronically on the radar screen, and thus avoiding parallax; the latter will be a series of radial marks against a transparent engraved scale. Do not make the mistake of assuming that errors arising from either operator or equipment will cancel each other out; although this may happen, it is just as likely that they will be additive, so always allow a wide margin of safety and, when changing course, make large radar visible changes.

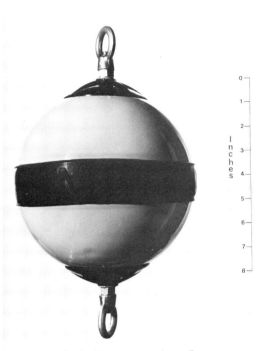

8.50   Spherical lens-type radar reflector

where it entered the water. Both light and radar waves are the same sort of energy, and are refracted or bent at the boundary of any substance through which they pass. Consider now a sphere of radar-transparent material with a radar wave applied from one direction; as the waves enter they will be converged internally toward the opposite side of the sphere. By disposing a number of spheres in a concentric fashion, successive bends can be made to converge the waves at a point on the circumference opposite the source. If a narrow horizontal reflector is now impressed on the outside of the assembly, the waves will be reflected from the inside face of this, back along a reciprocal path.

Radar Navigation

Apparent movement in the radar picture is in fact a composite effect of target movement and your own vessel's movement. It is quite hard to assimilate the effect which this has on the

Rangefinding

The very nature of radar allows range to be measured easily and accurately, as the boat does not affect the measurement and, if something appears on the screen, you can quickly establish its range. The two types of rangemarker commonly found are fixed range rings and variable range markers, whilst some expensive radars are fitted with both. With fixed rings, the operator can estimate the distance of single echoes in any part of the screen area, although there will be a reading error unless the echo is actually on a ring. The variable range marker will read more accurately the range of any one echo, but to adjust the control the operator will need a hand free.

Collision Avoidance and Plotting

Plotting is the established method of reducing risk of collision by keeping a record of the range and motion of selected targets. Selection is necessary because it is a manual process consuming both time and space. The operator systematically records the times, ranges, and bearings of special plotting sheets. But unless the radar is fitted with a compass stabilised display, a reflection plotter, and a variable range marker, the extreme instability of small craft reduces the accuracy of the plot to such an extent that you may find yourself involved in a radar-assisted collision. Even with all the equipment and skill required, in thick weather or at night by far the most valuable asset is a human mind, with its ability to concentrate continuously on the radar screen. In a busy estuary 10 moving targets within a mile is not unusual and, taking into account that a modern ship will cover a mile in 3 minutes, some idea of the problem can be imagined. If I add that your own vessel may be on a curved track—rounding a point for example—you can see that there would not be time to carry out sufficient plots and at the same time control the vessel.

It is however useful to consider the plotting procedure, as it is an aid to digesting the apparent effects of relative motion. A time between plots to suit the likely speed and range of targets must be chosen. Measure the range and bearing of the target, and transfer these to the plotting sheet, noting the time beside the mark; after the chosen time interval has elapsed, measure the range and bearing again and enter on the plotting sheet. This procedure is repeated and each mark joined together with a short line which should be arrowed to indicate direction. This must be done for every target likely to endanger your position. If the observations are equally spaced, the target's course and speed are constant; if not, they must be plotted until at least three aligned observations indicate its new course and speed. If the direction of the arrow on the plot is toward the centre of the screen, extend the plotting line until it passes the centre. The distance between the centre and this line gives the clearance between your vessel and the target. When you are in doubt, whether you are plotting or not, you can stop a small bat relatively quickly, thus removing the effect of your own boat's motion from the radar picture. Stopping on its own does not reduce risk, since you might well stop in the path of another vessel, so that continuous concentration on the radar picture, and a range scale capable of showing vessels close to you, are required. I am inclined to think that the 'intense concentration' factor is doing more for air traffic control than the 'occasional look' is doing for the maritime service. You must aim to be aware of all echoes and their movements, and if you do choose to try to plot echoes, pick the ones where the relative bearing remains steady and the range is closing.

Installation

Modern small radars consist only of a display and radome, and installation is much simpler than older types.

Effect of Topweight
I cannot over-emphasize the importance or minimising topweight in small boat installations and, as a radome is likely to be one of the higher and heavier things aboard, it will effect the boat's stability. Now that current consumption is so low, it is not uncommon to find radars fitted to partly open boats used for sport fishing. In addition to the sheer weight of the radome, there is the kinetic energy given to the weight by any dynamic force

8.51 a–d Suitable radar mountings

creating roll; if you should happen to encounter a sea where, perhaps just by changing course, the heeling period is resonant, dangerous roll amplitudes could occur. The rule must therefore be: the smaller the boat, the lower the height and weight, whatever the advantage in range terms of elevating the scanner.

8.51 c

8.51 b

Mounting the scanner

It is often desirable that the radome or scanner should be demountable, particularly where it is necessary to pass under bridges at varying states of tide. A low weight scanner will obviously be an advantage in this situation and a stowing shoe on the deck can be provided to secure this in its lower position, the cable length being tailored for this purpose. Nearly all radars house something in the scanner that will need servicing from time to time, so it also makes sense to choose a height where it can be safely serviced. If it is fitted on a mast bracket do not run the cables down inside the mast, as they cannot be supported and will chafe and stretch in service; they should be clamped to existing standing rigging or to a purpose-rigged jackstay beside the mast.

It is important to try to avoid obstructions which might give rise to blind sectors or false echoes. Obviously the masts are the most likely offenders; in my own boat the radome is mounted on the mizzen mast and there is a blind sector ahead and astern, this being the compromise I have decided to accept. On larger vessels the scanner can the aerials, which can cause the autopilot to switch from port to starboard at every revolution. Check this by rotating the scanner by hand with the autopilot switched on. The display produces the smallest external field although it is generally sited nearer to the compass. If you carry a radar spares kit including a magentron, it is important that it should have a fixed and marked stowage and that it be in situ when the compass is recalibrated after fitting the radar. If you replace a magnetron at sea, replace the defective unit in the spares kit, suitable labelled, keeping the same orientation. Such precautions are important on small craft because the separating distances are much less. If you sail with either unit removed for service, remember to allow for any difference that this may have made to the compass.

Display

A well oriented display within easy view of the helmsman is a great advantage, particularly when singlehanded. Try to achieve a position where the presentation is natural and not, for example, mounted on the after bulkhead of the wheelhouse, so that echoes from the starboard side of the vessel appear on the port side of the screen and vice versa. Some useful ideas (8.52a–c) for mounting displays are shown, but each particular vessel has its own limitations. Chapter 1 gives general guidance on electrical work, but I stress again that

8.51 d

be offset to starboard of the centreline thus moving the sectors to port, however on a small boat the asymetric weight of an offset scanner should not be considered (8.51a–d) show typical radar installations.

Magnetic interference

Before siting either unit, check for the possibility of magnetic interference by observing the compass when holding the radar units in their preferred positions. The radome, which will usually house the magnetron, must be a minimum of 2 metres (6½ ft) away from the compass, to keep deflections below 2°. An equivalent distance for the display is about 0·6 m (2 ft). The figures vary among manufacturers and are worth checking. Remember the proximity of the autopilot sensor, if any, as with many small radars the magnetron rotates on

8.52 b

it is important to minimise voltage drop in the wiring by having a cable with a large enough cross section area. Most radars will operate at 10% below the nominal supply but, if you allow this margin to be dissipated in cable losses, it means that when the engines are stopped the radar is reduced to operating without any safety factor; a real disadvantage if you have to lay off in fog or darkness for a number of hours.

8.52 c

8.52 a–c   *Various radar display mountings*

9 Communications Equipment

There were some that got the message in the
  old way,
And the flashes in the darkness spoke of you.
                              The Old Way
                              R A Hopwood

The history of radio communication goes back until it eventually blurs into the subject of communication by line transmission techniques and telegraphy. It is very hard to establish who originally applied electricity to signalling, as many workers were giving their attention to this problem simultaneously. Certainly the name of S F B Morse, an American inventor who devised the signalling code in collaboration with Alfred Vail in 1837, has been made almost immortal by its international acceptance and use. He produced a half-mile-long telegraph system in 1835, at New York University, which puts his work roughly parallel with Wheatstone and Cooke, who patented a practical telegraph system in 1837. At that time they were responsible for installing a telegraph signalling system between Euston and Chalk Farm stations in London.

There is of course a vast history associated with the development of line communication by telegraphy. However it continued on its own separate and sophisticated path when the fundamentals of radio telegraphy were first established by Clerk Maxwell's theory of the existence of electric waves in 1864, and Hertz's production of such waves in 1887. These events were quickly followed by Branly's invention in 1890 of a detector for Hertzian waves, the coherer. Marconi applied these principles to a system which used an aerial as one plate of a capacitor and the earth as another and subsequently applied the principle of electrically tuning the receiver and transmitter covered in the British Patent No. 7777.

Probably the next significant step was the introduction of the thermionic diode valve by Fleming in 1904. This was followed by L De Forest's three-electrode valve or 'triode' valve in 1906, which produced a means of amplification.

Line telephony, which was to provide many of the components for voice transmission by radio, had begun its emergence with Alexander Bell's discovery during experiments with line telegraphy, that vibration of a magnetised reed close to the poles of an electromagnet generated an alternating current capable of producing identical vibrations in the reed of a second similar arrangement. In 1876 he was granted a patent which covered the principles of telephone transmission.

The Bell electromagnetic system worked well as a receiver but was less efficient as a microphone and subsequently the carbon microphone was devised by Hunning. This combination of carbon microphone and electromagnetic earpiece until recent years has survived as a successful arrangement for both line and radio telephony.

In 1900 the Royal Navy were just commencing the installation of radio after trials during the previous year. The state of the communication art at that time is indicated by Winston Churchill, who has related how at the start of the South African war, the Commander in Chief was travelling to the scene of the action by sea, when news was received from a passing tramp steamer by a member of its crew holding up a blackboard with the words 'Three battles, Penn Symonds killed' written on it—very much line-of-sight propagation.

It is interesting to remember that the first transmission across water, in May 1897, was from a point on the South Wales coast to an island in the Bristol Channel, a distance of about three and a half miles. Mr W H Preece of the British Post

9.1   The Marchese Marconi's yacht Elettra

Office, lecturing at the Royal Institution in London on the 4th June 1897, stated that 'enough had been done to prove that for shipping and lighthouse purposes it will be a great and valuable acquisition.' Radio communication was almost from its invention applied to the needs of the seafarer; and from the development of communications equipment came many of the allied applications of what is presently called electronics and which we now take so much for granted. Marconi carried out considerable experimental work on board his steam yacht *Elettra* in the course of the early years of the development of communication by wireless (9.1), and in 1900 he formed the Marconi International Marine Co.

The introduction of radio to small boats could well have been the 250 W installation which was designed by the Radio Communication Co. for ships' lifeboats (RCC were taken over by Marconi Marine). One of these sets was fitted during 1927 to the Rosslare Harbour lifeboat (9.2). This was a radiotelegraph equipment, which meant that a skilled operator had to be carried and was the only

telegraphic equipment installed by the RNLI; however it did service until 1943. Radiotelephony was introduced to RNLI lifeboats in 1929 when five equipments were installed, one of which was in the Dover lifeboat (9.3).

Frequency Groups and Modulation

Communications is a very diverse subject, and as it has become rather littered with abbreviations I feel that the table of frequency groups and the services covered (9.4), together with an outline of the modulation systems employed, will help to make clear what must be difficult for many people to understand. It is of course intended only as a general guide and exceptions do occur.

Another major consideration is the method of superimposing the intelligence we wish to transmit on the outgoing signal. This process is called modulation and it may be carried out in a variety of ways. It is in fact quite possible to apply any form of modulation at any carrier frequency; however various requirements are imposed by the

9.2   Lifeboat fitted with early radiotelegraphy equipment

9.3   Lifeboat fitted with early radiotelegraphy equipment

type of intelligence to be sent and these together with current practice, engineering convenience, availability of techniques, etc. have produced a number of systems in common usage. In the second table (9.5) I have tried to summarise most of these by stating the service, the modulation technique and the common abbreviation.

The term simplex refers to an R/T installation which cannot simultaneously send and receive, and will generally use a single aerial with a changeover switch. A duplex system enables a two-way conversation to be carried on as the transmitter and receiver are in operation at the same time. Two aerials are used, one for sending and the other for receiving, and the receiver is fitted with a duplex filter which is tuned to reject the frequency of the transmitter. Such systems may be employed at any part of the frequency spectrum. At VHF, where it is required to use the public correspondence services, i.e. link calls via telephone systems, a duplex system is mandatory. Equipments with these facilities are fairly expensive and most smaller boats use a 6-channel simplex VHF R/T 10–20 watts output for that reason.

4 Frequency groups

Band	Frequency range	Wavelength	Service	Propagation
Very low frequency (VLF)	3–30 kHz	10,000–100,000 m	Long range telegraphy (world wide) Omega navigation system, echosounders, sonar	Strong ground wave
Low frequency (LF)	30–300 kHz	1,000–10,000 m	Long distance communication, broadcasting, Loran, echosounders, DF radio beacons, Consol, sonar, Decca navigation system	Ground wave
Medium frequency (MF)	0.3–3 MHz	100–1,000 m	Broadcasting, marine communications, DF radio beacons, Consol, Loran, amateur radio	Ground wave up to about 150 miles, skywave at night
High frequency (HF)	3–30 MHz	10–100 m	Directional broadcasting services, amateur radio, marine communications, weather facsimile transmissions	Lower frequencies as above, higher frequencies by skywave for longer hops
Very high frequency (VHF)	30–300 MHz	1–10 m	Communication between vehicles, fire, ambulance, police, aircraft, ships; television, local broadcasting	Short range communication by diffraction in built-up areas. Distances largely by line of sight
Ultra high frequency (UHF)	300–3,000 MHz	0.1–1 m	Aircraft navigational aids and landing systems, radar, microwave heating	Line of sight applications usually beamed
Super high frequency (SHF)	3,000–30,000 MHz and higher frequencies	1–10 cm and shorter wavelengths	Radar, microwave communication links for television, etc.	Line of sight applications usually beamed

Type of signal modulation	*Service*	*9.5 Signal modulation*
Signals without any form of modulation are called continuous waves (CW)	This type of wave is usually turned on and off by a Morse key or some automatic device and is used for simple transmitters, beacons or Decca Navigator system	
Signals modulated by a tone (MCW) Modulated carrier wave	Generally used for Morse or automatic sending, also used for telemetry, beacons and similar functions	
Signals modulated by moving the carrier frequency by a fixed amount (FSK) Frequency shift keying	Employed for weather facsimile transmission, teleprinters, telemetry, etc.	
Signals modulated by changing amplitude (AM) Amplitude modulation (DSB)	Extensively employed for telephony at all frequencies. In its simplest form produces upper and lower side bands equal to the highest modulating frequency in use. It is therefore sometimes referred to as DSB transmission (double sideband). In use for marine, general broadcasting, and aircraft communications at VHF	
Signals modulated in amplitude but with the carrier wave suppressed Suppressed carrier (DSB)	Very little advantage for the increase in complexity, and rarely used	
Signals modulated in amplitude but with both carrier and one sideband suppressed (SSB) Single side band	Great advantages technically in terms of air space and performance (see text). Used for marine, amateur and commercial applications	
Signals as in SSB but with a pilot carrier radiated at about the 25% level (SSB) Compatible AM	Used in the same systems as SSB above; particularly intended for occasions when an SSB transmitter is used to work a station where a special SSB receiver is not available	
Signals modulated by instantaneously varying the phase or frequency of the carrier wave (FM) Frequency modulation	Generally used at VHF for marine communications broadcasting	
Signals modulated by short bursts of the carrier signal (PM) Pulse modulation	Echosounders, Loran, radar	

Signal from several transmitters received in successive time slots (TM) Time multiplex

Omega navigation system

Propagation

The use of any particular frequency or type of modulation in the ranges outlined in the tables is, apart from the technical demands of the equipment use, influenced by the characteristics of the space through which the waves travel. Although all waves radiated will project part of their energy both skywards and along the ground; the extent of each component depends to some degree on both the frequency of the wave and the type of aerial. The different groups of frequencies listed have of course merging characteristics, and the following remarks are general rather than specific. A groundwave is, as its name suggests, a wave that follows the curvature of the earth radially from the transmitting aerial. The strongest groundwaves usually occur at the lowest frequencies (VLF) for several reasons, not the least of which is the type of transmitting aerial employed for practical reasons. A skywave is a wave which travels from the transmitting aerial in a skyward direction, and is reflected by the ionosphere to the point at which it is received. Reflection of such waves may occur when they reach the earth's surface again, and so they are reflected in a series of skips until attenuated by distance. Skywaves appear strongest at the higher frequencies, largely because the ionosphere more readily reflects waves in the HF group.

The specific groups of frequencies used for marine communications are:

1.5 MHz to 4.0 MHz	MF	AM or SSB
4.0 to 30 MHz	HF	AM or SSB
156 MHz to 162 MHz	VHF	FM

Although the exact extent of each band may vary slightly in different countries, the above groups are close enough to give an accurate guide.

In the MF band there is little or no skywave propagation during daylight hours, although a certain amount occurs during darkness. As the emphasis will therefore be on groundwave propagation, a vertical aerial will be required to effect the best results. This can be an inverted L

about 60 ft in length, a straight vertical wire, or a whip aerial, in which case it should preferably be loaded. Range in this band will depend on the transmitter power to some extent, but in general MF can be used up to about 250 miles.

In the HF band, generally only used by long distance sailors making use of extended range skywave propagation, the aerial will usually be somewhat shorter. Where HF is fitted, it is usual to carry MF equipment as well, the method commonly employed is to erect one aerial for each band. The HF aerial is very often a 3 m whip or part of the rigging. Range in this band using skywave propagation often extends well over 1,000 miles.

At VHF a fibreglass encased half-wave dipole is very often used, although a five-eighths wave configuration can be used which will give about a 3 dB gain. The first type is gnerally about 1.5 m (5 ft) long, and the gain aerial is about 3 m (9 ft) long. Both types are fixed with simple clamps and should be mounted as high as possible as the propagation at VHF is virtually line of sight. Range in this band is in the order of 10 to 20 miles.

Small Boat Installations Summarised

1. Fixed radiotelephone installation, amplitude modulated transmitter with carrier frequency range of 1.5 MHz to 4 MHz approx. Medium range communications, say up to 200 miles.
2. As above, but covering HF bands 4 MHz to 28 MHz. Long range communication, say, up to 1,000 miles.
3. Fixed installation VHF radiotelephone, frequency modulated transmitter, carrier frequency 160 MHz approx., channels 12.5 kHz apart. Short range communication, say up to 10 miles.
4. As (1) and (2) but designed for single side-band transmission. The advantages of SSB are outlined later in this chapter.
5. Emergency-only equipment with self-contained battery; transmission of distress or emergency messages only, on 2182 kHz or 500 kHz depending on the design.

There are obviously two separate parts of any radiotelephone, the transmitter and the receiver. The transmitter will be comprised, broadly speaking, of the following units:

1. A microphone to convert the acoustic pressure waves from speech into electrical signals.
2. An oscillator to create a carrier signal.
3. A power amplifier to raise the level of the carrier signal (2) so that it may be suitable for connection to an aerial for radiation.
4. A modulator to superimpose the microphone signal (1) on the signals in (2) or (3), according to the system in use.
5. A relay or similar device for disconnecting the receiver from the aerial when transmitting with a system (simplex) using a single aerial common to both transmitter and receiver.
6. A power unit to convert and stabilise the power from the boat's supply to a form suitable for electronic circuitry.

The second part of the equipment, the receiver, will be comprised of the following sections:

1. A RF tuning section which amplifies the signal at the transmitter frequency.
2. An oscillator and mixer section which converts the RF signals to a common intermediate frequency (IF) for convenient amplification.
3. An IF amplifier, which enables considerable amplification to be obtained with ease and also closely defines the selectivity of the receiver.
4. A detector or discriminator for amplitude modulated or frequency modulated signals respectively.
5. An audio frequency amplifier.
6. A loudspeaker or earpiece to convert the electrical signals from the audio amplifier (5) to audible acoustic pressure waves.
7. A power unit to convert and stabilise the power from the boat's supply to a form suitable for electronic circuitry.

Radiotelephones have become very complex in recent years, and must conform to a type approval specification laid down by the Ministry of Posts and Telecommunications in the UK, and equivalent authorities in other countries.

Alternative Equipments

Single sideband (SSB) equipments have been compulsory since 1973 for new installations. The change in the system was due to the increasing volume of radio traffic and thus the need to conserve air space. The double sideband (DSB) amplitude modulated transmissions which have served in the past will be continued for some years, and thus owners will still need information and service for their existing equipment. The general information given here, although primarily aimed at SSB equipment, will cover most aspects of the installation problems encountered with older equipment.

The trend to single sideband transmission can be best appreciated if we make a comparison with the old AM system. SSB trasmitters and receivers are by no means new, by definition. In fact most of the techniques, although refined by modern components and years of development, were in constant use by radio amateurs and industrial and military users all over the world years ago. In the world of shipping the reliability of transmission is a matter for concern, and with small craft in particular power conservation is also a necessary consideration. Better selectivity, frequency stability and signal to noise ratio play a significant part in effecting the desired improvements, and the use of SSB techniques allows improvement in all these areas.

In amplitude modulated (AM) transmission the outgoing radio waves consist of a carrier signal at the fundamental centre frequency and two sidebands. The two sidebands appear because when two frequencies are mixed, i.e. carrier and modulating signal, they produce other frequencies equal to their sum and difference. For instance, a 2000 kHz carrier modulated by a 1000 Hz (1 kHz) signal would produce two side frequencies of 2001 kHz and 1999 kHz respectively. As speech consists mainly of an instantaneous varying proportion of frequencies in a band roughly from 300 to 3000 Hz, when the carrier is modulated by speech it will produce sidebands of this order. The speech part of the signal is all contained in the sidebands, and

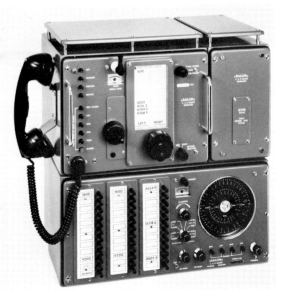

9.6   SSB Radiotelephone, the Sailor R110

the carrier contains no information but is merely there for the sidebands to beat against when received.

If we consider a conventional AM transmitter operated under conditions of 100% modulation, about 66% of the total power radiated by the transmitter is at the carrier frequency and thus the major part of the transmission conveys nothing in terms of intelligence. The remaining 34% of the transmitter power is equally divided between two sidebands, which are the parts of the transmitted signal actually carrying the information. As each sideband is the mirror image of the other, it is clear that only one is really necessary to convey the required information. This being the case, it will be

understood that with any amplitude modulated transmitter of the double sideband type, only about 17% of the total radiated power is fully utilised. For the same battery drain one can achieve six times the output power containing only intelligence by using a SSB system. The air space required is only half that required for a conventional AM DSB system because only one sideband is radiated. For the same peak power radiated with the AM DSB signal, a SSB system will give a signal to noise ratio which is eight times as great. It should, however, be said that SSB equipments are more complex and more demanding in all respects, and this does make them more expensive to manufacture, install and service.

The VHF communication service is only usable up to about 15 miles in small boats, where the aerial height obtainable is generally limited to 5 m. This has many advantages for local communication such as harbour control, etc. As the range obtainable is roughly limited by line of sight conditions it assists in clearing the hundreds of local calls from the precious air space of the lower frequency, long distance bands. VHF equipments are operated on specific channels and are crystal controlled transmitters and receivers, which greatly simplifies the operating procedure. A typical equipment in this class is the Mini Seavoice (9.7).

This is the relatively simple 6-channel equipment which is probably adequate for most small craft requirements. There are more complex VHF systems available for use where the public correspondence network will be used; these have to be duplex equipments and have two RF heads in

9.7   The Mini Seavoice, a low cost VHF R/T

9.8   VHF R/T, synthesiser type

the receiver, and employ either a duplexer or two aerials. Generally duplex equipments are fitted to cover all 26 channels; this is sometimes achieved with a synthesiser to effect an economy in the number of crystals. (9.8) shows an equipment of this type produced by Electronic Laboratories.

Where R/T equipment is not carried as a fixed installation, as perhaps in small boats or liferafts it is not practicable for one reason or another, specially designed emergency-only equipments are available. These come in various forms. The smallest types, of which the Safety Link is typical (6.12), operate on an internal battery to comply with the Ministry of Posts and Telecommunication Voluntary specification. The Marconi Lifesaver meets DTI specifications for use on commercial and fishing vessels, etc. and is of stronger construction to suit the requirements of the specification.

Lastly there is the type illustrated by the Marconi Survivor, which is intended for very severe conditions (9.10). It embodies a handpowered generator so that it may be operated continuously

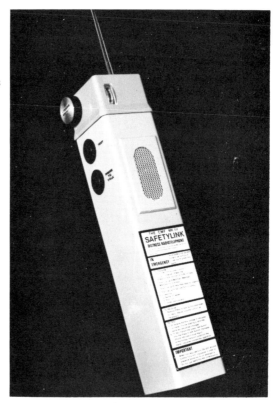

9.9 *Portable emergency transmitter*

9.10 *Hand-powered emergency transmitter*

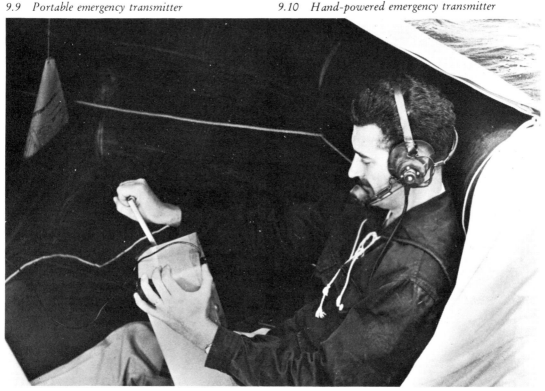

9.11 R/T aerial arrangement of fast powerboat

without relying on internal batteries. This type of equipment will be at the top end of the price and performance range, as it is designed and manufactured to meet rigorous DTI test procedures to ensure a good standard of reliability in extreme conditions.

Installation and Aerials

Many factors affect the siting and installation of radiotelephones and probably the supply to the equipment is as good a place to start a description as any. In chapter 1 electrical systems and the method of deriving cable sizes are discussed; also tables are given which will enable a suitable cable cross section to be selected. When running the cable make sure the length is kept to a mimimum and also that it is kept away from any leads which may carry interference from rotational machinery. The cable cross section should be chosen by making a 50% allowance above the current drawn

by the equipment in the transmit condition, so that the voltage drop in the cable run under these conditions is kept as low as possible, say 0.25 V. This will help to secure the full output from the transmitter. A double pole isolator should be installed at the end of the cable run from the distribution system so that a short flexible connection can be made to the equipment. This makes a useful terminating point for the installing engineer and saves time if the equipment is ever taken away from the boat for service work or at layup time, as removal is a matter of a moment.

When the site is being selected remember that there is always the possibility of sailing single handed, and that if the R/T can be operated while steering manually it could save you a few unpleasant moments at some stage. Another factor affecting the choice of site is the possible use of a R/T receiver that has a DF facility. Where this is to be used the loop and the receiver will need to be sited so that the receiver can be tuned with one

9.12   Whip and other aerials on Thurso lifeboat

hand on the loop handle while at the steering position. It is necessary for one's eye to quickly assimilate the loop reading, compass reading and null on the S meter. A bit of patience here, and probably some refitting of existing gear, will be well repaid.

Many small parts go into making a successful installation, and such items as miniature standoff insulators for the aerial downleads, deckhead feed-through insulators, etc. are available from most reputable marine agents.

On small craft of any type something of compromise has to be reached with the aerial system; (9.11) shows a Brooke Marine Ocean Pirate with the 2 MHz R/T aerials arranged for duplex operation, the receiver aerial being hung between the mast and the pulpit, and the transmitter aerial between the mast and the jackstaff. Another example of aerials suitable for motorboats are the fibreglass whip types shown in the photograph of the Thurso lifeboat (9.13). As explained in chapter

1, it was found that using two whips in parallel improved the radiation characteristics of the installation. The other electronic equipment visible in (9.13) is the Woodson SF folding DF loop which is very popular on small boats, the UHF communication aerials (the short vertical dipoles in the centre of the wheelhouse roof) and a Kelvin Hughes Type 17 radar scanner, which in this case has been mounted aft.

The simplest form of aerial for the 1.5 MHz to 4 MHz MF band, and by far the most consistently good, is an L-shaped array of total length between 10 and 20 m (30 and 60 ft). This is a relatively inexpensive aerial in all respects.

For a simplex system, the requirements are very straightforward. The transmitter and receiver will normally use the same aerial via an internal changeover relay or TR switch. Sometimes two aerials are used for reasons associated with either radio interference suppression or induction from the transmitter. In the case of the former the pickup of unwanted noise can often be reduced by using an aerial rigged in some particular position which may be further away from the source of the trouble. Another improvement can be made by screening the receiving aerial downlead from where it enters the deckhead, down to the receiver. Where aerials are common to both transmitter and receiver screening cannot be used other than exceptionally, as the capacitance of the screening at the bottom end of the aerial will reduce the amount of RF current flowing up the aerial conductor to charge the inherent aerial capacitance in the top section by which radiation is achieved.

If duplex facilities are required two aerials are a must and these may both take the form of inverted L types if convenient, as in the case of the Ocean Pirate (9.12). It should be stressed that good aerials mounted as high and clear as possible and of a length that brings them as close to resonance as possible in the band used for communication will vastly improve the signal to noise ratio.

For small motor boats, probably whip aerials are the answer, and several types are available. I have found that the top end loaded type or continuously loaded types give the best results. Although in many cases whip aerials are the only practical solution for small boats, there is no

9.13   R/T aerial arrangement on sailing yacht

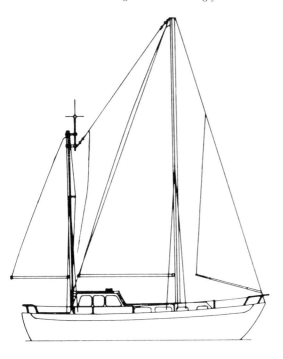

overriding case for having them. It should be understood that an unloaded whip aerial is only as effective as a piece of wire of the same length. As these items can be quite costly it will pay to try to fit a wire type aerial that will give a greater length and, if possible, height.

On sailing boats, undoubtedly the best policy is to insert strain insulators into one or more of the stays and to use these as aerials. This is very common practice; in fact my own boat has this arrangement which works very well. The line diagram (9.13) shows one possibility which has been used at various times with success.

For transmitters in the band from 1.5 MHz to 4 MHz, which are the MF band frequencies in common use, the aerial that can be rigged on any small boat is very often far from the theoretical ideal. To clarify this point, it is obviously out of the question to have a 'resonant' aerial at, for example, 3 MHz, as a whole wavelength at this frequency is in excess of 300 ft, and a quarter wavelength array is the closest approach we are ever likely to find the space for. If we are lucky enough on a sailing boat we might find a total length approaching this by using the fore and back stays; however, ideally the aerial should be vertical and thus the system would not have an effective height of anything like that required to achieve reasonable efficiency. An inverted L aerial is usually chosen for convenience at these frequencies, the total length being preferably about 60 ft. The transmission from such an aerial is by ground wave propagation and the polarisation is largely vertical. Its radiation resistance is about 10 ohms and its capacity about 200 pF. Sometimes the top element of this aerial is doubled, as is often seen on fishing vessels, and this generally improves the efficiency by increasing the capacity of the top of the aerial, thus increasing its effective length which tends to pull a current anti-node into the lower vertical part of the aerial.

In general, communications will be made over water and this, due to its low resistance, is many times better than overland transmission as the sea acts as the return path for the flow of RF currents. In the MF band, the earth system has considerable effect on the performance of the vessel's aerial system. The current distribution in a typical marine band aerial system is such as to be close to a maximum at or near the transmitter ground point. Any resistance in the boat's earthing arrangements is therefore a loss in series with the aerial system at a point where it will be most effective.

The basic installation requirement for a MF radiotelephone could be summarised as follows:

Very low resistance power supply leads
Good earth system (plate if not a metal hull)
Highest aerial possible, of length up to 60 ft.

As a typical marine aerial has radiation resistance of about 10 ohms, it will be clear that if the earth resistance should rise to anything approaching 1 ohm, about 10% of the power will be dissipated in the earth system.

While with boats having metal hulls it may be very easy to achieve a good low-resistance earth, on wooden or fibreglass vessels it is necessary to provide an earth plate. This may consist of a 16 to 18 s.w.g. metal plate about 3 square ft with a bolt through the centre. It is fitted by drilling the hull to allow the bolt to pass into some accessible place in the bilges. On wooden craft it will be necessary to screw the plate to the hull all round the edge. On fibreglass hulls it can be bonded to the hull and faired in, with the fibreglass covering only the edge of the sheet. The bolt protruding through the hull should have a doubling block on the inside to avoid local strain on the shell or planking. If the hull is steel, the earth connection may be taken to the closest point on the plating or framing to the transmitter. Care should be taken to see that this is a good clean joint, and that it is painted after the connection is made to prevent corrosion.

On sailing boats there is often a lead or cast iron keel which is bolted through the hull. An excellent earth can be established by drilling and tapping a keel bolt to take a suitable stud. From whatever earth is arranged, a good and substantial strip or braid, say 25 mm × 20 s.w.g. or equivalent, should be run via the shortest possible path to the earth terminal on the transmitter. It is better not to fasten this to the boat's timbers, and a suitable wiring batten should be provided.

I have encountered boats where somebody, possibly anxious to fit a radio for the smallest amount of money, has run the earth to a seacock or the engine, and has achieved some sort of operation. However, this sort of practice can

drastically reduce transmitter efficiency through a high impedance earth, and also increases the level of radio interference at the receiver.

Particularly when the earth impedance is higher than it need be, one encounters induction by the leakage of RF energy through the transmitter power unit supply leads. This will be manifest by possibly the engine warning lights or sometimes the cabin lights coming on when the transmitter is keyed. This effect can be easily recognised as the lights will vary in brightness as the transmitter tuning is varied. In some cases a cure can be effected by fitting filters in the transmitter power supply leads; however, the best approach will be to do something about improving the impedance of the transmitter earth, where it is evident that this is affecting performance.

Emergency Aerial and Earth for MF R/T

Possibly the cartoon impression of being cast away on a desert island with tattered trousers, long beard and buxom wench is rather far from yachting reality. However, even in this situation one would still have to contact civilisation to get a supply of razor blades.

Where a disaster of one sort or another has occurred, there are various things that can be done to effect temporary repairs where equipment or power supply damage is not too extensive. The emergency work would be divided into two sections:

Providing power for the equipment
Providing an aerial and earth.

The fundamental requirement for any equipment will be the necessary power to operate it. In any circumstances this must come from a storage battery or a generator of one sort or another. In certain circumstances the power supply itself may be in order but damage to the boat's wiring may have been caused by loose cargo, etc. When this has occurred temporary bridges of heavy wire over the damaged conductors or separate leads run straight to the battery will effect a temporary remedy. A pair of 6 m leads with bulldog clips on the ends are a great asset on such occasions, as speedy direct connections can be established. A simple but effective means of locating power can take the form of a lamp with holder and short leads.

Aerials and earths for MF equipment can be rigged in emergencies by approximating the length and height of the defective array, with rigging wire or indeed any convenient conductor. As in extreme cases it may not be possible to do this, the temporary aerial should consist of any available conductor connected to the transmitter aerial terminal and from this point taken vertically as high as possible. It does not matter if there is some length of wire trailing from the top of the support, although every effort should be made to keep the whole conductor elevated. The wire should not be allowed to contact any earthed component. An emergency earth can be improvised by taking a wire to the engine, keel bolts, or by lowering the anchor and connecting to the chain (it does not matter if the anchor is clear of the bottom). In fact any metal object—a bucket for example—could be used with success.

As it is highly unlikely that the temporary aerial and earth will have electrical characteristics close enough to the original for the transmitter to load into it, you must assess your own knowledge before going further. If you feel able to tackle some transmitter adjustment proceed as follows. Set the channel selector switch to the emergency channel, 2182 kHz. Set the meter to monitor aerial current and operate the transmitter (usually by squeezing the pressel on the handset). Watch the aerial current and swing the tuning control on the transmitter. If it is not possible to reach an aerial current peak within the range of the control of similar amplitude to the original reading, it will be necessary to adjust the PA coil in the transmitter. In some equipment, it is possible to select the inductors from switches placed on the front panel. In this case it is only necessary to adjust each switch until a maximum is reached. Where, as with many equipments, the PA tuning is within the cabinet, it will be necessary to withdraw the transmitter from the case. The PA coil can be easily recognised; it will be a fairly large air spaced spiral of heavy wire with numerous tapping connectors, often of the push-on type. Each connector will be associated with one of the channels available to the user. The practice is for position 1 on the channel selector to be the emergency frequency and this connector should be

identified. It should be moved along the coil one turn at a time for about five turns on either side of the original position. The transmitter will have to be pushed back into its case to close the safety interlock between each adjustment. Each time the connector is moved the tuning control is moved through its range, and the direction in which the aerial current reaches a peak is usually easy to find. The transmitter should, of course, only be operated for the brief period required to swing the tuning control. There is the possibility of tuning the PA to a harmonic of the distress frequency, and this can be avoided by moving the coil tap first in the direction which increases the number of turns in circuit. If no peak is found when moving in this direction then the first peak encountered which leaves the maximum number of turns in circuit is the fundamental tuning point. Examination will be the only way to establish this, and therefore if in doubt return the tap to its original position and accept that you will be radiating at least something although with a considerable reduction in range. Remember that you will get better range after dark, and that the silence periods of three minutes after every hour and half hour increase your chances of being heard.

To check that you have RF current in the aerial, take an insulated screwdriver and touch it on the aerial terminal while transmitting; small sparks will appear where it touches the aerial. If the equipment is SSB it will be necessary to switch to pilot tone or whistle into the microphone when making this test.

Perhaps I have assumed the worst—it could be that the microphone is damaged or a lead broken in its cable. As such connections need soldering usually, such a fault could still make life difficult. If it is necessary to send an urgent message and the transmitter shows no sign of modulation, see if the pilot tone on SSB equipment will give an RF output, or if DSB establish the presence of the carrier (by the screwdriver test if necessary). If any sort of signal is available at the aerial, get out the Morse code and send your message by keying the transmitter with the 'press to talk' button—even if you are no good at Morse there is a good chance someone will recognise SOS. Send intermittently to conserve power and give a five/ten second dash after each group of three SOS. This will enable a bearing to be taken of your position by ships or aircraft.

One could also consider several improvisations for radiating a radio distress signal, from bits and pieces having nothing to do with transmitting in the ordinary sense. Although such measures are in normal circumstances illegal, in the cause of saving a life the law is far from being an ass. In an extreme case a metal spar or indeed the anchor chain could suffice as either aerial or earth conductor, and a means of generating a very rough signal could be a petrol engine with the aerial lead touched to a sparking plug as a means of keying Morse. A magneto rotated by hand with the case earthed and the HT terminal connected to the aerial would also produce quite effective results, especially after dark. We are in fact talking about an improvised spark transmitter that would interfere with just about every receiver irrespective of the frequency it was tuned to, so there would be a good chance of being picked up. Just about everything that conventionally generates interference could be used—for example a battery electric razor—preferably with the suppressors removed. Simply connect one brush to earth and the other to the aerial. I must again stress that such measures should not be resorted to other than in the direst of emergencies.

Lightning Conductors

Most modern boats have aluminium alloy masts or require only a connection from the bottom of the mast to a suitable earth plate to give such protection as can be reasonably achieved. For this purpose a separate earth plate of at least 0.5 sq. m in area should be provided as close as possible underneath the mast to be protected. If two or more masts have to be protected, fit such a plate under each mast. These earth plates should be completely separate from all other earths in order to minimise damage in the event of a strike; also so that interference is not introduced to the radio, etc. by pickup in the protecting conductor. Conductors from masts to earth plates should consist of several heavy gauge insulated wires taken directly to the plate with no sharp bends. Where high voltages are encountered sharp bends or points produce a corona discharge which due to the ionisation of surrounding air, makes an easy path for a heavy discharge to follow. The

likelihood is that with any excessive length or sharp bend a strike would flash over between the base of the mast and the keel.

Where a wooden mast is used, a spike projecting at least 150 mm above the top should be fitted. This should be at least 12 mm in diameter with a heavy insulated conductor about 100 sq. mm in section clamped to the bottom end. This conductor should be suitably cleated to the mast and taken to a through-deck bolt, thence to the earth plate.

10　Meteorological Equipment

And the coming wind did roar more loud,
And the sails did sigh like sedge
And the rain poured down from one black cloud
The moon was at its edge.
　　　　　　　The Ancient Mariner

The vagaries of the weather impinge on all yachtsmen, but although to some this may mean that when conditions are bad a weekend is lost from the boating calender to others in the midst of a voyage of any distance it can mean discomfort and danger. A great yachting interest in meteorology, and the continual search for higher efficiency, have brought to the market many interesting measuring instruments. Motor yachts in general do not usually have much meteorological equipment apart from the barometer, probably because diesel oil or petrol has a more consistent power output than wind. Sailing vessels, being considerably slower, strive for greater efficiency and to achieve this very often fit devices for monitoring wind speed and direction. Such units are often quite sophisticated, with remote monitoring of measured or computed parameters.

Several manufacturers produce equipment of the type described above, and several different principles are involved for transmitting the wind direction indication, although all use a rotating cup head for wind speed measurement. The instruments shown here have excellent presentation and are styled so as to be complementary with other equipments in the makers' ranges of products. This makes an aesthetically pleasing layout relatively easy to achieve; small fibreglass consoles are available to simplify cockpit mounting

All modern racing yachts have discrete sailing characteristics which may be defined by a polar diagram showing for each value of true wind speed V_t the best possible speed for each point of sailing, whether close hauled, reaching or running before the wind. The characteristic example (10.1) shows the typical performance of a yacht for a true wind

speed V_t of 7 knots, indicating for the windward leg that the best speed made good to windward (V_{mg}) would be at an apparent wind angle β of 40° relative to the ship's head. The abbreviations are clarified in (10.2). Further reference to the polar diagram (10.1) will provide the following table of performance:

Apparent wind Angle β	Ship's speed V_s	Speed made good windward V_{mg}
40°	2.6	2.0
50°	2.8	1.4
60°	3.0	0.5

Deriving the performance curve for each point of sailing and for various values of true wind speed is an essential requirement for serious race tuning, and being able to define and accurately steer at the best angle β is of paramount importance.

Brookes & Gatehouse manufacture a quality equipment, the Hengist, for monitoring apparent wind direction (10.3), utilising a two-dial display. One dial is an all-round 360° display, useful for sail trimming when sailing free and for steering before the wind. The other is used when sailing close hauled, the entire scale being occupied by the two sectors from 10° to 50° on either bow. The apparent wind angle can be easily observed with an accuracy of 1°. The complementary Horsa wind speed indicator (10.3) is calibrated to 60 knots on a non-linear scale, which is made more 'open' at the lower end for clarity. The masthead pickup unit for both instruments comprises a small weathercock vane and a rotating cup anemometer, both devices assembled as a single unit and readily detachable. The vane is mounted on the shaft of a

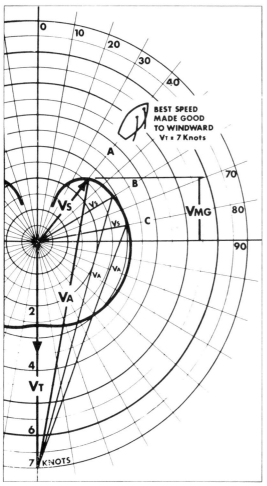

10.1 Boat speed vs wind speed

watertight electrical transmitting unit. A DC system of transmission is used, employing high grade wire-wound potentiometers which consume only 0.08 A from the boat's 12, 24, 32 or 36 V supply. The lifetime of the transmitting unit is expected to be between three and ten years of continuous operation. An internal oil-filled damping device is fitted to minimise fluctuations in turbulent wind conditions. The control unit on/off switch has two 'on' positions, in one of which additional damping is added to the circuit of the close hauled indicator to reduce hunting of the pointer due to the movement of the masthead in a seaway.

Weather Facsimile

I may well be accused of kite-flying for even mentioning the weather facsimile service, as at the

moment the equipment is pretty expensive. However, as demand increases the price will come down and facsimile transmission will be used for other communications as well as weather data, thus further justifying the use of this particular medium. It is a means of conveying information which is extremely economical in terms of air space. Although it is a very old method of picture transmission, it has much in its favour; indeed it was used for the original moon pictures from unmanned craft. The data is reproduced on present day machines by using a surface coat burnout paper of the Teledeltos type as used in many recording echosounders.

The meteorological services of many countries now use this particular method of transmission; it is certainly the most efficient way of obtaining the latest weather maps. It also means that the weather map received aboard your boat is an exact replica of that drawn at the relevant met centre (10.5), and much greater detail than is provided by radio forecasts can be accurately communicated. The Admiralty *List of Radio Signals Vol. III* has a section giving details of facsimile transmissions throughout the world. The information transmitted includes such data as surface analysis and prognosis, forecasts, observed ice formation, wave analysis and prognosis, etc. The parts of the world not yet covered by these transmissions are not great and in fact few yachtsman use these areas extensively.

The special receivers (10.4) for this type of transmission are very selective; in addition, because of the nature of the transmitted signal, which is frequency shift keyed, a greater level of noise immunity is achieved. It may well be possible to receive intelligible maps by this means when all

10.2 Wind speed vector diagram

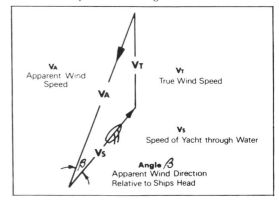

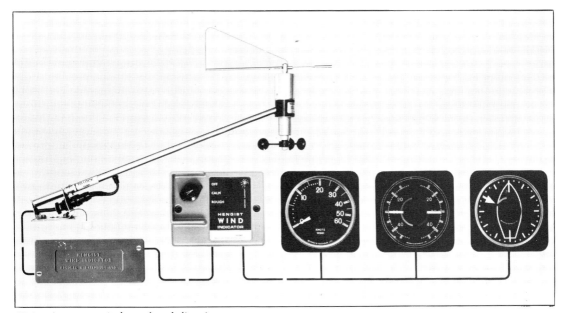

10.3 *Apparent wind speed and direction system*

other forms of communication have failed. For those who are interested in this equipment and its use, there is a booklet available from HMSO: No. Met 0.515 entitled *Instructions for the Preparation of Weather Maps.* This gives information on the symbols, etc. that will be encountered. Until market expansion enables reasonable price reductions, weather fax will be used mainly on the luxury type of yacht. However, a few of the serious competitors in the racing world have used the equipment. No doubt there are also many enterprising marinas who will eventually install such equipment and provide photocopies of the lastest weather chart for a modest fee.

The World Meteorological Organization has a specification to which all weather fax transmitters conform. Briefly, the transmitter consists of either a rotating drum or a flat bed on which the chart to be transmitted is fastened. The chart is suitably illuminated and scanned by moving an aperture or rotating the drum. A photo-electric cell picks up the picture information produced by scanning and converts it to electrical signals which are used to modulate the transmitter at the met station. The scanning density is normally 96 lines/in. (about 3.8 mm). The normal drum speeds are 60, 90 and 120 r.p.m. The slower the speed the longer the chart will take to reproduce. Typically a 22 in. chart will take about 18 min. to be reproduced at 120 r.p.m.

To receive the signal successfully a good quality receiver is necessary which has special output circuits to enable the picture information to be extracted. As this in general will not be available from the ship's R/T receiver, many equipments currently on the market have the necessary receiver embodied in the equipment. The receiver has to have excellent stability and is usually crystal

10.4 *Weather facsimile equipment*

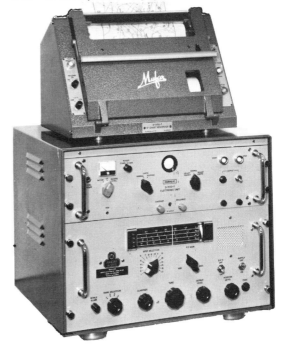

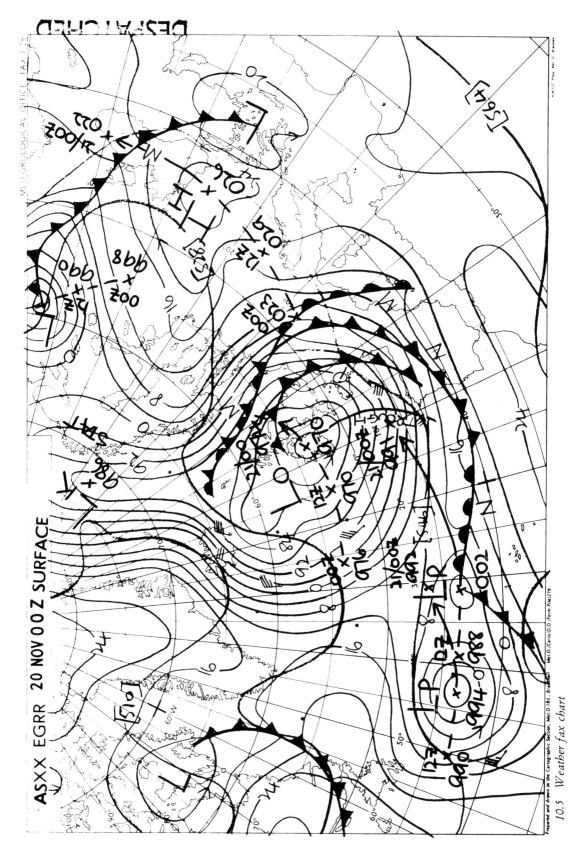

10.5 *Weather fax chart*

controlled. The signal has a mean frequency modulation of 2550 Hz and shifts to + 400 Hz and – 400 Hz to reproduce white and black respectively. These figures refer to the HF band, the frequency shift being ± 150 Hz in the LF bands. It will be understood that the limits imposed by the foregoing details put stringent requirements on the abilities of the receiver. In order to produce a faithful reproduction of the transmitted picture it is necessary to ensure perfect synchronism. This is achieved by having a very stable frequency generator embodied in the receiver which provides accurately timed signal for the synchronous motors that drive the stylus and recorder paper. It is necessary to arrange the phase of the received signal relative to the paper in order to make sure that the left hand edge of the picture starts on the left hand side of the paper. This can

be done manually or automatically, although not all machines are fitted with automatic phasing.

The aerial for the equipment does not have any special requirements. In general, however, the aerial for the fax receiver should be as far as possible from the R/T transmitter aerial and DF loop, and should also be sited as high and clear as possible. It will also help if it resonates at roughly the frequencies most likely to be used. Because of the mechanics involved, even the smaller units currently available weigh in the order of 30–40 kg. Mounting and stowage must therefore be undertaken with due care.

A typical weather fax chart with some of the common symbols is shown (10.5). This originated at the Bracknell weather station, and is reproduced by permission of the Controller of Her Majesty's Stationery Office.

11 Stabilisers

Never more sailor, shalt thou be,
Tossed on the wind ridden, restless sea.
                    Walter de la Mare

Until a very few years ago, stabilisers for small craft were just not available. The present position is that there are several on the market, and three types, all by companies of high repute, are outlined in this chapter. Much can be added to personal comfort and cargo security by decreasing the roll rate and amplitude of small craft in rough weather. As a roll acceleration as low as 0.1 G is sufficient to induce motion sickness, it will be appreciated that even in relatively calm weather much can be done to make the average yacht more comfortable when underway.

Over the years a vast number of roll reduction devices have been tried, for example bilge keels, outriggers, movable weights, fluid transfer and large solidly mounted gyroscopes. Most worked to some extent; however, the results achieved did not justify the effort until dynamic fin stabilisers were introduced. With big ships a very complex control system is used which compounds signals due to roll acceleration, roll angle and rudder position. This is necessary to cover the extended roll frequency spectrum that may be encountered with bigger craft. Sensing roll acceleration or rate only has been found to adequately cover that part of the roll frequency spectrum around the natural hull resonance of smaller vessels, even with the lower frequencies encountered in following seas.

The whole aim of small craft stabilisers is to provide damping of most of the roll angle and rate at or near the boat's natural roll frequency. Before considering the various equipments available it is as well to recognise what stabilisers are able to achieve, and why they are used for roll reduction rather than for the reduction of pitch and other composite ship motions.

Reduction of ship motions other than roll involves the use of considerable power to produce significant effect. In fact stresses within the structure of the vessel created to stabilise these effects could reach proportions that would cause damage or failure and are thus somewhat impracticable. Stabilisation of roll can be justified as follows:

In certain sea conditions rolling can reach large amplitudes.
Rolling can dislodge gear, which can be dangerous, and is most uncomfortable for passengers and crew.
Provided care is used in fitting, the stresses introduced to the hull structure will not be excessive.
The power requirements of a device to reduce roll are within the limits of practicability for small craft.

From the graph (11.1) it will be seen that the vessel will only achieve large roll amplitudes over a relatively narrow range of wave periods. To produce a force equal in amplitude but of need to be designed to cover this range and produce a forece equal in amplitude but of opposite sign to the sea forces initiating the motion. When this is achieved a minimum roll is produced. It should be understood that as stabilisers work by detecting the commencement of a roll and amplifying this to produce enough power for corrective measures to be applied, there must always be a small residual rolling motion. Although complete suppression will therefore not be achieved, reduction of roll by as much as 90%

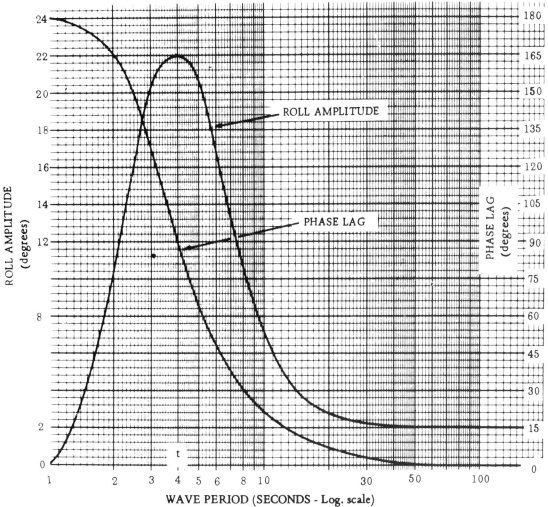

11.1   Relationship of roll amplitude to roll period

could be possible under conditions where the wave periods coincide with the natural roll period of the vessel; i.e. a 30° roll could be reduced to 3°.

Buoyancy and gravity act through directions and points indicated in (11.2), which shows a cross section through a typical hull. The hatched area is equal to the displacement. The pressure due to the displacement appears to act about a point called the centre of buoyancy (B). The weight of the vessel acts about a point called the centre of gravity (G). The metacentre (M) is the centre about which the centre of buoyancy acts. When the vessel is inclined the centre of buoyancy is displaced (B₁) and moves about the metacentre. This creates a condition where the forces due to gravity acting downward and the forces due to buoyancy acting upwards are displaced horizontally from the centre

11.2   Forces of buoyancy and gravity acting on a hull

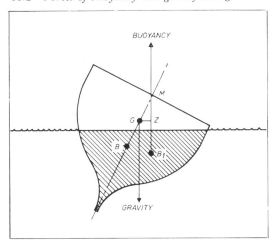

of gravity. This condition causes the vessel to commence a roll towards the upright position. Due to inertia the centre of buoyancy passes the centreline of the vessel and carries it past the upright position so that the vessel rolls a number of times before coming to rest. This roll is damped out by frictional losses between hull and water and the energy absorbed by generating a surface wave; although the amplitude diminishes, the period between peaks remains constant (11.3). This constant factor represents the natural rolling period for a particular vessel.

In calm water any disturbance imparts energy to the vessel and causes it to roll at its natural frequency until it has discharged the energy received. If a continuous train of waves are made to impinge on a vessel it will behave in a manner which will depend largely on the frequency of the incident waves (11.1) shows how the amplitude of the roll will change as the wave period is varied. The graph shows the likely response of a vessel having a natural rolling period of 4 sec. and subjected to wave periods between 1 and 100 sec.

Where the wave period is long the vessel tends to follow the wave almost exactly. As the period shortens, the roll amplitude increases as the natural roll period of the vessel is approached. At this point the roll amplitude exceeds the wave slope and the vessel's roll begins to lag behind the incident waves. It will be seen that when the exciting waves have the same period as the vessel's natural period, the roll amplitude will be considerable. The roll of the vessel at this point will be about a quarter of a wave period behind the incident wave, and thus the vessel will reach its maximum roll angle as the crest and trough of each wave passes. There obviously are, then, almost

11.3   Roll damping

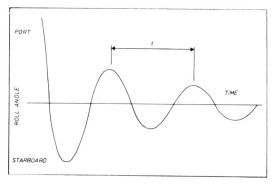

quiet sea conditions which, if the swell is concident (resonant) with the natural roll period, will give extreme discomfort. Any vessel is thus able to apparently amplify the wave slope to which it is subject. The extent to which it does this is called the amplification factor. When underway at cruising speed there is typically a ratio between the wave slope and the roll amplitude of 6.

The stabilisers described all work on the movable fin principle as this is the only type there would be enough room for on small craft. The fins are positioned by a hydraulic or pneumatic system in accordance with data provided by a control unit. The control units employ a velocity gyroscope which measures the sign and velocity of the roll and gives a signal proportional to the latter. In some systems this is compared with the fin position signal and an increase or decrease fin incidence signal is applied to the actuator on the fins.

One unit uses pneumatic power in a force balance arrangement and the second type uses hydraulic power with pre-set proportional incidence ratios using electronic control gear. A third type employs hydraulic control throughout including a hydromechanical gyroscope. The object of the all-hydraulic and all-pneumatic systems is to improve reliability and serviceability by reducing the number of skills demanded of personnel.

The existence of three different makes, all with slightly different principles, would seem to indicate that there must be a 'best' one. If this is so, it is very hard to find as all are very well engineered and have achieved practical success.

The principal difference between the equipments described is that one uses a force balance arrangement; that is, a system where fin position would automatically be limited as a function of water velocity over the fins by their inherent torque requirement. The argument for this arrangement is that without touching any controls fin angle is automatically increased or decreased as the speed and other requirements of the vessel alter. The other two utilise a fin position system, in which the fin incidence is directly proportional to roll velocity. The argument for using this method of control is that even below the point of cavitation the fin moment does not vary directly in proportion to angle of attack. This is difficult to account for in a pressure balance system as the

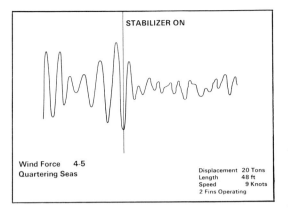

STABILIZER ON

Wind Force   4-5
Quartering Seas

Displacement 20 Tons
Length   48 ft
Speed   9 Knots
2 Fins Operating

11.4–5   Stabiliser performance trials

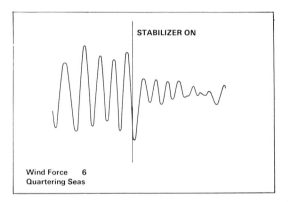

STABILIZER ON

Wind Force   6
Quartering Seas

same pressure may occur for more than one angle of attack. As stabilisers are used more extensively at fixed cruising speeds, I feel that for small boats the arguments are possibly to academic as all types appear to work well.

Installation of the fin units is of course carried out with the boat out of the water. The pneumatic unit requires only small holes through the hull and has the actuators outboard. The hydraulic units require a larger hole but have the actuators inboard, which on balance may prove better for servicing as the boat would not need to be slipped for attention to the fin actuators. The choice would depend very much on the individual case as the standard fin sizes for each type are also different. As all of the units described here are very well made; I could only recommend that all types are examined against a particular vessel's requirement. The EMI pneumatic and the Sperry hydraulic types can work without any call on the boat's electric supply—all control is air or oil operated and the pump or compressor is mounted

to drive from the engine. This complete independence from the electric supply may be an additional deciding factor for small craft. Electrical indicators are used, but consume only a few tenths of an amp and do not prevent normal operation when a supply is absent.

In general, craft down to about 10 m in length and in the speed range of around 7 to 25 knots are possible candidates for stabilisers of the type described here. The power to provide the righting torque is derived from the boat's engine in all cases. The engine causes the forward motion of the vessel and thus when the fins are angled with respect to the flow of water over the hull, a torque is developed at the root of the fin to effect a righting moment. As the speed of the vessel increases the righting moment also increases where the fin angle remains constant. At the higher speeds the planing condition is approached; pitching and pounding rather than rolling then become the major problems. In fact the stabiliser fins do reduce rolling even in the zero incidence aspect as they act in the same way as bilge keels. Some typical results for the EMI pneumatic system show the degree of improvement that can be achieved (11.4, 11.5). The improvement in comfort is a very real one and in my view very worth while. A two-fin system layout is shown in (11.6).

The immediate thought comes to mind concerning the possibility of damage to anything that 'sticks out' underneath. In order to reduce this likelihood to a minimum, the fins are fitted within the half breadth and depth of the hull and this gives a measure of protection when berthing alongside or accidentally taking the ground. The EMI fin dimensions are shown in (11.7) and a complete fitted fin is shown in (11.8). The fins should generally be positioned in the middle third of the boat's length. If mounted too far forward or aft they tend to produce some steering forces, and this could prove to have a most unhappy effect on autopilot operation. This position often means that the fin stocks are in the engineroom, which is very convenient for installation purposes. Retractable fins are available for large vessels; however the equipment cost, space required and fitting expense makes them impracticable for small craft.

The Vosper Mini-fin and Maxi-fin installations consist of a pair of fins, or in some cases two pairs,

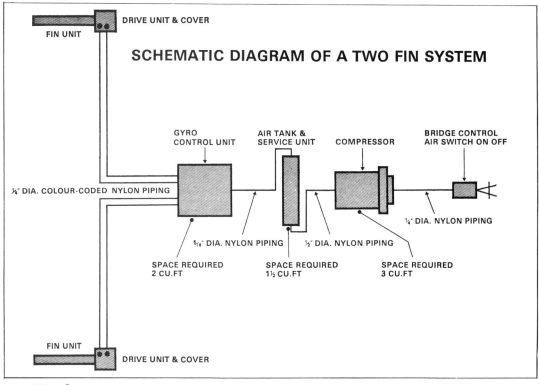

11.6   Two-fin system

11.7   Fin dimensions for EMI system

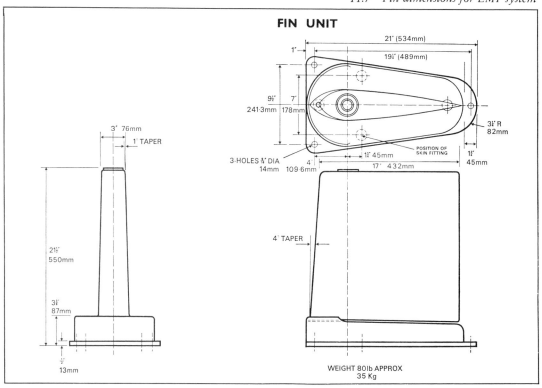

mounted on stocks projecting through the hull. The stock is rotated by two single-acting hydraulic cylinders in response to electrical signals recieved from a gyro control unit. Twin oil pumps driven from the boat's engine, an oil cooler and tank complete the equipment. A Vosper fin and actuator assembly in cut-away form are shown in (11.9). The Maxi-fin is an up-rated version of the Mini-fin, capable of withstanding the increased loads imposed by application to larger, faster craft.

The Vosper stabiliser unit mounted inside the hull is an aluminium bronze or steel casting. The stainless steel stock extends through a conventional packed gland, and turns in a water lubricated nylon bearing. Four different standard sizes of fin, moulded in reinforced nylon with a bronze or steel insert for mounting on the stock, are available to allow for matching to the different stabilisation needs of craft of various sizes and speeds. In craft of wood or fibreglass construction aluminium bronze castings are used, steel castings being fitted in steel or aluminium vessels.

Each stock is coupled to a pair of single-acting hydraulic cylinders of very simple design, which continually rotate the fin in response to gyro control signals. All bearings in the stabiliser unit are of the dry or pre-packed type requiring little lubrication. The hydraulic solenoid valve is the key to the operation of the hydraulic cylinders since it controls the flow of oil in response to the electrical signals from the gyro control unit. This is a wet-armature valve having a response 10 to 15 times better than conventional solenoid valves. The hydraulic control block, consisting of a stack of manifold units, including the solenoid valve, is mounted rigidly on the stabiliser unit and is already assembled when the unit is delivered. It is only necessary to connect the hydraulic control block and cylinders to the pump circuit, including oil reservoir and cooler, with flexible hoses or suitable piping.

The hydraulic oil supply comes from a pump unit consisting of a coupled pair of gear pumps, one for each stabiliser unit, with a V-belt pulley between them or direct drive, arranged for mounting on the main engine (on one engine in twin screw craft). The oil cooler is a miniature unit requiring a 3 gal./min. flow of water, which would normally come from the engine's water cooling system. The oil reservoir has a capacity of 5 gal.

11.9   *Vosper fin and actuator*

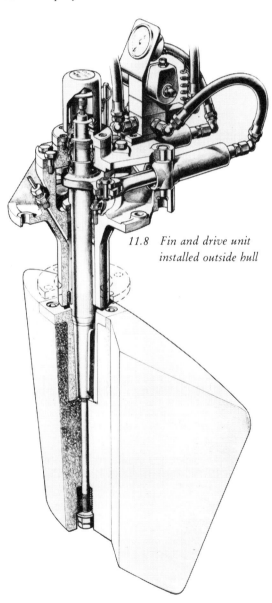

11.8   *Fin and drive unit installed outside hull*

The gyro control unit consists of a rate gyro specially developed by Vosper Thornycroft Controls Division, which senses rate of roll and transmits a corresponding electrical signal to a static switching circuit which operates the solenoid valve. A potentiometer on the fin stock provides a feedback of fin position which is summed with gyro output. This control system is extremely simple and no special skill is needed to set it up. The electrical supply needed is 12, 24 or 36 V DC, which must be stabilised to within ± 10%. There are electrical connections to the control panel from the solenoids, feedback potentiometers and DC supply.

In the EMI stabiliser system the fins are a standard size and the number of fins fitted is arranged to suit the dynamic characteristics of each vessel. The necessary calculations for arriving at a satisfactory solution for any particular vessel are given later in this chapter. The smaller vessel will require normally only one pair. The fins themselves are of fibreglass, and as the actuators are outboard, no moving parts pass through the hull.

The fins are operated by means of double-acting cylinders. The piston in each cylinder is mechanically coupled to a lever attached to a drive dog which turns the fin. No resetting mechanism is used, the required fin angle at any one time being obtained by balancing the hydrostatic force generated by the fin against the pressure in the cylinder. This arrangement has the advantage that the control settings are not critically dependent on the speed of the vessel. The air supply is obtained from a compressor which will usually be belt-driven from the main engine, and the power absorbed from the engine amounts to about 2% of its rated horsepower.

A velocity gyroscope rotates about a beam axis and its supporting gimbal pivots about an upright axis. A constant velocity air jet is applied to serrations in the rim of the gyro wheel which causes it to rotate at constant speed. Any movement of the vessel about its roll axis will cause a corresponding precession of the gyroscope about its vertical axis; it is mechanically linked to the pressure control unit which provides two pressure signals at its output. With no gyro input signal these output pressures will be equal and at about 30 p.s.i. As the gyroscope moves, the output

pressure signals change in order to compensate for the movement. An input signal corresponding to full output will cause one pressure to increase from 30 p.s.i. to 100 p.s.i. and the other to decrease from 30 p.s.i. to zero airflow.

The fin base is fixed rigidly to the hull. The piston mechanisms which control the fin are of the double acting type and are fitted in this unit, which also houses a water lubricated bearing on which the fin pivots. The pneumatic supply to the mechanisms is provided via skin fittings. A small external cover streamlines the fin base and protects the pistons and driving elements of the fin (11.8). Immediately inboard of the skin fittings, stop valves are fitted in order to safe-guard against the damage or failure of an external pipe of fitting. The fin itself is a symmetrical hydrofoil whose angle of incidence may be varied by up to 30° in either direction from the streamline position. It produces a lift of approximately 500 lbs ft at a speed of 10 knots when the angle of incidence is at maximum. The plan area of the fin presented to the water is approximately 0.3 sq. m.

In assessing the requirements for a stabiliser installation irrespective of make or type it is necessary to take into account the following factors on any particular vessel:

Righting torque per degree of inclination
Natural rolling period
Waterline beam
Hull form
Type of hull, i.e. wood, steel, fibreglass, etc.
Available space for fins, control unit and compressor or pump.

The righting torque figure enables the number of fins to be calculated for any particular vessel. In order to achieve a reasonably accurate figure it is advisable to average the results of three or four inclining tests. These can be carried out by using a spring balance and a block and tackle attached to the superstructure or mast at a known height above the waterline and to a stout anchor point ashore. An inclinometer is set up on the boat and the tackle pulled up to produce an inclination of say 15°–20°. The weight is then read off the balance scale and divided by the inclinometer reading. The righting torque per degree of inclination can be calculated as follows, where

X   degrees is the angle of inclination

W tons is the weight causing the inclination

R   is the distance from the waterline to the point where the weight is acting, in feet

T   tons ft the righting torque per degree of inclination

Righting torque per degree equals $\dfrac{WR}{X}$ tons ft per degree.

The natural rolling period can be established by building up a roll of about 10° while the boat is moored, the ropes being suitably slacked for this purpose. This sort of roll amplitude can easily be induced by a number of people rocking the boat so that one complete roll cycle can be timed.

The number of fins required for any particular boat depends on the righting torque, which can be established for the EMI units described in this chapter, by way of example, from the formula below, where

N is the number of fins

T the tons ft per degree righting torque

B The waterline beam in feet

Number of fins will equal $\dfrac{25T}{B}$

It is unlikely that N will resolve into an exact multiple of 2, in which case the next multiple of 2 above or below the calculated figure should be used. It is possible to use an odd number of fins but is not recommended as steering may be adversely affected. Obviously, in all cases where the figure less than 2, one pair of fins if fitted.

The precise position of fins on the hull is not important provided certain details are carefully observed. One of the main points to bear in mind is that it is the function of the fin units to apply considerable force to the hull, and as this force is transmitted to the hull at the point of entry of the fin root it is essential that such strengthening as may be necessary is carried out with care. The guides for fin positioning are as follows:

They should be mounted near the mid-section of the hull; this is often the engine compartment which is very convenient.

They should be mounted such that when the fin

is tilted to its maximum angle, a heel of 15° in calm water will not bring any part of the fin out of the water.

When the fins are in the streamlined position they should be mounted so that they are parallel to the direction of water flow at that point on the hull.

The base of the fin should be tangential to the hull at the point of contact.

The installation of the Vosper stabilisers is shown in the following series of photographs. Part of the bilge keel is cut away and the hole for the stock bored (11.10). This hole is pilot drilled first and then extended and enlarged through the reinforcing pad inboard, after this latter has been fitted. The pad must be thicknessed to allow the barrel of the main unit to project $\frac{1}{8}$ in. (3.2 mm) outside the hull (11.11). The stock is then inserted to check that the fin will align normal to the planking (11.11). The inboard pad is fitted to the hull, bored and countersunk to fit the fillet on the main bearing housing (11.12). Outside the hull the doubler plate is fitted and bedded (11.13). This plate is rolled to fit the curve of the hull and its bore filed to a snug fit on the projecting barrel of the main housing. The fin is shown in the process of assembly to the stock. It is of course important that the main housing unit be fastened so that the fin will be parallel to the waterline plane at cruising speed.

Where the hull is not constructed of wood as shown in the preceeding photographs the structural treatment is varied to suit the hull material. In a fibreglass hull a wooden block of suitable dimensions is glassed in (11.14). This should be as large as possible, to dissipate the local stress at the fin stock over a wide area of the skin. This is particularly important with fibreglass as a combination of stress and water can be calculated to considerably shorten the structural life of the hull. A doubler plate is fitted outboard as with wooden hulls.

In a steel hull (11.15) the bearing housing is bolted to a seating ring and shell pipe which are in turn welded to the hull with reinforcing fillets and webs as necessary in each case. As above, local reinforcing is carried out by means of a doubler plate outboard. In a steel hull all these components will be of steel: a similar arrangement using marine aluminium alloys

11.10–19   Installation of Vosper stabiliser system   *11.11*

11.12   *11.13*

would be suitable for an aluminium hull.

In (11.16) the completed Vosper fin installation is seen from outside the hull, and (11.17) shows an inside view. In (11.18) the oil reservoir can be seen at top right, and just below it the oil cooler. To the left of the gate valve in the middle of the picture, the oil filter is clearly visible. The oil pump which provides the hydraulic power for moving the fins is installed as shown (11.19), and driven off the main engine. The mounting plate should have slotted mounting holes so that the driving belt can be correctly tensioned.

I believe it will be clear from the photographs above that the work on the hull is of a nature that needs the attention of a shipwright.

The Sperry Rand Dol-Fin is entirely hydraulic,

including the gyroscope which was developed especially for the system. A fin together with its actuators and the control panel is shown in (11.20). The gyroscope consists of a rotor which spins at 12,000 r.p.m., mounted in a gimbal which supports ball bearings on the rotor shaft. Each end of the gimbal is supported by pivot bearings. A spring wire shaft passes through one pivot bearing to which is fastened a simple flow control device activating to greater or lesser extent the flow from two jets, which thus depends on the angular displacement of the gimbal. In the steady state of zero displacement two identical pressures are produced by the jets. When the gimbal is displaced a differential pressure is created which may be as much as 125 p.s.i., and this is applied to the fin

11.14

11.15

11.16

11.17

11.18   11.19

positioning valve spool on each of the actuator assemblies, upsetting the force balance on the spool.

In operation oil is pumped from the reservoir via a filter where maximum pressure is defined by a relief valve. Fluid is also directed to the supply parts of the fin positioning valves. The spool in those servo valves is force balanced by means of a spring at each end, and this balance is upset by signals from the gyroscope which are applied to either end of the spool.

The valve spring on one end is terminated by an adjustable stop while the opposite end is connected via a spring linkage to the fin so that when the fin is in the position demanded by the gyroscope the system is again in force balance. Should the fin motion be stopped because it requires more torque than the cylinder can produce through the lever arm, all oil flow would go over the relief valve. This provides a means of preventing the generation of excessive fin lift at high boat speeds and also helps to prevent fin cavitation.

An interesting feature of the actuator housing is that it is pressurized to prevent water entry in the event of shaft seal leakage; also the part of the mount that pierces the hull has been cast in a high pressure fibreglass laminate, which means that it is compatible with any hull material.

Tests were conducted by Sperry in three sea states: a 3 ft running chop, a mixed sea with complex waves of 3 to 5 ft, and a very rough sea with waves running to 8 to 10 ft high. The boat was practically immovable in the 3 ft chop but rolled ± 6° with stabilisers turned off. The effective period of the waves changes as the velocity of the boat with respect to the waves varied. As expected, the system was most effective heading into the waves, when the effective period of the waves was closest to the natural period of the boat, which was 3.4 sec.

Peak roll angle was reduced up to 75%. More significantly, especially from the standpoint of passenger comfort, average roll rate was reduced as much as 90%. Even in the case of waves coming from dead astern the average roll rate was reduced 70%, although roll angle was then hardly reduced at all. Roll rate reduction was created by almost total damping of roll at the boat's natural frequency, but roll amplitude was governed by the long effective period (27 sec. per cycle) which was beyond the capability of the system. In purely subjective terms the reduction in roll rate reduced

11.20 Sperry Rand Dol-Fin stabiliser

11.21 Trim tabs

passenger discomfort to the point where a voyage could be made comfortably rather than remain in port.

As far as the 8 to 10 ft waves were concerned, about all that was learned was that the stabilisers effectively damped motion at or near the boat's natural frequency. The effect of the stabilisers was quite evident in reducing high frequency rolls propagaged by the smaller waves superimposed on the main 8 ft waves, but the only way to avoid passenger discomfort due to the main waves was to return to port.

Trim Tabs

Many planing hulls, due to poor weight distribution, are somewhat reluctant to take up a planing attitude. Also, the smaller types of hull in particular have a tendency to veer when the trim changes slightly due to crew movements. In order

to extend the range of speed over which a hull will sustain its planing characteristics, the addition of trim tabs has become an accepted practice. The tabs may be raised or lowered from the helmsman's position by remote control, effected in some types by hydraulics and in others by electrical arrangements. The object is to produce a controllable amount of hyrostatic reaction at the transom, with a near-vertical resultant force to tip the hull forward into a planing position, so that the highest speed/power efficiency can be achieved.

The units I have seen all seem to use stainless steel for the tabs. Stainless steels are highly active materials from the corrosion aspect, even the so-called passive ones, and especially when used with aluminium. As many hulls and outdrives are of aluminium construction, I am a bit sceptical about the degree of corrosion that occurs after installation. I have also seen some glass reinforced nylon jacks. Nylon is hygroscopic and as a result swells when wet even if reinforced with glass. It would, therefore, be in the interest of boat owners looking for underwater units to make sure that the materials used to manufacture the tabs and actuators will suit the hull material and the rigours of a marine environment. For guidance on this subject consult the notes on materials in chapter 1. The whole construction of trim tabs must be very substantial as extremely high transient loading may occur. Clearly the method of attachment to the hull must also be substantial, fairing pads being provided as necessary to streamline the heel of the transom into the tabs. A typical set of trim tabs is shown (11.21).

With outdrives, especially twin drives, transom space is often limited and fitting may be more of a problem, particularly as cavitation will take place if the tabs are brought too close to the propellers. As the tabs are loose to some extent, and immersed, there is a likelihood of radio interference being caused by the intermittent contact of components. Both parts of the tabs should be connected together and to the boat's ground system.

Electrically operated trim tabs consume in the region of 5 to 10 A when adjustment only is taking place; it is therefore not necessary to consider this item when making calculations for assessing the size of generator/battery combinations.

12 Magnetic Compasses, Steering Monitors and Gyroscopic Compasses

But the principal failing occurred in the sailing
And the Bellman perplexed and distressed
Said he had hoped at least, when the wind blew
*   due east*
That the ship would not travel due west.

The Hunting of the Snark
Lewis Carroll

Magnetic compasses in the form which most of us have come to accept started their developed life as Lord Kelvin's 'improved' compass in the 1850–1900 era. The photograph (12.1) shows Lord Kelvin handling one of his 'new devices'. I often think what a golden age for science and invention that period was: Faraday and Marconi and many other prominent scientists and engineers were devoting all their energies at that time to techniques which are now at the will of even the dinghy sailor. The following extract of a note by Arthur Hughes comes from the Kelvin Hughes archives and is dated late in the nineteenth century. It shows how personal were the relationships between the instrument makers and shipmasters of that time.

I served my time as an apprentice, seven years in nautical instrument making at 59 Fenchurch Street, and in contact with the last of the sailing ships at London Dock. The masters were personal friends of the instrument maker, and I remember being sent with Mr Hughes's compliments to greet them on arrival. They would send their gear ashore—charts, books and instruments, with their pets, monkeys and parrots, and the cellars at Fenchurch Street were full of junk of shipmasters who sometimes forgot where it was. We used to say that three things were missing when a sailing ship got home—the liquid out of the spirit compass, which they drank and replaced with water, the steel chain out of the chain boxes on the binnacle' and the mercury out of the barometers, which the master used to dose the sailors.

12.1 Lord Kelvin at the compass

Seafaring has of course rather changed since the days of press gangs and swash-buckling shipmasters with pet monkeys, and compasses have been refined and tailored to the requirements of the leisure sailor. One thing that has changed very little in all this time, however, is the source of energy responsible for turning the cards in all magnetic compasses— the earth's magnetic field.

Both polar and sectional views are shown in the idealised view of the earth's magnetic field (12.2). On the section it will be noted that the field is only approximately horizontal at the equator, and a progressively higher vertical component is introduced as the latitude increases. Owing to irregularities in the magnetic structure of the earth, the poles referred to magnetically do not coincide with the geographic poles. Also, they are areas rather than discrete points, and constantly move their positions; this is commonly understood and is referred to as variation. This particular effect is of course not involved with the installation of a compass on a boat, but some background is given in order to make plain some of the effects that will be encountered. The particular sign and amount of variation may be found on the charts of the area in question. Sometimes charts will show lines joining places of equal variation, called isogonic lines. These are only accurate for the date stated on the chart due to the steady migration of the magnetic poles, and the annual change is normally quoted in order that the variation at a later date may be

computed. As the magnetic poles are displaced from the geographic poles, it follows that the magnetic equator is also displaced from the geographic equator. The magnetic equator may be defined as a line joining points on the earth's surface where the magnetic vector is horizontal, and is sometimes called the aclinic line. At all other places the earth's magnetic vector has both a vertical and horizontal component. The angle of this vector to the earth's surface on the N/S line is called the angle of dip. Places of equal dip are joined by isoclinic lines.

It will be seen that the compass card will be acted on by both horizontal and vertical forces over most of the earth's surface. Since a compass card is largely constrained in the horizontal plane, it responds mainly to the horizontal component of the total ambient field. As this includes fields created in and about the vessel's structure, we must consider this very carefully.

Compass design

In recent years small boat compasses have reached maturity and have crystallised into two main categories:

> a) the heavily damped, ungimballed type for use in fast boats (12.4).
> b) the more conventional type with internal or external gimbals, and fairly fast response (12.3).

The hemispherical type has many features that make it a natural choice for many small boats. The card image is particularly clear, and easy to read without heavy concentration, and there is no grid or aft lubber line to confuse the eye. The shape precludes the use of an azimuth sight, but anyway the compass in a small boat is not likely to be placed where a sight could be used to advantage. No doubt this has given rise to the increased popularity of hand bearing compasses. Personally I am always nervous of any compass that is not fixed and calibrated.

Electronics have been applied to the measurement of the earth's field for the purpose of producing autopilot signals or convenient forms of steering read-out, and one can now obtain a fluxgate or Hall effect compass with a digital display. But none of these developments will alter

12.2   Earth's magnetic field

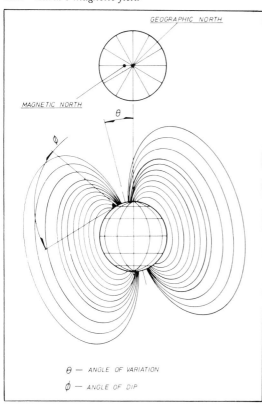

θ — ANGLE OF VARIATION

∅ — ANGLE OF DIP

12.3   Conventional steering compass

the basic necessity for a good, properly calibrated mechanical compass, as reliability and freedom from any form of external primary power source give it an integrity as yet unsurpassed.

The magnetic system in a conventional compass is so constrained by gimbals and card-magnet shape, that it responds preferentially to the horizontal component of the earth's magnetic field. However, the vertical component cannot be completely eliminated, and it tends to make the card tilt north side down in the northern hemisphere, and south side down in the southern hemisphere. In the course of manufacture the bowl can be made large enough to allow for the tilt, alternatively weight can be added to the card to balance it. If weight is added, the compass can only be used in the area for which it was intended without further attention by an expert. A further disadvantage of such compensation is that it takes the centre of weight away from the pivot, making the compass more sensitive to accelerations caused by boat movements, particularly when the course

steered applies motion in the east-west plane.

To reduce the effects of movement, the compass is usually filled with a mixture of pure alcohol and water; various additives are used to adjust the viscosity of the fluid to suit the individual manufacturer's requirements. In recent years eddy current damping has been applied to at least one commercial compass. This is a principle which has been applied for some years to the moving coil meters used in yacht instrument consoles. Eddy current damping is achieved by simply placing a magnet near an electrically conducting mass; any relative movement between the two components will induce currents in the conducting medium, and such currents are effectively 'short circuited' by the presence of the mass at the moment of induction, so that the net effect is that 'eddies' of current are produced which are a heavy electrical loss. This loss is reflected in mechanical terms through the magnetic coupling to produce damping on the movement. The degree of damping is effected by the size and power of the magnet, the conductivity of the mass, and the spacing between the two components.

The idea of eddy current damping may seem wonderful for those of us whose compasses develop bubbles in the fluid every season, but it is not yet widely accepted, and for many years fluid-filled compasses will be with us.

Another point to remember is that without a liquid in the bowl the whole weight of the magnet and card system is on the pivot. The presence of a fluid reduces the weight on the pivot system by the displacement of the card and magnets, and it also acts as a lubricant and, as nothing in this life is

12.4   Ungimballed, heavily damped grid compass

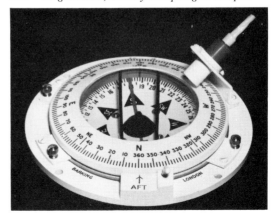

free, gives us other design problems. Changes in temperature expand or contract the fluid, and therefore some part of the compass bowl must vary its geometry in sympathy with temperature, or a leak is bound to occur.

This problem is usually alleviated by incorporating a corrugated diaphragm into the bottom of the bowl. The nature of the fluid must of course also be such that its viscosity (and therefore damping characteristics) do not vary with temperature to any significant extent. As a rough-and-ready check on the damping characteristics, good all round performance can be expected if it will pass the following simple test.

Pull the card through 90° degrees with a small magnet; remove the magnet and allow the card to swing back and note the time taken; a figure of between 3 and 6 seconds to the peak of the overshoot, and a total settling time of 10 seconds, would be considered satisfactory, particularly if only one overshoot occurs.

The size and shape of the bowl must also be considered in conjunction with dimension of the magnet and card system, as the fluid mechanically couples the two components by friction. Obviously if coupling exists, motion from the boat will be transmitted to the card. It can be observed by turning the bowl sharply while observing the card; a good compass will show little, if any, deflection. Less than 10 degrees could be taken as a satisfactory figure.

Pivot Friction
The bearing on which the card is suspended can give rise to error, although (as I have mentioned earlier) with a liquid-filled compass this is not so noticeable, as the immersion of the card and magnets leaves a smaller weight of the pivot. This effect, combined with slight vibration when under way, makes the problem minimal. However, *some* sticking will occur under static conditions, and this can be checked by *slowly* rotating the case clockwise to establish the degree of deflection obtained before the card seeks its original position. Repeating the above measurement in an anticlockwise direction will indicate the band of error. This is a severe test, as the degree of leverage against the pivot is very low under small error conditions.

Illumination

To facilitate reading during the hours of darkness, a small light source is usually fitted. Quite a low level of illumination is all that is required; where direct electric lighting is fitted, a small resistor is often provided to reduce the light for night use.

In this application 'Betalights' have much to recommend them. These devices consist of a minute radioactive source, configured to excite a small cell of tritium gas; thus ionised, the gas emits a green or orange glow depending on the type. The package consists of a small glass capsule and, so long as it does not leak, it will last 10 years or so with a reasonable light output. The small extra cost of betalights is easily covered by saving the expense of wiring to a conventional electric lamp. Another advantage is that of avoiding possible error from the field surrounding the lamp wiring.

Accuracy

The ultimate standard of accuracy is dependant on many factors, and it is useful to consider some of the things that one can do to get the best results. When you buy a new instrument, it is likely that the error existing between the magnet system and the card markings will be within plus or minus one degree. With any given compass the error will always be in the same direction, and it is corrected by slewing the bowl mounting during adjustment. Accuracy is also affected by the ease with which compass readings can be taken; clearly if the compass is mounted too high you will have to crane your neck to see it, and by the time you drop on to your heels the boat will be on a different heading.

One should be realistic about the accuracy to expect; it is one thing to measure minute angular changes on the shop counter, but quite another to select a compass that will allow good judgement to be applied to an oscillating card when the boat is heaving about at sea. I suggest you will do well to get within 5 degrees. This standard of error can perhaps be better imagined as the angle subtended by two points a quarter of a mile apart observed from 3 miles. Although this is probably the best that you will achieve, it does not necessarily imply that after a run of thirty miles you will certainly be several miles off course. Steering is a continuous process, subject to continual correction by the helmsman, and over a distance many errors will be equal and opposite, so that the skill of the helmsman could prove more important than the reading error of the compass. Very accurate readings are usually only required for position fixing, in which case it is better to average a few readings.

Siting

The position chosen for the compass is very much part of the results you will obtain from it. Apart from the necessity of being able to read it clearly and quickly, you must also have a position which will avoid the two most common siting defects:

a) The compass is placed so close to electrical equipment that the deviation is affected by switching the equipment on or off.
b) the compass is placed so close to ferrous material that a comparatively small change in the magnetic characteristics of the material makes a significant change in the deviation.

The engines and console instruments are the likely sources of magnetic interference, and steel hulled yachts will need special attention. For all types of construction the following remarks will apply. The ferrous parts of hulls, engines, etc. are composed of various materials which may be more or less magnetically retentive. In fact some items may be of alloys which possess both high and low magnetic retention to some degree. For convenience when considering corrective measures, we can resolve the entire structure into two components, one hard and retentive and the other soft and non-retentive. The ambient field interference due to the hard component will be permanent and irrespective of the direction of the ship's head will have a constant effect on the compass. The soft component, however, will vary the ship's heading. The various factors making up the total deviation can be reduced to basic elements, or coefficients.

Before detailing these, let us take some general points on the positioning of a compass. It will often be found right in the midst of a cluster of engine controls and meters that often have permanent magnets embodied in their structures,

with the obvious dire effects on calibration. It may well be that a centreline position is not possible, in which case one will have to have the next best thing. However, a site must be chosen which is as near the centreline as possible and clear of disturbing magnetic fields caused by such things as steel stanchions or beams, electronic equipment (radar in particular), meters, canopy frames, etc. A preliminary magnetic check (as for an autopilot sensor) should be made on the position chosen for the compass as follows, using a small pocket or hand bearing compass and a wooden rule. First place the rule fore and aft through the proposed location, and move the pocket compass along the rule for a distance of 30 cm (1 ft) on either side of the intended position. The needle must show no appreciable change in field direction over this distance. Repeat with the rule athwartships and again with it placed vertically. If all checks show little or no change in the field direction the site can be expected to give good results. When this test is carried out care should be taken to see that the ship is in normal seagoing trim with all tools, deck gear, anchors, dinghy, etc. in their proper stowages. In difficult installations or cases of doubt, the experience of a qualified compass adjuster is impossible to replace. In steel hulled vessels it will also be advantageous to take a vertical field measurement with a declinometer. The vessel should be turned about on its moorings about for three or four hours before any adjustment begins. The declinometer should be set up dead level ashore at some known undisturbed are and the weight adjusted to balance the indicator to zero. The instrument may then be set up on board at the proposed site for the compass and the vertical component of the vessel's field measured and compensated before swinging takes place.

Adjustment

I have already emphasised that there is no replacement for a qualified compass adjuster; however, for those who feel competent to make reasonable adjustment a brief outline of magnetic errors and the means of correcting them is given here. This has been done particularly to assist with magnetic sense units which may be fitted in addition to the magnetic compass. Optical compasses and magnetometers associated with automatic pilots need reasonable calibration and they might well be adequately corrected by a competent yachtsman (chapter 7).

The following describes the most commonly encountered errors, symptoms and means of correction. A deviation table should be placed in a readable position close to each instrument. A good and inexpensive method of doing this is to cover the calibration chart with a sheet of $\frac{1}{8}$ in. Perspex retained by small brass screws.

In order to make clear the nature of particular coefficients, I have drawn a boat shape with a magnet superimposed, which represents the magnetic effect on the compass which must be cancelled by a corrector magnet of opposite polarity and properly positioned (12.5, 12.6). I have drawn beside each an impression of the error curve that the individual effects would cause. It will be understood that any particular boat will have present a number of error-causing magnets and the actual curve found will be a composite of several effects.

The basic coefficients are A,B,C,D,E and heeling error. These may be variously introduced by either the hard components, in which case permanent errors are introduced, or by the soft components having magnetic poles induced in them, giving

induced errors (IE). Each error may also give a positive (easterly) deviation or a negative (westerly) deviation. This will depend on how the particular error-causing magnetic field was created in the first place.

Coefficient A error is constant in sign for all courses and it may be westerly (—A) or easterly (+A). It is not easy to correct and may be minimised by placing the compass on the centreline of the vessel.

Coefficient B errors create deviations which vary by the sine of the vessel's compass course. In general, if the error is a permanent one the field will be distorted as shown (12.5). In the positive sense it gives rise to zero deviation on N/S courses westerly deviation on westerly courses, and easterly deviation on easterly courses. As this error is caused by permanent fore and aft magnetism it may be corrected by fitting a small permanent magnet fore and aft and adjacent to the compass. The proximity of the magnet should be adjusted until the error is at a minimum. The error may be positive or negative and the corrector magnet polarity will need to be reversed as appropriate.

If the error is induced it gives rise to the same effect but is caused by an induced vertical magnetic effect. The correction procedure in this case is to fix a vertical bar of soft iron (Flinders bar) in line fore and aft with the compass. Where the compass is sited forward of midships the bar should be fastened in front of the compass to compensate for the mass of soft compenents in the boat aft of the compass position. When the compass is fitted aft the corrector bar will be behind the compass.

Coefficient C errors, if permanent, create deviations that vary as the cosine of the vessel's course (12.6). The error will be zero when heading east or west and at a maximum when on north or south headings. It is due to an athwartships field, which again may be in a positive or negative direction. It is corrected by placing a small permanent magnet athwartships and adjusting its position relative to the compass as described under B errors. In the positive sense the errors will be easterly when on northerly headings and westerly when on southerly headings.

If the error is induced the effect will be the same as with permanent C errors, but again it will be caused by a vertical field in the ship's structure produced in the soft components. It is not a

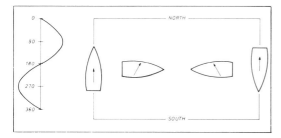

12.5   Coefficient B error
12.6   Coefficient C error

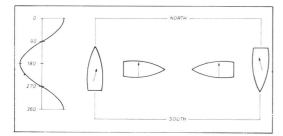

common error in a well positioned compass and is corrected by rearranging the Flinders bar so that it lies between the fore and aft and the athwartships line, thus compensating for induced B and C errors.

Coefficient D errors create deviations that vary as the sine of twice the vessel's course. The maximum deviations will occur on NE, SE, SW and NW headings. This type of error is created by soft components in the horizontal plane about the compass position, and is corrected by attaching soft iron spheres to the compass on suitable brackets so that they cause an equal and opposite effect. If the D error deviation is positive (easterly on NE headings) it is corrected by positioning the soft iron spheres athwartships. Before correction it is usual for the boat to have a negative D error; however errors of this type are corrected by shipping the spheres in the fore and aft line.

Coefficient E errors create deviations that vary as the cosine of twice the vessel's course. They are caused by unbalanced, diagonally placed soft iron components. This situation is further degraded by the compass being offset from the centreline. The maximum deviations occur in north, east, south and westerly headings. The compensating soft iron spheres should be lined up to 45° off the port bow to correct +E errors and 45° off the starboard bow to correct —E errors. In fact a single pair of spheres can be used to correct both D and E errors, being slewed to a position that satisfactorily compensates both.

Heeling errors, under a (hopefully theoretical) condition of permanent list, would give rise to deviations varying as the cosine of the vessel's course. It is important because it will make the card very active in rough weather and trying to steer with the card constantly moving is very tiring. Deviation will again be zero on east and west and a maximum on north and south. It is caused by a vertical field within the vessel and may be positive or negative: it may be cancelled to some extent by a vertical corrector magnet. The procedure is to take a vertical field measurement with a declinometer as described above. This is necessary because it is obviously inconvenient to carry a constant angle of heel for the purposes of calibration. The vertical magnet or magnets must be placed symmetrically under the compass so as not to introduce other errors.

If the north pole of the vessel's field is downward heeling error will cause a compass deviation toward the high side; conversely if the northpole is uppermost the deviation will be toward the low side. This type of error is also caused by induced magnetic alignment of the soft components in the structure as correction is done with permanent magnets the calibration will not hold good for all latitudes.

Although this effect is probably not serious in other than steel hulled vessels, it may become noticeable where an autopilot sense unit is involved. A simple way of checking this is to steer automatically on an N/S course. The effect of heeling error is to make the steering gear responsive to rolling motions of the vessel, and this effect is at a maximum on north or south courses. If it is noted that without being off course a steering movement takes place in sympathy with the boat's rolling movement, the possibility of heeling errors will bear further investigation. Obviously a better mean course will be held, and current consumption, wear and tear will also be considerably reduced by eliminating such errors. I have noticed on one or two occasions that after a radar aerial has been fitted on the wheelhouse top, and the compass religiously swung afterwards, the autopilot sense unit is either forgotten or given the roughest of checks. The autopilot, although it balances normally and appears to steer well in calm water, is never the same again, due to the large

12.7 Compass with bearing sight

external field from the magnetron in the radar.

To summarise magnetic compasses and their correction briefly, the equipment and procedure are as follows. The equipment required is minimal, and in some cases where the compass is sited so that an all-round view is obtained a sighting ring may be attached to the compass. The Sestrel Moore compass (12.7) can be supplied with such a sight. As introducing one correction may cause interaction with another it is important to carry out the work in the order given here. On the great number of small craft made from non-magnetic materials (timber, aluminium, fibreglass) the permanent type of error is the only one encountered to any great extent, and it is reasonable to assume that with care in compass siting little trouble will be found. With the steel hulled vessel more care and experience is needed, and some very odd effects will be found on occasion.

The adjustment procedure is as follows:

1. Estimate the induced coefficient B and length of Flinders bar, fastened as necessary.
2. Set spheres midway in their brackets.
3. Swing the boat to establish the deviations on NE, SE, SW, NW. The spheres are then both adjusted to remove the D errors. One or both of the spheres may in fact have to be removed completely, or even on occasion lined up fore and aft.
4. Heeling error must now be checked. The declinometer method of measuring the vertical component has been described above. The compass will have to be removed for the check to be made in the exact position of the compass card. When the corrector has been placed in order to balance the declinometer the vertical component will still not be completely compensated, because of the soft iron components disposed athwartships and the possible modification of the effect by the soft iron spheres. However it should reduce heeling error to an acceptable level. If persistent problems are encountered here it would be wise to get professional advice.

5. Deal with errors B and C. One or other will show a greater error and should be corrected first. Very often B errors are greater, and are removed by steadying the vessel on an east or west heading; magnets are then fixed in the fore and aft line to balance the disturbing field. The C errors are balanced in exactly the same way, by steadying the vessel on north or south and placing the magnets athwartships.
6. The ship's head should now be steadied on NE, SE, SW and NW and any deviation found should be removed by repositioning the spheres.
7. Run through the B and C error checks again and readjust magnets if necessary.
8. Swing the boat very slowly and make a correction graph.

In order to get a bearing for reference purposes, by far the best method is to take a magnetic bearing from a chart of some conspicuous mark. If possible, but sadly these most useful points are not available everywhere, tie the boat to a dolphin fitted with a swinging truck and by reference to the appropriate chart the best results will be obtained. By using time azimuth tables astronomical bodies may also be used. This may be convenient or necessary on very long voyages, although it will require the use of a very good time standard, and some experience.

12.8 Magnesyn repeating compass

Remote Reading Units

During the 1940s the need for a remote reading compass for aircraft became apparent and the Magnesyn type was developed for this purpose. There are now several examples of this type of equipment on the market of which the Neco unit is typical (12.8). I have been told on occasion, and indeed I have seen published information suggesting that this type of unit is difficult to correct. Let me straight away point out that this is absurdly untrue. Possibly it stems from the incorrect belief that 'compasses are adjusted'. This is loose terminology; it is the compass site that is adjusted to produce conditions at the compass that approximate as closely as possible those that would obtain if the compass was placed in a completely clear position subject to an undisturbed field. All devices sensing the direction of the earth's magnetic vector will respond to any local field disturbance in the same way as a conventional compass. By the same token, the site can be corrected for the effects of ambient fields using exactly the procedure described earlier. In fact the remote reading compass has the advantage that the master compass unit can be positioned where the ambient field disturbance is at a minimum. All the points discussed earlier concerning the siting of compasses may be applied to the master unit of the Magnesyn.

As information on how these units work seems to be sparse and as a result few people are keen to take on repairs, I will describe the principle of operation. Many of these compasses were available from government surplus stores and most were sold in perfect condition with a small static invertor. The Magnesyn master compass is a special form of liquid compass with a toroidal coil disposed concentrically with its magnet system. The magnet system is pivoted on a bearing arrangement with very low inherent friction, and is damped as is a conventional compass by filling the magnet chamber with an oil of suitable viscosity. The magnet system is free to couple with the earth's field and takes up a position of alignment with the horizontal component of the ambient field. A high power permanent magnet system is employed to achieve a close coupling with the high permeability core material on which the toroid is wound. The toroidal coil is tapped at the 120° and 240° points, thus dividing the coil into three equal segments electrically. These coils are usually sectioned at least every 30° in order to assist with distributing the turns evenly, which is a critical part of their manufacture. The current consumption is typically 100 mA at 28 V 400 Hz. The accuracy achievable should be better than 1°; in fact the surplus units were accurate to 0.25° per unit. This means that a simple master and slave system would produce readings accurate to 0.5°.

The 400 Hz AC power supply may be obtained from a static or rotary invertor powered from the boat's supply. Some of the static invertors I have encountered had a poor waveform and no regulation, and were generally not so satisfactory as the original rotary type of convertor that was designed for the job. The latest commercial units, however, do not suffer from this problem.

The magnet in the master compass causes a flux to be set up in the toroidal core material which will originate in line with the magnetic poles and be equal and opposite in the two halves of the core, disposed on either side of the polar line. The AC excitation causes an alternating flux to be set up in the toroidal material which on one half-cycle assists the flux due to the magnet in half A and on the other half-cycle assists the same flux in half B. The combined effect of the flux due to the permanent magnet and the AC exciting wave will thus cause the core material to saturate on both the positive and negative-going half-cycles. This will produce energy at twice the frequency of the supply voltage (this energy is called the second harmonic component). If the magnet is moved relative to the fixed taps on the coil, it will be understood that the magnitude of this harmonic energy on adjacent taps will vary with rotor position. The fundamental frequency voltages are also present on the taps, but these do not vary in value as they are due to the supply component only, which is not affected by the magnet position.

If we now imagine a condition where a second coil and magnet system is connected in parallel to the master unit and provided with a suitable housing to prevent the second magnet coupling with earth's field, it will be clear that the fundamental voltages will be perfectly balanced at the tapping points regardless of either magnet position. However, if when the system is operating one of the magnets is moved, it will produce an unbalance in the harmonic energy between the units. This unbalance will cause currents to flow which will produce restoring torques to bring the second magnet into alignment. This is in principle the means by which the Magnesyn repeater follows the master unit.

When testing suspect Magnesyn units do not use a conventional ohmmeter to check coil resistances as direct current passed through the coils can cause damage. It is much better to use a bridge with a low power AC source.

The troubles normally encountered with this type of compass are:

Sticky pivots
Invertor not working
Broken connections in terminating plugs
Liquid leaking from the master unit

None of these things are noticeably worse than anything that might occur with a normal compass, and conventional repair techniques are employed. On a 12 V supply a typical Magnesyn compass system will consume about 0.5 A. Many of the units that I have seen also embody a corrector box which is mounted on the master unit.

Another remote reading compass gaining popularity is the digital type. A typical example is that manufactured by Data Marine, who have specialised in all types of instruments with a digital presentation (12.9).

The heart of the system is a specially constructed liquid filled compass, having in its base a lens system with a light source and ten small photo-transistors. A special digital encoding disc is mounted under the conventional compass card and this provided signals to drive the circuitry in the display head. More than one readout may be

connected to the same master unit; also the degree of brightness may be varied to suit the ambient light conditions. This type of compass needs about 1.2–1.5 A to power it on a 12 V supply. Its accuracy is within 1° and this is the smallest angular increment indicated. Correctors are fitted within the master unit to enable the compass adjuster to make any necessary arrangements to compensate for the usual siting problems. As optical encoding devices are not extensively used in the small craft marine world at the moment, I will give here a simplified explanation of the operating principle for the sake of clarity.

The encoder card is illuminated by a lamp which has a slit mask between it and the disc. This produces a narrow beam of light across the encoder disc, and the photo-electric cells will be activated sequentially dependent on the position of the encoder disc. The output from the photocells is amplified to operate a series of electronic 'gates', which are devices whose outputs change state when the inputs coincide. It will be understood that if the photocells are illuminated with a predetermined code-an output will be passed to the readout from the gate which will coincide with the position of the compass card. If the number of photocells is arranged in conjunction with a suitable encoding disc, the number of coincidental situations can be arranged to suit any particular requirement.

As these equipments are all of small size I feel that the owner would be well advised to take advantage of factory service where possible. Conditions in a factory service department are obviously much better for accurate work than any likely to be found aboard even the most luxurious yachts.

A third type of remote reading device is the steering monitor. This unit considerably reduces the strain of watching a conventional compass, and deviations are indicated on a large clear meter on a left or right of pre-set course basis. A typical example manufactured by Brookes & Gatehouse is shown (12.10). The compass sensor is on the left of the picture and the indicator is shown bottom right.

12.9   Digital remote reading compass

Gyroscopic Compasses

Perhaps only the larger yachts will be able to

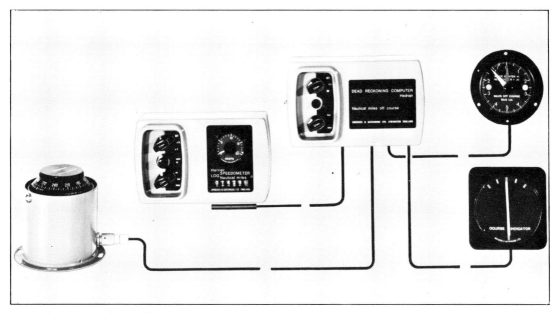

12.10   Steering monitor and DR system

consider fitting gyroscopes. However as the size and power requirements of these equipments continues to reduce, the long distance yachtsman will no doubt consider such a valuable navigational aid more seriously. For this reason, and the fact that I feel more progress is possible in this direction, I include some background material in gyroscopes and an example of the excellent instruments available.

A gyroscopic compass indicates true north with an accuracy generally better than 0.5° under normal conditions. The repeaters are all capable of fulfilling the same standards, and as electrical signals are available for follow-up drives the system can be used to provide signals for many other functions associated with navigation, for instance in the computing aspect of navigation, which must become better instrumented as time goes on.

Leon Foucault, the French physicist, gave the gyroscope its name when he used such a device to demonstrate the rotation of the earth *circa* 1850. By definition the gyroscope is a spinning mass, universally gimballed and constructed so that its centre of gravity and the intersection of its cadan axes coincide. The gyroscope has the ability to release considerably greater directive energy than the magnetic compass because of the higher energy input to the system. This energy is stored in the rotating mass which gives the

system its inertia, imparting to the spinning mass a tendency to maintain the direction of its plane of rotation. The physics of this aspect have been known and used for some time: Newton's second law of motion states that any rotating body resists any change in its angular momentum. This property of inertia is well demonstrated by the earth itself as its spin axis continually points to the pole star. A second property possessed by a gyroscope is that of precession—the change in axial direction that occurs when a torque is applied.

These properties, with the rotational and gravitational fields of the earth, form the basis for the north-seeking gyroscopic compass. Considering what happens to a free gyroscope situated at the equator will help to clarify the operating principles. If the spin axis is horizontal and pointing N/S, the gyroscopic axis will exhibit no apparent changes as the earth rotates. If the gyroscope is initially oriented with its spin axis horizontal and pointing E/W, the gyroscope spin axis will apparently rotate 360° in one day about the gimbal axis.

If this free gyroscope is made pendulous it becomes north-seeking by virtue of the effect of the torque applied about the gimbal axis. The basis of a practical gyrocompass then is a gyroscope with its spin axis horizontal and mounted within a pendulous gimbal system. If we assume that the spin axis is pointing east, as the earth rotates this axis will appear to move upwards at the east end, and the weight of the pendulum will cause a torque to be applied about the gimbal axis. This causes rotation of the gyro spin axis about the vertical precession axis, thus diminishing the angle between the spin axis and the meridian. This action will carry the spin axis past north towards west until the north end of the spin axis begins to tilt downwards. When this occurs, the applied torque reverses. The spin axis then moves eastwards until the original orientation is attained. This oscillation motion is critically damped in a practical gyroscope and the spin axis settles pointing N/S.

As soon as we mount our gyroscope on a boat it becomes subject to acclerations from pitching, rolling, changes in speed and course, etc. The boat's speed is in addition or subtraction to the earth's rotational speed, and this also introduces an error that will vary with latitude. Although expensive several types of small gyroscopic

compasses are available. The Sperry unit is shown (12.11). The following is the basic technical data of the Plath unit, which is fairly typical

Outer diameter 420 mm, height 570 mm, weight 30 kg

Mechanical freedoms: pitch ±50°,
                                    roll ±50°
                                    A error correction ±5°

Accuracies: indication error at sea ±1°
                     static error ±0.2°
                     follow-up of servo loop ±0.1°
                     lag error n=12° per sec. ±0.3°

Consumption: during run-up 200 va
                        duration operation 160 va
                        each repeater 25 va

Deviations after mains breakdown for up to 3 min. ±2°

Transient time about 4 hours

Max. rate of turning speed 360° per 25 sec.

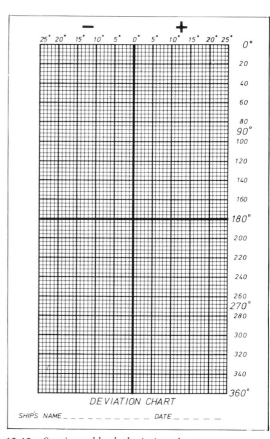

12.11 *Sperry gyrocompass*

12.12 *Specimen blank deviation chart*

13 Speed and Distance Recorders

Day after day, day after day,
We stuck, nor breath nor motion,
As idle as a painted ship
Upon a painted ocean.

The Ancient Mariner

Probably the earliest known attempt to estimate distance or speed at sea was made by the Romans, who used a type of water wheel fixed to the hull of a galley which carried a drum filled with pebbles. Every time the wheel revolved one pebble fell out into a tally box. By counting the number of pebbles in the box an estimate of distance travelled could be made.

Of the early methods of estimating speed and distance, the best known are the Dutchman's log and the common log. Both methods have been in use since the fifteenth century. The Dutchman's log gives a fairly accurate method of finding a vessel's speed. Two points on the hull are chosen and the distance between them accurately measured. A small float or similar object is then thrown as far ahead as possible and timed accurately as it floats past the two marks. The success of the results depends on the accuracy of observation and timing.

The common or ship log was first used about 1578 and consisted in its early form of a piece of wood attached to a line and thrown overboard to lie like a 'log' on the water. The wood was roughly triangular in shape and weighted on one of its points to keep it floating upright in the water. In use it is heaved overboard well clear and to windward of the ship, both the lines attached are then paid out for about 10 or 20 fathoms to carry the log beyond the disturbed wake of the ship. This part of the line is called stray-line and where this joins the log line proper, a piece of bunting is inserted. Beyond the bunting the line is marked by a knotted cord every 47 ft 3 in. where a 28 seconds sand glass was used for timing (very like a miniature hour glass). The length of line between

the knots has the same relationship to a nautical mile as 18 seconds has to 1 hour; thus the speed could be read out in knots as the line was run out, by nipping the line quickly the instant the sand ran out of the glass. When the log line was nipped the bone peg securing it in the log ship pulled away, allowing it to be retrieved with the heaving line.

The earliest record of a successful towing log is of one produced by Edward Massey and fitted in HMS *Donegal* in 1805. Trials carried out in the Bay of Naples were very successful. The device consisted of a shallow rectangular box with a float plate on its upper side which contained the register. The dial was exposed and calibrated in tenths, miles and 100 mile sections. The rotator consisted of a thin metal tube coned at the fore end and carrying flat metal vanes set at an angle. the rotator was attached by a rope about six feet long to a universal joint on the first spindle of the register. The whole mechanism and register were towed under water, which meant hauling in the log when readings were required.

In 1849 Rev E Berthon of Fairham produced an improvement of the pressure log described by the Vicompt De Vaux in 1807, and a trial model was installed on the HMS *Dauntless* in 1850. In 1876 the Kelway log was introduced, utilising a rotator extending through the bottom of the ship.

I have mentioned only a few of those who spent considerable time and effort in producing speed and distance recorders although it would be easy to list at least twenty who have made some contribution to the present state of the art. World War One gave considerable impetus to the development of the pressure type log, partly for use in submarines and partly in an attempt to overcome the need for a log line. The sugmerged type of hull log using a small propeller protruding through the bottom was also developed during and after this war.

Small craft now have a choice of several different types of log equipment, and invariably one or more logs are fitted no matter what other navigational aids are carried. In fact an increasing number of navigational aids now require a log signal to operate them. Science has enabled the navigator to fix his position with considerable ease and certainty, and has made it possible for him to see through fog and cloud, but there are times in bad weather or in poor visivility when navigation by dead reckoning depends on skill, and at such times distance run is vitally important.

Of the many equipments on the market, most small craft types seem to employ an impeller, possibly because it has had a long time since Archimedes to reach its present state of definition. Many other methods of recording speed and distance are known and some are employed for bigger craft. Advanced technology has only just begun to filter through for small craft. This may be because of the cost barrier; new technology is expensive and often needs skilled attention for some time in post-development. The various principles of operation used for all sizes of craft are:

Impeller (electromagnetic pickup or mechanical cable drive)
Electromagnetic (Faradat effect)
Acoustic Doppler
Pressure differential hydropneumatic

All of the different types have a common problem—that of maintaining constant unvarying contact with the surrounding water. Some have a lower susceptibility than others (the Doppler type for instance), but in general a degree of integration is used to provide steady readings and give reasonably accurate results. As aeration increases with speed, the effect is to read low at higher speeds. This is usually a fairly well defined constant for each boat and therefore can be allowed for in setting up. This requires many runs up and down a measured distance after installation, at three or four different engine speeds, making an initial compensating adjustment to the log at cruising

speed and producing a correction graph for the other speeds.

The siting of all underwater transducers is of great importance. All, except some pressure types and the cable drive variety, are electro-mechanical transducers, and therefore it is necessary to be consious of the usual things that will degrade not only the log but possibly some other related equipment having nothing at all to do with water speed. Basic rules are:

Keep all wiring screened and bonded to ground—not to the R/T earth.
Keep all log wiring clear of other wiring.
Cleat any wires in bilge space to a suitable batten and not to planking.
Do not fit close to engine, struts, A-brackets, echosounder transducer, water inlets or outlets.
Remember, when servicing is needed, the more awkward the site, the more it costs in time.
All types should be fitted in the laminar flow region of the hull.

I should expand the last statement by explaining that the water touching the hull is not stationary, due to friction between the hull and the water, but moves at a speed somewhere between the surrounding water's movement and the vessel's speed through the water. In the water closest to the hull, due to its shape and minor projections or indentations, an area of turbulence exists. Beyond this region the water can be regarded as flowing in a laminar fashion which will be sufficiently stable to enable speed measurement to be taken from it. In practice a compromise position must be found which will be influenced by the type of boat. For example, in most sailing boats the water is most turbulent in the forward third of the hull and also in areas close to the waterline. As with echosounders, the middle third of the length is the most likely place to get good results. Look for the echosounder transducer: there may be more than one on a sailing boat. Pick a site which avoids the turbulence from its fairing block, etc.; if the unit you are fitting projects underwater, as does an impeller for instance, you must also avoid siting it ahead of the echosounder transducer or you will find that although the log works well the echosounder now suffers from the air bubbles released by the log unit, giving reduced sensitivity and spurious readings. Obviously there is not an unlimited area to use and generally what is available has to be shared by all manner of skin fittings for bailers, inlets, outlets, echosounders, logs, sonar, etc. I could only summarise by advising you not to fit any electronic transducers in line astern either with each other or with any other underwater fitting. Fit flush wherever possible, and in all other cases streamline with fairing blocks.

In fast power boats considerable problems are encountered with aeration, and it is doubtful if the middle third of the hull does more than touch the water occasionally at sea. As there is usually considerable cavitation, the water ahead of the screws is also very broken, the result being that instruments relying on water contact are not good at high speed. In these cases the equipment is fitted as low as possible just aft of the middle third. With slower displacement craft, say up to about 15 knots or so, the middle third area will generally produce good results.

These problems have been alleviated in some larger vessels by making the transducer long and retractable; i.e. when in use the sensing head is lowered so that its business end is roughly 12 in. (30 cm) clear of the hull. However projections of this type need guards, and some compromise is usually necessary. Particularly with small craft, anything sticking out will be very quickly knocked off.

As with all equipment, and especially that which will be fitted under water, it is necessary to pay due attention to materials. Many skin fittings are made of bronze and this will not be suitable for all vessels, particularly steel or aluminium hulls (see chapter 1). In general beware of any underwater combination of two different metals within its own structure, or of a metal different from that employed elsewhere on the craft's wetted area. If absolutely necessary, this problem can be reduced by cathodic protection in some cases. The underwater end comes in roughly three different versions:

Fixed type
Removable with open slide skin fittings
Removable slide fitting with seacock.

There can be no doubt that the latter is to be preferred. The first type, while offering the advantage of low initial cost (it may be only 25% of the price of the last type), has the advantage that any small accidental bump will make slipping necessary, and the cost of this together with a replacement unit will instantly prove the point. The second type does allow removal of the slide while afloat, but inevitably some water will enter in the process of screwing on the sealing cap usually supplied. For space reasons in small craft it may not be possible to fit the seacock type, although such units are the only first class job.

On sailing boats it is sometimes not possible to fit the impeller unit in an undisturbed area coincident with adequate access and heeling to either side; in such cases two impellers may be used with a gravity changeover switch, in much the same way as an echosounder transducer arrangement.

Depending on the design of the instrument, pulses from an impeller type may be used in two different ways to give a readout of speed and distance. Firstly, all the pulses will need to be amplified, and having been raised to a processable level are integrated and directly monitored by the speed readout. This signal is then used to control a pulse generator with a counter readout (usually electromagnetic) to register distance run.

The second type employs a binary scaler to pulse the distance recorder directly, and the output from this circuit is used to clock a pulse rate to voltage generator to indicate speed (13.1). Statistically the binary type should be more accurate, but as the accuracy of the readout depends greatly on the rest of the equipment and its installation, I feel that provided both are well engineered, and there are no operational advantages to be gained with either principle.

One digital system claims an accuracy of $\pm 1\frac{1}{2}\%$ on distance run, while another analogue system claims $\pm 5\%$. My view is that unless confirmed by a same-day check over a measured distance before and after a particular event conducted at the same speed, it would be unwise to count on an accuracy better than $\pm 5\%$ for equipments within the small craft bracket, as many factors such as weed, possible distortion of the underwater unit, or other external variables could easily reduce the accuracy even beyond this limit. Checking the log two or three times a year and whenever suspect is just as important as swinging the compass, although it

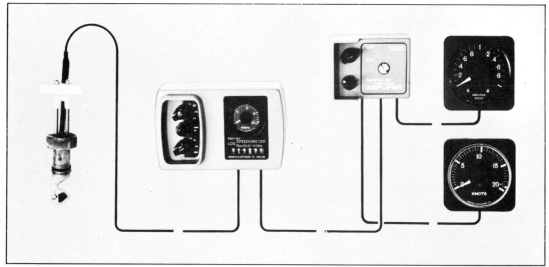

13.1   Log system

requires a lot less effort.

In general it will be found that electric impeller log readings are quite linear at speeds over about 1 knot. This because of the increase of frictional losses, etc. in the impeller below this speed relative to the motive force applied to the blades. However, do not assume this will apply until you have checked, as quite a small obstruction under the hull—even the fairing block for the echosounder transducer— can drastically alter the local flow pattern at different speeds. It will be understood that I am referring to the flow pattern over quite a small area—most small impeller units are only about 1 in. (25 mm) in diameter. Most of the units on the market also provide for a repeater or second readout to be available at a location remote from the main instrument. This is of course most useful for sailing boats and power craft with flying bridges.

When selecting a unit for your particular boat, the following points need considering:
Will it be internal battery powered only?
If not, it must not ground the boat's battery supply via the impeller unit. Isolation can be checked before purchase by a continuity meter, or even a battery and bulb, which should be connected between the metal parts of the underwater unit and the supply terminals inside the unit, with the on/off control in the 'on' position.
Will it create radio interference (even if you have

no radio at the moment)? Freedom from radio interference can be assessed before fitting by examination only: desirable features are a balanced screened feeder to the transducer, all electronic circuitry screened within the case, and an interference filter in the supply leads.
If you are making a purchase from an unfamiliar source you could justifiably ask for these components to be pointed out to you.

Electromagnetic Types

It is well known that a conductor moving in a magnetic field will have an electromotive force induced in it. This discovery was fundamental in establishing the theory of electromagnetism; indeed, Faraday found that a similar effect was created in fluids. In 1832 he had tried, on that occasion without success, to measure the voltage induced across the Thames by tidal movement of the water in the vertical component of the earth's magnetic field. Large electrodes were lowered from Waterloo Bridge, but the only signals detected were due to galvanic and thermal effects. Wollaston subsequently measured tidally induced voltages in the English Channel in 1851. In 1917 two Americans, Smith and Slepian, patented a device for measuring the speed of a ship relative to the sea. This was achieved by creating an alternative magnetic field in the water from an inductor within the hull and measuring the voltage induced between two suitably placed electrodes.

The Seaspeed Magnetic Log (13.2) uses the Faraday effect and indicates speed, and distance down to 0.01 nautical miles. The transducer is virtually flush with the hull, the maximum projection being only 3 mm. This not only eliminates weeding up and the possibility of mechanical damage common to the impeller and pressure types, but improves accuracy and linearity caused disturbances due to its own mass. The electromagnetic log is inherently linear in response, i.e. its output signal is directly proportional to mean velocity for practical purposes. This goes further than imagined at first sight: if the log signal is not linear—and many other types are not, in the fluctuating flow conditions under the hull—the output signal cannot be a true mean velocity. Accuracy is not affected by temperature, density, conductivity, salinity, etc. (as are pressure or acoustic types, for example; and as the output signal is electrical it has no mechanical conversion to make, with attendant acceleration, inertial and frictional errors.

Doppler Logs

The acoustic equipment shown (13.3) is based on the discovery in 1849 by Christian Doppler that relative motion between an object transmitting or receiving a signal causes an apparent change in frequency (a railway locomotive whistle's apparent change in pitch as it approaches illustrates this principle). The frequency shift is proportional to the velocity of the moving object in relation to a

13.2   Seaspeed Magnetic log

13.3   Doppler sonar log and transducer

stationary surface. With the Doppler speed log, sonar energy transmitted from a boat is returned from the seabed or from small particles in the water, and the relative frequency of the returned signal is compared to the transmitted frequency and the boat's velocity computed from the difference (13.4).

The unit described here is a top grade unit which would be too expensive for small craft, but as I expect to see more of this sort of technology in the small craft bracket, I have outlined some of the problems that exist. Clearly a device of this type has great advantages from the small craft aspect as the absence of impellers and probes greatly improves reliability and reduces replacement cost. Two pulsed sonar signals are transmitted ahead and astern from a small transducer (shown at the right hand side of (13.3) and averaging the two signals largely cancels errors due to pitch and roll. A strong return signal is received from the seabed up to a depth of about 500 ft, and beyond the 500 to 600 ft region the system automatically locks onto the return signal from the water mass, the sonar energy being reflected from the small scatterers present in seawater. The electronic gating is set to observe the acoustic return only from the undisturbed water below the ship, thus excluding the effects of turbulance and boundary layers. The result is a highly accurate and reliable indication of the true velocity relative to the bottom up to 500 ft, and to the water mass at all greater depths. Operation is not affected by turns or manoeuvres. This pulsed sonar Doppler log is the only type of equipment capable of giving ground speed up to depths of 500 ft (83 fathoms or 160 m). Imagine—all coastal navigation free of drift calculations!

In order for the motion of a boat to cause a

frequency shift in a sonar transmission, the beam must have a directional vector aligned with the motion of the boat. Without delving into the mathematics of this it will be clear that changes of trim will affect this vector and cause large changes in apparent velocity. A 3° trim change would cause a change in indicated velocity of 5% where a single forward facing transducer is used. To reduce this error the transducer is arranged in a Janus configuration consisting basically of one transducer facing aft and one facing forward, both disposed to have the same vector in the line of motion (13.3). Using this form of compensation the error would be less than 0.2% for the 3° trim change.

Doppler sonar systems can be designed to operate on the continuous wave (CW) principle or by pulse transmission. In a CW system a continuous signal is transmitted by the transducer, and usually a separate receiving transducer placed near the transmitter receives continuously. Energy is scattered in all directions by particles in the water as well as on the bottom; that scattered in the direction of the receiver is accepted and processed. The Doppler shift measured is dominated by the strongest return signal, which may be from the bottom return or from air bubbles or other scatterers between the transducer and the seabed. In the absence of such scatterers, the strongest signal received will be from the seabed and a true bottom referenced velocity measurement can be obtained. As the water becomes deeper and the number of scattering particles increases, the scattered signal begins to dominate. Because this is a weak signal, the transmitted energy in the vicinity of the receiver soon dominates all returned energy and the system ceases to operate. The receiver is now accepting only the relatively high levels of energy from the sending transducer and zero velocity is indicated. This point is reached in CW Doppler sonar at depths between 100 and 200 ft in good conditions.

This is an important point to bear in mind as a number of cheap CW Doppler logs intended for small boats are making an appearance, and I have yet to see one that makes it clear that there is a limitation to the performance.

To eliminate the restrictions' due to CW operation, the pulse Doppler sonar was designed. An example of this type of equipment is that manufactured by the Marquardt Co. of Amercia (13.3). The principle is to transmit a short burst of energy with the receiver off, and at a

13.4 Doppler sonar log system

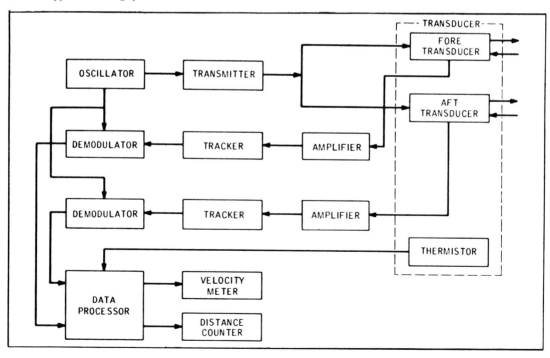

predetermined time to turn the receiver on to accept the returned energy. As the receiver is off during the transmit period a large amount of transmitter energy can be used without the danger of the receiver locking onto the transmitted signal. The receiver circuit is so arranged that signals have to reach a pre-set threshold level before they are processed; also that signals are received only after a pre-set time period after the transmit pulse. By blanking off the layer of water close under the hull electronically the speed is measured relative to the ground or water some distance clear of the hull. The signals that perform these functions are called blanking signals and various arrangements can be used. The vessel's velocity relative to any specific water layer can be measured by selecting a suitable

time constant for the blanking signals. The only limitation to this water speed measurement is the strength of the signal returned from the water.

To summarise the relative merits of the CW and pulse systems, CW is limited to depths of less than 200 ft but will operate in depths of less than 2 ft over relatively hard bottoms. Pulse systems can operate in the bottom return mode to depths in excess of 1000 ft, and will operate in the water return mode at almost any desired depth. Water return operation is generally not possible in the CW system; however pulse systems are limited in depth of operation due to the minimum time required to send out and receive a discrete return. The accuracy of the CW system is theoretically superior to that obtainable from pulse systems at

Sec	3 min	4 min	5 min	6 min	7 min	8 min	9 min	10 min	11 min	12 min	13 min	14 min	15 min	16 min	17 min
0	20,000	15,000	12,000	10,000	8,571	7,500	6,667	6,000	5,455	5,000	4,615	4,286	4,000	3,750	3,529
2	19,780	14,876	11,921	9,945	8,531	7,469	6,642	5,980	5,438	4,986	4,604	4,275	3,991	3,742	3,522
4	19,565	14,754	11,842	9,890	8,491	7,438	6,618	5,960	5,422	4,972	4,592	4,265	3,982	3,734	3,515
6	19,355	14,634	11,765	9,836	8,451	7,407	6,593	5,941	5,405	4,959	4,580	4,255	3,973	3,727	3,508
8	19,149	14,516	11,688	9,783	8,411	7,377	6,569	5,921	5,389	4,945	4,568	4,245	3,965	3,719	3,501
10	18,947	14,400	11,613	9,730	8,372	7,347	6,545	5,902	5,373	4,931	4,257	4,235	3,956	3,711	3,495
12	18,750	14,286	11,538	9,677	8,333	7,317	6,522	5,882	5,357	4,918	4,545	4,225	3,947	3,704	3,488
14	18,557	14,173	11,465	9,626	8,295	7,287	6,498	5,863	5,341	4,905	4,534	4,215	3,939	3,697	3,481
16	18,367	14,062	11,392	9,574	8,257	7,258	6,475	5,844	5,325	4,891	4,523	4,206	3,930	3,689	3,474
18	18,182	13,953	11,321	9,524	8,219	7,229	6,452	5,825	5,310	4,878	4,511	4,196	3,922	3,680	3,468
20	18,000	13,846	11,250	9,474	8,182	7,200	6,429	5,806	5,294	4,865	4,500	4,186	3,913	3,673	3,461
22	17,822	13,740	11,180	9,424	8,145	7,171	6,406	5,788	5,271	4,852	4,489	4,176	3,905	3,666	3,454
24	17,647	13,636	11,111	9,375	8,108	7,143	6,383	5,769	5,263	4,839	4,478	4,167	3,896	3,659	3,448
26	17,476	13,534	11,043	9,326	8,072	7,115	6,360	5,751	5,248	4,826	4,466	4,157	3,888	3,651	3,441
28	17,308	13,433	10,976	9,278	8,036	7,087	6,338	5,732	5,233	4,813	4,455	4,147	3,879	3,644	3,435
30	17,143	13,333	10,909	9,231	8,000	7,059	6,316	5,714	5,217	4,800	4,444	4,138	3,871	3,636	3,428
32	16,981	13,235	10,843	9,184	7,965	7,031	6,294	5,696	5,202	4,787	4,433	4,128	3,863	3,629	3,422
34	16,822	13,139	10,778	9,137	7,930	7,004	6,272	5,678	5,187	4,774	4,423	4,119	3,854	3,621	3,415
36	16,667	13,043	10,714	9,091	7,895	6,977	6,250	5,660	5,172	4,762	4,412	4,110	3,846	3,614	3,409
38	16,514	12,950	10,651	9,045	7,860	6,950	6,228	5,643	5,158	4,749	4,401	4,100	3,838	3,607	3,402
40	16,364	12,857	10,588	9,000	7,826	6,923	6,207	5,625	5,143	4,737	4,390	4,091	3,830	3,600	3,396
42	16,216	12,766	10,526	8,955	7,792	6,897	6,186	5,607	5,128	4,724	4,379	4,082	3,822	3,593	3,389
44	16,071	12,676	10,465	8,911	7,759	6,870	6,164	5,590	5,114	4,712	4,369	4,072	3,814	3,586	3,383
46	15,929	12,587	10,405	8,867	7,725	6,844	6,143	5,573	5,099	4,700	4,358	4,063	3,805	3,578	3,377
48	15,789	12,500	10,345	8,824	7,692	6,818	6,122	5,556	5,085	4,687	4,348	4,054	3,797	3,571	3,370
50	15,652	12,414	10,286	8,780	7,660	6,792	6,102	5,538	5,070	4,675	4,337	4,045	3,789	3,564	3,364
52	15,517	12,329	10,227	8,738	7,627	6,767	6,081	5,531	5,056	4,663	4,327	4,035	3,782	3,557	3,358
54	15,385	12,245	10,169	8,696	7,595	6,742	6,061	5,505	5,042	4,651	4,316	4,027	3,774	3,550	3,351
56	15,254	12,162	10,112	8,654	7,563	6,716	6,040	5,488	5,028	4,639	4,306	4,018	3,765	3,543	3,345
58	15,126	12,081	10,056	8,612	7,531	6,691	6,020	5,471	5,014	4,627	4,296	4,009	3,758	3,536	3,339

depths of less than 25 ft; however the accuracy of a CW system degrades at depths greater than 25 ft because of water mass return. The accuracy of a pulse system can be maintained at all depths. A single transducer may be used with the pulse system, but two separate transducers are usually required for CW operation. Difficulty is encountered with CW systems when air bubbles caused by the wakes of other craft of the boat's own propeller are present in the sonar transmission area.

Several facts about Doppler sonar are commonly misunderstood. The shape of the sea bottom does not affect the Doppler shift because this occurs at the transmitter and receiver, not at the reflecting surface. Doppler shift is caused by relative motion between the transmitter or receiver and the transmitted signal. The shape of the reflecting surface will affect the amplitude of the return but not the frequency. Secondly, changes in the speed of sound due to various strata being at different temperatures and salinity do not affect the Doppler shift because changes in the wavelength of the signal travelling towards the bottom are very nearly the same as those changes which will occur when the signal returns to the surface.

In spite of advanced technology, the sales of towed logs are constantly increasing, as for the serious navigator they are extremely reliable instruments requiring no electric power and which when fouled can be untangled, repaired or replaced without slipping the boat. Thomas Walker & Son Ltd, who produce these logs have a history dating back to the 1800s in the design and manufacture of ships logs.

For the purposes of calibration the table above gives time and speed over the measured nautical mile.

14 Navigation Systems

Navigation was always a difficult art
Though with only one ship and one bell
And he feared he must really decline for his part
Undertaking another as well.

Lewis Carroll

Developments in electronics have enabled great advances to be made in navigating equipments, many of which are described in this chapter. That bastion of mechanical ingenuity, the chronometer, has already been given an electronic 'inside'. No doubt it will not be long before the sextant is also given suitable electronic transducers so that it will interface with an electronic computing device.

Marine chronometers are highly developed and many use either tuning forks or quartz crystals to achieve a very high level of accuracy. As there are no critical mechanical parts, this type of instrument needs no gimbals and is not subject to acceleration errors. Very precise radio time signals are now available at frequent intervals day and night, and thus chronometers can be checked and corrected at much shorter intervals than was possible when attention was first given to producing a timepiece accurate enough for navigational purposes.

In 1713 the English Board of Longitude offered a prize of £20.000 for a discovery that would allow longitude to be determined at sea with a maximum error of 30 miles. In 1761 John Harrison produced a successful chronometer that won this award. It was understandably the result of many years' work, and incorporated a temperature compensated balance wheel. The basic design was further developed by John Arnold and virtually perfected by Thomas Earnshaw (1749–1829), and in fact chronometers based on Earnshaw's design are still being produced by Mercers of St Albans, England.

Thomas Mercer is now the only chronometer maker in the UK. They were established in 1858 at Clerkenwell in London, the same year as the British Horological Institute was founded. About 1870 Thomas Mercer moved the firm to St Albans, and before he died in 1900 with many international awards to his credit, he was acknowledged to be one of the principal chronometer makers in the world. To ensure accurate timekeeping in the early days, an apprentice would travel to London by train and check each chronometer against a master clock at the Horological Institute. Later a Bell system was installed, enabling direct contact with Greenwich to be obtained. Today the quartz crystal chronometers are checked against a broadcast frequency held to international standards and the minimum accuracy of the quartz crystal type of instrument is to within 0.01 seconds per day, whereas the accuracy of the mechanical chronometer is within 0.5 seconds per day.

Radio Navigational Systems

The most exotic guidance systems in use at the present time are the various military inertial equipments. Accuracy is paramount and cost a secondary consideration. Next down the scale comes the satellite system with associated computing equipment. Both, I feel, are still in a state of development to some extent, and by their nature will always be somewhat costly. Omega looks promising and although very expensive at the moment, could be brought within a reasonable cost bracket eventually. It is a hyperbolic grid system, as are Decca and Loran. The Loran system differs from Omega and Decca in that it is a pulsed system, using a time rather than a phase lattice. I have devoted chapter 4 to radio direction finding and will only mention it here in terms of comparative performance. A summary of the various systems appears towards the end of this chapter.

Decca

The Decca Navigator system came into use late in the last war, during the invasion of Europe, and may be considered a medium range system with good accuracy. Typical ranges of 400 miles by day and 250 by night may be expected; at night skywave pollution restricts the useful range. The system has developed its chains of stations now covering most of Europe and some other areas. A fix is obtained by reading two co-ordinates off the meters on the readout unit (14.2) and referring to a special lattice chart. It is a very quick operation and the elegance of the system may be extended by adding an automatic plotter, in which case positional information is available instantaneously. Once correctly set up the equipment will give a continuous record of position. Accuracy is dependent on the distance from the transmitter and the angle of cut of the lattice lines. Under favourable conditions positions correct to within 50 yds when up to 50 miles away from the transmitting stations are typical. Clearly bearing or radial type aids such as Consol could not produce this sort of accuracy at any similar range. However the price has to be paid for this accuracy: the equipment cannot be purchased outright, and part of the rental goes to service the very large number of transmitting stations maintained by the Decca company. The system does not have deep-sea or world coverage, and while this equipment may be used on any type of vessel it is clearly only economical on commercial vessels, where accuracy can be reckoned in real money terms. For yachting one of the other systems will generally be employed.

The diagram (14.1) illustratres the way lanes are created by the combined signals from two Decca transmitters. The Decca Mk 21 navigation receiver is shown (14.2), and part of a chart showing the Decca lattice overlay is illustrated in (14.3) by courtesy of the US Hydrographic Office.

Consol

The Consol system of radio navigation originated with the German *Elecktra*, later named *Sonne* system. The operating frequency is in the region of 300 kHz. A multilobe pattern of radio signals is radiated by switching and phase shifting signals applied to a series of aerials spaced by an integral number of wavelengths greater than two. This function produces equisignal lines relative to the station's position and the navigator locates himself relative to these lines. The advantage of the system is that the only equipment needed to obtain fixes is a receiver, preferably with a narrow band filter, and a Consol chart of the area (14.4), or Consol tables to convert the count to a bearing from the station.

The signal from a Consol station consists of a long tone signal interrupted by the station call sign in Morse. There is then a short pause and the counting cycle begins. Dots or dashes will be heard for a period followed by a continuous note called

14.1   Phase locked transmission

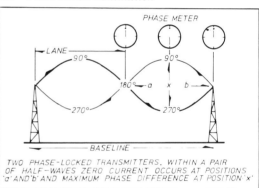

TWO PHASE-LOCKED TRANSMITTERS. WITHIN A PAIR OF HALF-WAVES ZERO CURRENT OCCURS AT POSITIONS 'a' AND 'b' AND MAXIMUM PHASE DIFFERENCE AT POSITION 'x'

14.2   Decca Navigator readout unit

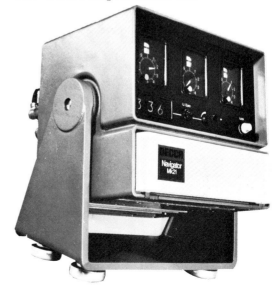

14.3   Decca lattice chart

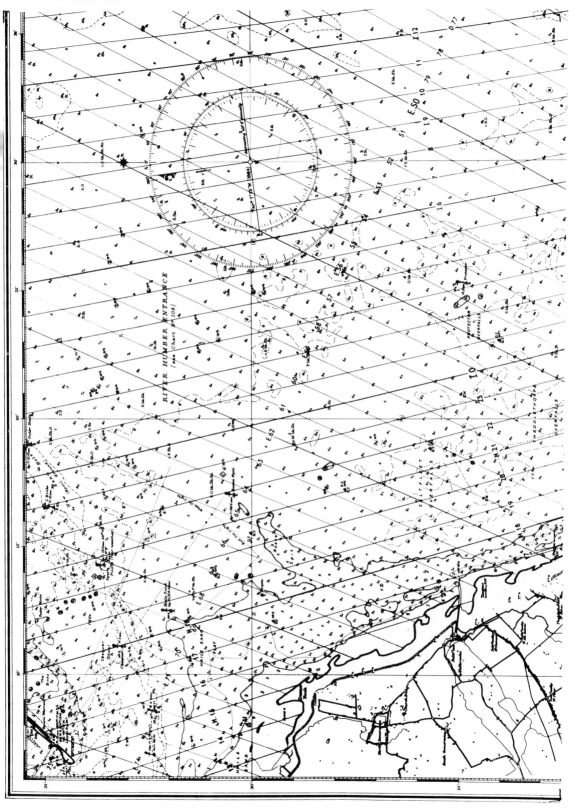

the equisignal; at the end of this signal a further number of characters, of the opposite type to those preceding the equisignal, will be heard. The number of dots and dashes should add up to 60, but it will often be found that some of the characters are lost, in which case the count is corrected as in the following example;

Equisignal	number of dots	22
	number of dashes	34
Total number of characters		56
Number lost		4
		60

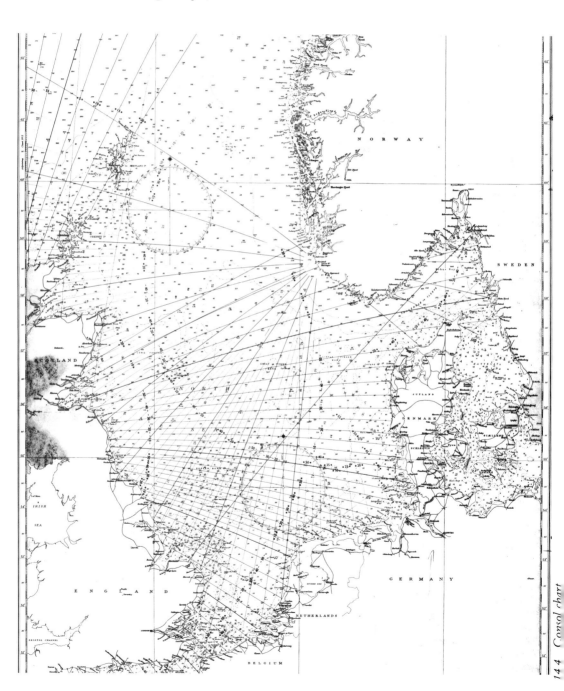

144 Consol chart

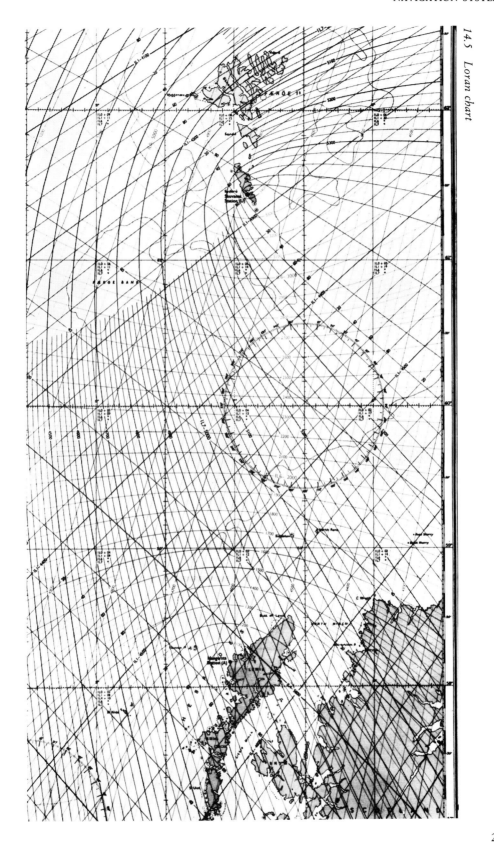

The number of lost characters is divided equally between dots and dashes. The number and type of characters before the equisignal should be referred to the Consol chart or table for position finding purposes. Several counts should be taken and averaged before referring to the chart. If wide variations in count are experienced it will indicate that the bearing is unreliable. In the above example the characters to consider for bearing reduction are 22 dots plus half the number of characters lost, i.e. 24 dots.

To obtain an unambiguous fix from Consol bearings it is essential to know the boat's position to within a 20° sector from the station, and normally the DR position will give this. Alternatively a straight DF bearing of the station can be taken. The Consol system will normally give a range of about 1,000 miles by day and about 1,500 by night; however, its accuracy is not all that good—errors of 12 miles are not infrequently encountered at distances beyond roughly 300 to 400 miles.

Loran

The Loran system was developed at the Massachusetts Institute of Technology during World War Two to provide a 24 hour all-weather navigation system for ships and aircraft. By 1946 it had become quite advanced and was being adapted for civil use. Loran is a long range system of navigation which depends on the transmission and reception of pulsed radio signals from pairs of land stations. The frequencies used are much lower than those used for radar, and this enables a considerable range to be achieved.

As it exists today the system provides means for locating a vessel at any given moment without reference to compass or log, by plotting on special charts with a parabolic lattice overlay. The navigator locates himself by plotting at least two position lines, the intersection of which is the vessel's position. The Loran receiver is operated by superimposing the traces on a cathode ray tube, to measure the difference in the time of arrival of two pulses sent out in synchronism from different points. By reference to Loran charts (14.5) this time difference will give a position line. By using a second pulse rate or pair of stations a second position line is established which gives the vessels

position by intersecting the first line. The accuracy of the fix is better in the area between the stations on the baseline (14.6) and can be as good as 0.1 miles in this position. At night and on the edge of the line distribution the error may be as much as 2 miles. Each station of any pair is usually separated by 200 to 400 miles. The frequencies employed for the Loran A system are in the region of 2 MHz at the lower end on the marine communication band. Using this part of the frequency spectrum both groundwave and skywave propagation can be exploited to give a range of about 700 miles by day and about 1400 miles by night.

The Loran C system operates on the same principles, on a frequency of 100 kHz. The receiving equipment is arranged to display not only pulse time difference but also to compare the phase of the two received signals. The average accuracy of the Loran C system is about $\frac{1}{8}$ mile and the groundwave range typically 1200 miles. It combines the advantages of long range with high accuracy.

The aerial used for the Loran receiver may be a simple wire aerial, although the usual precautions are necessary to avoid interference from machinery and induction from the R/T transmitter aerial, as with other communications equipment. The receiver is basically a good communications receiver without an audio output stage. In its place is connected an accurate time measuring oscilloscope, to enable the operator to measure the interval between pulses to the order of 1 microsecond or better.

The Loran transmitter pairs operate with one station acting as a 'master' station and the other as a 'slave' accurately synchronised to its master.

14.6 Hyperbolic pattern created by two phase locked transmitters

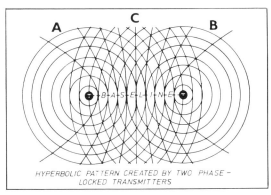

HYPERBOLIC PATTERN CREATED BY TWO PHASE-LOCKED TRANSMITTERS

Referring to (14.6), the two transmitters are shown at either end of a baseline. If a second line drawn bisecting the baseline in perpendicular fashion, it will be readily understood that at any point on this centreline C a pulse sent out simultaneously from A and B would reach the centreline at the same time. It also follows that at any position other than on the centreline the signal from the nearer transmitter would arrive first; also that the further the vessel is from the centreline the greater will be the time difference between the two received pulses. In fact, to make sure that the master station pulse arrives first each slave pulse is delayed by a pre-set amount. The master pulse is then always easy to identify and the time differences increase continually from a minimum at the slave transmitter to a maximum at the master transmitter. The lines of constant time difference form hyperbolic curves which are computed to take into account the earth's curvature and eccentricity. The navigator has access to all this information in quite a painless way: he simply buys charts with the appropriate Loran lattice on them. In fact no knowledge of the system is required in order to use it well.

Loran transmitter pairs are normally some 200 to 400 nautical miles apart; exceptionally, however, this distance may decrease to 100 n.m. or increase to some 700 n.m. where a particular geographical situation demands it. Transmitters are so disposed that signals from at least two pairs are receivable in a particular area, to facilitate fixing a position by the intersection of the position lines. Economy is sometimes effected by making one master transmitter common to two slave transmitters. These common transmitters are double pulsed, in that they send out two sets of pulses which have their own discrete identity. For practical purposes a double pulsed transmitter may be considered as two separate transmitters on the same site.

Radio waves are affected by the medium in which they travel, and at the frequencies in question can travel by both groundwaves, travelling parallel with the earth's surface, and by skywaves, which travel up to the ionosphere where under favourable conditions they are reflected back to the receiving area. I do hope that all this talk of skywaves and ionospheres will not put anybody off using Loran. In fact, once you have familiarised yourself with it, the system is very simple to use.

Since the paths of skywaves and groundwaves are of different lengths, the trasnmitted pulse can appear at the receiver as a series of pulses (14.7). The groundwave signal will have the shorter path length and therefore will always appear first in the series. The single-hop E layer reflection will be next. Sundry multiple-hop and F layer reflections beyond one-hop E layer are not considered reliable enough.

It is possible to match any pair of pulses within range of the receiver, but to obtain navigational information it will be necessary to select the proper pulses. If groundwave signals can be received from both the stations in a pair, they should be used for preference, even if they are considerable weaker than the skywave pulses. (In the log enter GW against the fix to indicate its quality.) It is bad practice to match a groundwave pulse with a skywave pulse. If only one groundwave is receivable it is better to match the two E layer one-hop skywave signals (note SW against the fix) and apply skywave correction to the position lines.

Skywave correction compensates for the groundwave path being shorter than the one-hop E layer skywave path. Loran position lines on charts are derived on the assumption that the signals travel via the groundwave. Correction therefore reduces a skywave time difference reading (SW reading) to the equivalent groundwave reading, so that charts with single system of lines can be used for both purposes. Skywave corrections are normally tabulated from 250 n.m. to 1500 n.m. The former is the lower limit of certainty for skywave readings: the latter is the useful limit of the range. Readings on skywaves are inherently less accurate than those derived from groundwaves. The skywave corrections in microseconds are entered on the charts at the intersections of lines of lat. and long. The sign before the figures denotes whether they should be added or subtracted from the observed reading. Where it is stated that the correctional values are changing rapidly, it will be necessary to interpolate in order to avoid unnecessary errors. In order to assist with the problem of identification of skywave and groundwave (14.8) gives an impression of what is likely to happen with skywave signals by comparison with groundwave signals. Further evidence for identification comes from:

The approximate known ship's position

relative to Loran transmitters
The appearance of signals under observation
The spacing of the pulse under observation
relative to the other pulses displayed.

Most navigators use as many checks as possible and take fixes as frequently as possible, and if the same practice is applied to Loran navigation the problem of identity will be greatly reduced. Mistakes in identity will be obvious by a sudden inconsistency with respect to previous fixes.

Two inherent characteristics of skywaves are, first, that they are subject to fading, which falling away and reappearance of the signal may on some occasions be quite rapid, cycling less than one minute. At the other times the cycling is very slow and the signal appears quite steady, like a groundwave, for several minutes. Secondly,

skywaves will split into two or more humps which fade more or less independently. Splitting may be a source of error when making skywave readings as the leading edge of the signal could be momentarily faded, which would give the pulse an apparent shift of several microseconds. Generally speaking the greater the distance to the transmitter the steadier the skywave signal. Of the skywave signals that will appear, the one-hop E layer signal will be generally much steadier than the rest.

Groundwaves are generally steady in amplitude and always free from splitting; if, however, the signal is weak it may appear to flicker from noise. In particularly violent weather the vessel's rolling may result in the groundwave signal varying somewhat in amplitude. When this happens all the signals displayed should vary together.

The range of Loran signals is affected in much the same way as R/T signals as they are both in the 2 MHz area of operation. The basic factors are:
Time of day
Geographical region
Ionosopheric conditions
Signal path (land or sea)
Background noise
Directional effects of the Loran receiver aerial.

Fortunately none of these things needs to be a great problem. The first four items will become a matter of experience in a very short while.

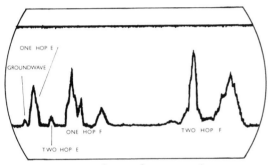

14.7   *Skywave and groundwave reception*

14.8   *Skywave and groundwave diurnal effects*

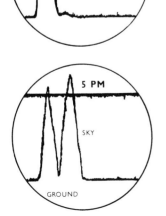

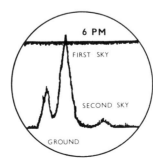

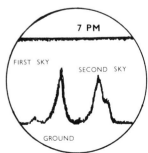

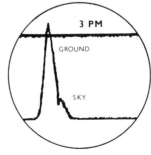

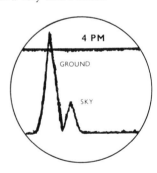

Background noise is suppressible in the extreme by turning off the offending item, and if due to static will have to be worked through or left to pass. The possibility of directional effects caused by the vessel's rigging or structure of the Loran aerial are easily checked on the completion of installation by using any pair groundwave signals, sailing in a circle and noting the signal strength with respect to heading.

Identification of Loran stations is by two characteristics: pulse rate and operating frequency. Receivers are normally fixed tuned at pre-set frequencies to simplify operation. The pulse rates are also pre-set and may be selected via a panel control. To effect an economy in air space a number of pairs of stations operate on the same frequency; however, each pair has a different pulse rate. Signals from all the Loran stations on the same channel can appear on the screen at the same time provided they are within range. By selecting the correct pulse rate for the station pair it is intended to use, the signals from this appear stationary while the others will 'drift through' the traces, and can be ignored. Sometimes ghost pulses will appear beside the stationary pulse on the screen; these may be at the same frequency but at a different pulse rate. Such pulses flicker faintly and the sweep line extends through their bases.

Each pair of Loran stations has an identity symbol with three digits. The first digit gives the channel frequency, the second gives the basic pulse recurrence rate, and the third gives the specific recurrence rate. These symbols are used on Loran tables and charts; the word 'rate' stands for emissions from a pair of transmitters, for example Loran Rate 2S4. Frequency channels are:

1. 1950 kHz
2. 1850 kHz
3. 1900 kHz
4. 1750 kHz

Basic pulse recurrence rates:

H (High) $33\frac{1}{3}$ per sec.
L (Low)   25   per sec.
S (Special) 20   per sec.

Specific recurrence rates for station identification:
0, 1, 2, 3, 4, 5, 6, 7

For example, the group 2S4–2120 indicates:
2 = Frequency 1850 kHz
S = Special recurrence rate 20 per sec.
4 = Specific recurrence pulse rate
2120 = Loran position for the station
Other common abbreviations used in the Loran system are:

T   tabulated reading in microseconds
TG   reading of groundwave match
TS   reading of skywave match
TSG reading of skywave/groundwave match.

Loran transmitters are, although rarely, fallible, and when the synchronization between the two stations in the pair is lost the signals are made to blink on and off or move backwards and forwards along the trace as a warning against their use for navigation for the time being.

The accuracy obtained depends on:
1. Synchronization of Loran transmitters
2. Skill in matching and identifying signals
3. Certainty of skywave correction when used
4. Position relative to Loran transmitter
5. Accuracy of charts and tables
6. Calibration of indicator unit

In the case of (1), if synchronization error exceeds 2 μsec., one or both stations will blink their transmissions. By practice (2) and with reasonable care and judgement it should be possible to match the received signals and read the indicator to within 1 μsec. (2). On bad signals affected by noise, it should still be possible to obtain a match to within a few microseconds.

The ionosphere (3), from which the skywaves are reflected, constantly varies in height above the earth and therefore the correction tables are average values. Skywaves are most valuable at distances in excess of about 700 miles, where with care in reading and correction an average error of 2 μsec. is achievable.

The best position (4) from the accuracy point of view will be on the baseline between the transmitters as the lines of position are closest at this point (14.6). The worst positions are next to the baseline extensions, where line separation can be several miles per microsecond, even within the groundwave range of the transmitters. About 25 μsec. from the baseline extension must be considered an area of poor reliability for groundwaves, and likewise for skywaves for a distance of 200 μsec. Experience and common sense will give a fair indication of probable error.

Charts and tables (5) for Loran are prepared by the US Hydrographic Office. Those showing Loran lines and depth information are, in my opinion, the most suitable for small craft (a quick look at the depth sounder on each fix does worlds for the confidence, or otherwise). Admiralty charts, although large, do give the user confidence, although other reputable sources are available to the yachtsman.

The calibration (6) of the instruments that have so far come my way has been good. However, great care should be taken to treat the equipment as a precision instrument.

Typical Loran equipment is shown in (14.9) and (14.10) with manual pulse matching and automatic respectively.

Omega

This all-weather, day and night, world wide navigation system has been developed for the US Navy over about 20 years. Recently it has been available for use by merchant shipping. The American company Northrop Inc. has produced the commercial version shown (14.11) which is a solid state, single frequency phase locked superhetrodyne type, with whip aerial and coupler for reception of Omega signals.

The system comprises a network of only eight VLF land based transmitters providing a world wide hyperbolic form of electronic lattice within which position can be determined with an accuracy of ±1 n.m. in daylight and ±2 n.m. at night. When all eight transmitters are operating at full power each will have a range of between 5000 and 6000 miles, so that as many as four or five will be available for navigation purposes for any one area.

Omega transmitters, being phase locked to universal time, provide a signal field where the

phase is always constant. Thus the measured phase difference of a pair of signals observed at a given location depends solely on how much further the observer is from one station than another. Also the same phase angle measurement will be observed at all points which have the same difference in distance from two stations. The locus of such points is a contour of constant phase which is fixed on the surface of the earth with respect to the positions of the two transmitters. Because the relative phase of every pair of signals observed at any point on the earth defines a known contour containing that point, the intersection of two such contours, established by different pairs of stations, defines the location of the point (14.12).

Omega stations all transmit on three basic frequencies, 10.2, 11.33 and 13.6 kHz, and always in the same order, with the duration of each transmission varying from 0.9 to 1.2 sec. depending on the station. A typical sequence is shown in (14.13). The basic 10.2 kHz transmissions generate hyperbolic lanes 8 n.m. wide on the baseline, and in order to initially position the boat within this system the navigator must know his position to within ±4 n.m. Omega is a lane counting system, and once the lane count is established and the equipment is running continuously no reference to other equipment or systems is necessary.

The full system is planned to operate with eight stations, with an interval between each transmission of 200 m sec.; the entire transmission cycle will thus repeat itself every 10m sec. with the start of the 10 sec. cycle synchronized to universal time. The signals will be of different amplitudes depending upon the observer's distance from the various transmitters, so that the time sequence of transmissions and the relative signal strength can be used to identify the Omega signal.

The signal strength of the various stations may also be recognised by either the relative sound level or the amplitude of the various signals shown on a recorder. Incorporated in the receiver is the required timing, phase measuring, lane counting and digital readout for determining position lines. Four stations can be tuned simultaneously, providing six available lines of position and allowing display of any three selected lines.

Considerable activity is taking place with Omega development at this time and already there are a

14.9   Loran A manually operated receiver
14.10   Loran A and C receiver with automatic digital readout

14.11   *Omega 1 receiver*

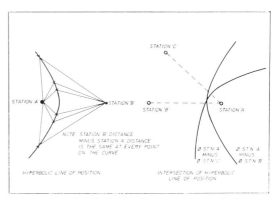

14.12   *Position fixing by Omega phase locked transmissions*

number of smaller equipments available, such as the Plath Omega receiver (14.14). My own feelings are that this system of navigation will be widely adopted in the future by all sections of the marine fraternity. No doubt special small craft versions will appear in due course.

Skywave corrections, which are taken from US Naval Oceanographic Office tables, are then applied and corrected position lines plotted on an Omega chart, a typical time to obtain a fix being about two minutes. The Omega charts (14.15) are overprinted with a lattice of numbered lanes (in much the same way as Decca and Loran charts) one of which will correspond to the number indicated on the receiver to indicate the line of position. The lower digits indicate the position between the lane.

Of the two units which have so far come my way, the aerials in both cases have been a fibreglass whip with a special coupling unit at the base. The makers supplied this inclusive with the equipment price and no difficulty was experienced in mounting it. It should, as with other receiving aerials, be kept as far as possible from the R/T transmitter aerial, and be given a good earth.

Inertial Navigation

Although very expensive, and needing a constant power input of about 300 W, some specialized applications are apparent, for example positioning a submersible working from a support vessel. Three mutually perpendicular accelerometers define movements in the horizontal plane as apparent from a gyroscopically stabilized platform. The accelerometer outputs are integrated to obtain

speed, a second integration yielding distance run. A mini-computer is used to derive co-ordinates based in terms of movement from an entered position. The system needs no external signals for operation, although drift occurs which needs correcting at regular intervals by reference to some other system. Accuracies of 1 to 2 n.m. are possible. Installation needs expert knowledge.

Satellite Navigation—Navsat

The present navigation satellites have been operational since 1967 and were launched by the US Navy. The system is known variously as NNSS, Transit or Navsat. The cost of shipborne equipment has dropped considerably; for example, the Walker Sat-Nav 801 (14.16) costs about the same as Omega and the current consumption is 2 amps. The system uses 5 longitudinally spaced satellites in polar orbit with periods of about 108 minutes, these remain above the horizon for 10–20 minutes. The satellite transmits on two frequencies, 150 and 400 MHz respectively. These transmissions serve the dual purpose of providing doppler information, and retransmission of stored orbital data received from ground tracking stations every 12 hours. Position is derived by measuring the doppler shift of the received signal with respect to a precision reference frequency. The satellite signal will exhibit zero shift at the point when it is closest, taken together with a burst of position information transmitted every 2 mins, it is clear that by relating this to a time reference, position can be derived. All functions are

231

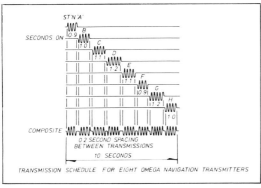

14.13   *Omega transmission sequencing*   14.14   *Omega receiver*

Comparison of radio navigation systems

	Consol	Decca	Loran A	Loran C	Omega	Navsat
Frequency	200–400 kHz	70–130 kHz	2 MHz	100 kHz	10.2 and 13.6 kHz	150 & 40
Signal type	CW	CW	Pulse	Pulse	Time multiplex	Doppler data
Range	1200 n.m.	400 n.m. day 250 n.m. night	700 n.m. day 1400 n.m. night Coverage mainly in northern hemisphere, especially around North America	1200 n.m. Coverage mainly in northern hemisphere	5000 World coverage	World wi
Average accuracy	4 n.m.	$\frac{1}{4}$ n.m.	2 n.m.	$\frac{1}{8}$ n.m.	$\frac{1}{2}$ n.m.	200 metre
Time required for fix	10 min.	30 sec.	2 min. manual 30 sec. auto	2 min. manual 30 sec. auto	30 sec.	From 15 to about hour
Position line created by	Rotating beam pattern	Phase comparison of signals	Time comparison of signals	Time and phase comparison of signals	Phase comparison of signals	Fix indic lat & lon satellite c received
Remarks	Not very accurate, but can be used with any receiver having BFO; low cost	Automatic high accuracy in good conditions; range limited by skywave pollution; rental only	Large bandwidth required for pulse transmissions; skywave does not seriously degrade accuracy	High accuracy and long range available; medium cost	Only eight stations required to cover the world; expensive	Cost com to Omeg

performed by an integral microcomputer and position is displayed as Lat and Long.

The information available from this system is not continuous, and is therefore more suitable for ocean navigation. The time between fixes varies with latitude and can be over an hour. However, it is accurate to something like 200 metres and between fixes, with usually constant courses and speeds in open waters, simple DR will mean a high standard easily meeting most requirements. The aerial is usually a short dipole housed in a plastic cover. Installation is straightforward and could be handled by many boat owners.

Navstar

This is a new system which should be in operation by 1987. The system will comprise 24 satellites with a 12 hour orbital period, which should give any vessel anywhere in the world a view of at least six satellites at any time. Unlike the Transit system, position is determined by timed pulses (like radar). Various other important features are available; for example, time, course and speed can be computed and, as these satellites are continuously visible, the accuracy of fixes is within 10 metres, thus covering all but the most critical work. Power required, cost, aerial used, and installation are similar to Navstat.

Comparison of Radio Navigation Systems

Many factors are involved in the choice of equipment for each installation, and to make comparison as simple as possible I have listed the salient features of each system. See page 232.

14.15   Omega chart

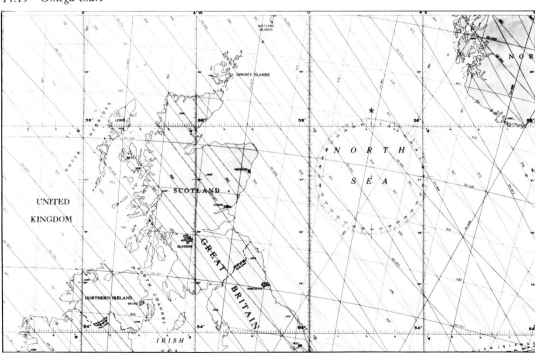

14.16   *Walker Sat Nav*

15 Ancillary Appliances

The time has come the walrus said
To talk of many things . . .
     Lewis Carroll

There are a number of equipments available which do not fall strictly under the headings of previous chapters, and of these few give rise to exceptional problems either during installation or service. For the sake of interest I have selected some of these and described them in the following pages.
(15.1) shows a completely portable type manufactured by Marconi Marine powered by four standard torch batteries which have a useful life of about 10,000 operations of 10 sec. duration. The range of this unit is about 350 yards under normal conditions. Permanently installed equipment gives more output power than the portable type, and can include facilities such as a foghorn and intercommunication with other parts of the boat. Although it may be that an intercom on a small boat may not get much use, a moment's thought

15.1   Marconi Marine's 'Viking IV' transistorised loudhailer

will recall how, when at the wheel, communication with anyone on the foredeck is always in sign language because of wind or engine noise. Also, of course, being able to hail the lock keeper or pilot and hear the reply from inside the wheelhouse is helpful.

Even in relatively calm weather it is necessary to have some means of clearing spray from the wheelhouse windows. The Kent Clearview Screen has become widely accepted, and the small craft version with an integral motor in the centre boss is illustrated (15.2). As an alternative some might prefer a straight-line marine wiper such as that manufactured by Wynstruments Ltd (15.4). A version suitable for small boats has been designed to be suitable for fixed, sliding or hinged windows and can be supplied with either fixed or variable speed drive. This company also produces a heavy duty pendulum type wiper, and also a marine duty screen washer. Installation of all the above is simple, all the motors used have metal housings, and an adequate level of radio interference suppression is generally not difficult to achieve.

As most small boats are left for long periods without attention, it is not uncommon to find automatic bilge level sensors and associated pumps, to cover the possibility of a fault in some part of the underwater area or fitting. In my view the non-contracting type of detector which employes a small ultrasonic transducer will give the best reliability. If contacts are used there is always the possibility of problems with electrolytic action and/or current leakage.

Pressurised automatic water systems are now almost a must for everything except the smallest craft. A typical installation on a 35 ft cruiser is

15.2   Kent clearview screen

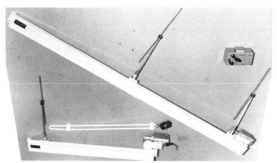

15.4   Straight line wiper by Wynstruments Ltd

15.3   Water system pressurisation unit

are available it may be possible to fit a desalinator (15.5) such as the Sea Still (G M Power Plant, Ipswich, Suffolk). This device makes use of waste heat from the main engine or auxiliary generator, and by evaporation extracts the salt from raw seawater. The unit is entirely automatic in operation and would require the heat generated by an engine of between 60 and 100 h.p. working at almost full power to operate at its maximum efficiency and discharge about 10 gal. per hour. Such units are by no means commonplace and for this reason perhaps a little more information is not out of place. The unit has its own heat exchanger which is piped in parallel with the engine heat exchanger, and the fresh water in the engine cooling circuit is circulated through the Sea Still heat exchanger and back to the engine. This continues unless the amount of heat being absorbed by the Sea Still is less than the engine is giving off. If this occurs the thermostat in the outlet side of the Sea Still heat exchanger lifts and passes part of the water back to the engine's heat exchanger for

shown (15.3); the unit is very compact and is made by Peters & Russell Inc. for use on a 12 V supply. The current drawn by these units is of course intermittent, and although it may instantaneously reach 10 A or so, averaged over 24 hours it is not generally significant. The pump shown will provide water for toilet, galley and deck wash; it is a diaphragm type and has the capacity to serve several outlets simultaneously.

Although surrounded by seawater, fresh water for washing and drinking may be inconveniently remote. Where space and the power to operate it

15.5   Sea Still desalinator by G & M Powerplant

further cooling before re-entry to the engine. Part of the hot seawater circulating in the still is tapped off through a make-up feed regulating valve to take the place of the fresh water discharged. Cold seawater is pumped through the condensing coils in the interior of the still and then allowed to run out over the side, carrying with it the brine deposits accumulated in the base of the still. The pumps can be operated from the engines, or may be electric if this is more suitable to the application.

The control unit of the Sea Still is very simple, and when switched to automatic will not operate the still until the heating medium and the water in circulation have reached a sufficient temperature to produce water that has reached the pasteurisation point. A warning cell is fitted to give a remote indication of salinity and shut the still down automatically when excessive salinity of the discharged water occurs, so that the cause can be investigated.

Food eaten afloat will invariably be slightly different, because the facilities available in small craft for preparation are not usually very extensive. When at sea both the time available for the task and the weather have a great bearing on what one eats. Probably a really important item for the cruising yacht is a fast and efficient method of producing hot drinks or soups. In this respect a low voltage kettle or immersion heater is invaluable. An electric frying pan is likely to consume a fair amount of current, although there can be little doubt about the variety of dishes one can produce with such a utensil. The 3 kW baby cooker produced by Belling has already been used with success on small craft, and where the power is available it is excellent for all conventional forms of cooking. The cost of this unit is very low and it does have the advantage of built-in hotplates.

In the higher cost bracket a microwave oven can often prove a valuable piece of equipment. In recent years there has been a considerable increase in interest in microwave cooking, mainly because of the speed of heating. Until very recently little information has been available on the subject in an easily digestable form. Vessels of about 40 ft upwards would be capable of finding space in the galley area. It would also only be suitable for those craft fitted with 110 V or 240 V alternators or AC shore supply.

There may be a temptation to use an invertor to supply the power from the boat's batteries. If this is tried great care must be taken to see that the waveform of the supply is a reasonable sinewave and also that the frequency is within 3% as microwave ovens employ reactance type regulators which will not work within their design range where the form factor or the frequency are different from the prescribed parameters. The cheaper invertor units employ a switching principle to produce a squarewave output and these types are not suitable. The more expensive sinewave output types would be suitable, but due to the efficiency the primary current of such units would not be in a range that could be considered elegant from a small craft point of view.

From the technical aspect various constants are beginning to appear, such as frequency, maximum power leakage for operational safety, etc. The frequency most commonly used is 2.45 GHz, which has been found to be a good compromise for uniformity of heating. At frequencies much in excess of this the depth of penetration into the food falls off, and at lower frequencies the heating pattern becomes rather patchy. Because the food is heated throughout immediately rather than by the conventional process of conduction from the outside to the inside, the greatest advantage comes in re-heating partially cooked or fully cooked food. This would be acknowledged by anyone coming off watch at 2 a.m. and being able to select a meal of their fancy from a choice of three or four possible dishes, and at 2.03 a.m. to sit down and eat it piping hot. The times are roughly those for an oven with a 600 W RF power output, which would be the biggest practical size suitable. Incidentally, it is essential not to heat frozen foods too quickly in the early stages. As melting takes place hot spots will appear due to the irregular load distribution of ice, water and food, all of which have differing absorption rates. However thawing time is reduced to about one-tenth of that required with a conventional cooker. Because of the vast difference in the application of the energy, the effect on the food is also rather different. Nutritional examination shows better retention of the natural juices and vitamins in the food when cooked with microwaves. One other difference is that as the heat is so much more uniform, no crust or surface browning takes place naturally. This has been regarded as a major objection to acceptibility; however by brushing the food with a solution having a high loss, a hot film is created at the surface, which gives acceptable browning.

It is essential to avoid the use of metal dishes, plates or cooking foil. Metal objects reflect microwave energy, causing a mismatch condition which can damage the magnetron that provides the power. The dishes that may be used are china, plastic (preferably polypropylene) or glass. The new heat resistant plastic ovenware will also be satisfactory. The dishes will only become heated by conduction from the food, and it is possible to cook the food on the table utensil. Another point worth noting is that microwave energy appears to have a sterilising effect which destroys certain bacteria.

It is usual for some of the cooling air from the magnetron to be blown into the oven cavity to reduce condensation on the oven walls. The oven is usually made from stainless steel and remains cold in operation, thus causing steam from the food to condense on the oven walls. It is therefore quite normal for a slight draft to be appearent from the oven door gauze.

With a well designed microwave appliance there is very low radiation risk; however the rules are different and must be understood and adhered to. The major risk is exposure of the operator to microwave energy. Manufacturers are required to embody safety switches on the oven door to prevent this, and also to suppress stray leakage from the magnetron heater cathode connection, any ventilating ducts and the door seal. Never tamper with safety switches or any other part of the oven, and if the unit ever receives any form of physical stress have it checked for leakage. If it fails to function for any reason, call in a microwave oven expert.

Heating Equipment

The safest fuel for heating systems on boats is diesel. In the course of the average season one hears of several boats being destroyed by fire. Since no case that I have encountered in the course of my working life had its origins in a diesel air or water heater, I feel that their safety record sets a standard by which other systems will be judged.

Water heaters
It is not generally realised that a water heater running on diesel fuel may sometimes provide a better space-heating alternative. For the larger vessel, a system can be devised where running hot water is available for galley and heads, while cabin heating is simultaneously achieved by means of conventional radiators. The plumbing could be arranged to use waste heat from the main engine or, optionally, the water heater unit can warm the engine in cold weather. Owners with experience of diesel engines in cold climates will appreciate this point particularly.

Webasto manufacture a wide range of heating appliances, the smallest water heater (15.6) having an electrical consumption of about 70 watts for the heater itself, and about 40 watts for the water circulating pump, these figures must clearly be taken into account when working out battery capacity. Its heat output is about 32,000 BTU's per hour (as a rough and ready guide, this is equivalent to three large domestic electric fires running for one hour). Its consumption of diesel fuel runs at about 1 litre per hour (4 hours for one gallon). All the heating units are controlled via thermostats, and a programmer which determines a cycle of events for ignition. By switching the unit on, both the combustion air fan and the water circulating pump are started. The air fan runs for about 15 seconds (to clear away any gases that have accumulated since the last running period) and, at the end of this period, the high tension spark ignition and the fuel are switched on; as combustion becomes established, a photo electric sensor switches off the ignition circuit. The hot gases produced pass through a heat exchanger, through which the water to be heated is drawn by the circulating pump. On leaving the heat exchanger the exhaust gases are ducted overboard. The thermostat is normally set to 80°C (176°F) and by closing the solenoid valve in the fuel supply, the heater will cut out automatically when this temperature is reached. It should be noted that the air fan will run for two or three minutes after the heater has extinguished, in order to remove any products of the combustion period that remain.

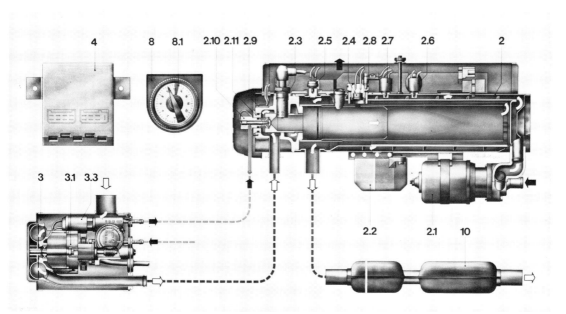

15.6	Webasto water heater
2	Heat exchanger
2.1	Water pump
2.2	Glow plug controller
2.3	Glow plug
2.4 to 2.7	Control function thermostats
2.8	Overheat sensor
2.9	Ring heater on burner for cold start
2.10	Fuel atomiser
2.11	Atomiser mounting ring
3	Combustion air pressuriser
3.1	Air and fuel pump motor
3.3	Magnetic valve
4	Electronic sequence control
8 to 8.1	Temperature selector
10	Exhaust silencer

Installation

With all heating equipment I strongly recommend that you use an technician of the manufacturer. A stock of all the right bits and a knowledge of all the small details often combine to make the job cheaper than doing it wrong yourself. If you do decide to have a go yourself, find the local boat heater wizard and pick his brains.

When selecting electrical equipment for your boat, I have found that it pays to go for the model with insulated return electrics, a clearly marked earth terminal and fitted radio suppression equipment. If such features are not available, it is likely that the item was not intended for marine use.

Air heaters

This is probably the most common form of heating in the small craft industry; indeed, it could be said that the Webasto HL3003 (15.7) has become an industry 'standard'. The heat output from this unit is 12,000 Btu/hour, which in domestic terms is roughly equivalent to a large three bar electric fire. The consumption is about 45 watts, and the fuel consumption about 0·5 litres (2 pints) per hour. The air flow amounts to about 6 cubic metres (65 cubic ft) per minute, making it ideal for vessels in the 9 to 14 metre range. More recently a unit for smaller boats has become available, the HL20, which operates on similar principles but has a pressurised exhaust, thus simplifying installation by allowing a smaller diameter exhaust duct to be used. Unlike most other heaters, it can be mounted in the area to be heated. This has several advantages: for example, it is easily accessible for service work, and heat directly radiated by the unit warms the area. In many smaller boats (my own is an example), the amount of space anywhere is limited and it may well prove an advantage to mount the unit in the wheelhouse. Generally all air heaters should be mounted as near to the area to be heated as possible, and should have complete

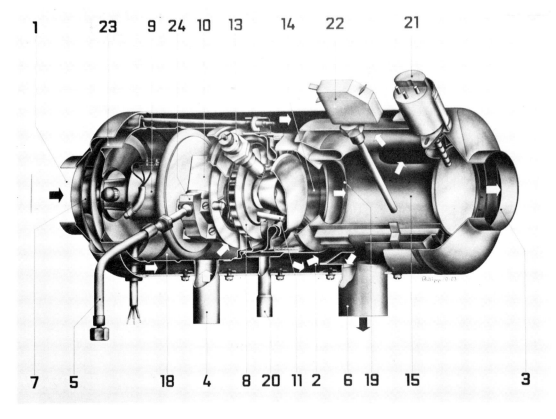

15.7   *Webasto HL 3003 air heater*
 1   *Fresh air inlet*
 2   *Division of air passages*
 3   *Hot air outlet*
 4   *Combustion air inlet*
 5   *Suction connecting piece*
 6   *Exhaust gas outlet*
 7   *Fresh air blower*
 8   *Combustion air blower*
 9   *Electric motor*
10   *Fuel pump*
11   *Fuel atomizer*

13   *Glow plug*
14   *Main combustion chamber*
15   *Heat exchanger*
18   *Intake housing*
19   *Flame baffle*
20   *Oil drainage pipe*
21   *Overheat thermostat*
22   *Flame detection thermostat*
23   *Motor holder*
24   *Connecting piece*

protection from the weather. Special grommets are available to seal ducts and pipes at bulkheads. The electronic control unit should be protected not only from the usual marine environmental hazards, but also from excessive heat, either from the heater unit or the engines.

By employing the right accessories in the ducting system, the heating air may derive fresh air from outside the boat, or air drawn from inside at a point remote from the heater output, which has clear advantages when the weather is very cold.

The air used for combustion must not be drawn from any habitable space, and the intake should be suitably positioned so that it does not draw in exhaust gases either from the main engines or the heater itself. The electrical work is not extensive, and outside of the general context of chapter 1 the only thing to remember is to size the cable cross section to minimise voltage drop in the starting mode, which will avoid starting difficulties when batteries are low.

15.8   *Norvent Viking showing main components*

Air Conditioning

As I live on the east coast of England, I normally think in terms of how to keep warm, but I realise that there are some people who have a problem

keeping cool. Mechanical refrigeration is the only means available, and this consumes a fair amount of energy, which implies that it will not be available for the smallest boat. Where a shore supply or generating capacity is available, it is possible to obtain an air conditioning unit small enough to fit on boats of, say, 12m (37 ft) and upwards. The unit illustrated in (15.8) is the Viking supplied by Norvent of Newcastle, a water-cooled compression type unit, completely self-contained; the power required is about 2kW at 240WAC. The principle of operation is based on the propensity of substances such as Freon or Methyl-chloride to vapourise when subjected to heat or a reduction in pressure. In practice, this change occurs in an evaporator designed so that it will have considerable contact with the air to be cooled; by reducing the pressure, heat is extracted from the air to vapourise the refrigerant. This is then pumped away and liquified in a condenser, which is water-cooled to reduce size and increase

15.9   *Oil-fired heating installation*

15.10   Francis marine anchor winch

efficiency. Other small equipments are becoming available (originally intended for long distance lorries) in which the refrigerant pump is engine-driven and only the air blowers are electric; this approach may ultimately reduce the electric power required for small boats to an acceptable level.

Winches

Electric hauling equipment has much to offer the small boat owner (15.10). Aside from the mundane chore of raising the anchors and pulling in mooring cables against the wind, many unusual tasks can be made easy to manage single handed. For example a temporary derrick can be rigged with tackle and spar for shipping or landing heavy gear. The sunken dinghy can be raised by hauling alternately on fore and aft lines so that the gunwales are above

the water, when bailing will quickly clear the problem. If you have inadvertently taken the ground and the next tide produces insufficient water to enable you to float clear, by running out a couple of heavy anchors, or in rivers possibly a cable to a tree, considerable strain can be applied in the refloating direction. By re-trimming, floating loose gear off in the dinghy, etc. it is generally possible to get clear.

Installing any hauling equipment means that great care must be taken to spread the imposed load over a wide area of the vessel's structure. The base of the equipment should be on a large wooden pad and bolted right through a deck beam. Some equipments I have seen use motor car starter motors with one side of the battery terminals connected to the casing. Avoid this type at all cost as electrolytic action will occur in the deck timbers and mounting bolts which can lead to problems all over the hull.

Motors employed for this job are usually the series type, which exerts the highest torque at the lowest speed; also its speed is to a large extent dependent on the load. As the motor slows down under load the current drawn rises, and if the maximum torque capability is to be realised the supply cables must be very large in cross section.

... 'He ended; and his words their drooping cheer
Enlightened, and their languished hope revived,
The invention all admired, and each how he
To be the inventor missed, so easy it seemed
Once found, which yet unfound most would
    have thought
Impossible; yet, haply, of thy race,
In future days, if malice should abound,
Someone, intent on mischief or inspired
With devilish machination, might devise
Like instrument to plague the sons of men

Paradise Lost
John Milton

Glossary

ABERRATION A defect in an optical or electron lens or microwave lens or mirror system, which causes a lack of definition at all points except one in the focussing plane.

ABSORPTION Dissipation of energy in the medium through which it is travelling.

AERIAL An electrical element from which electromagnetic waves are radiated into space or received from space.

AFTERGLOW The slowly decaying glow remaining in the cathode ray tube phosphor after excitation has ceased.

AMPERE HOUR (AH) The term used to define the storage capability of batteries. The quoted figure normally applies at the 10 hour rate, i.e. a 40 AH battery could sustain a 4 A discharge for 10 hours.

AMPLIFICATION The degree of magnification achieved between the input and output terminations of a mechanical or electrical device.

AMPLITUDE The maximum value of any periodic occurrence whether it has electrical or mechanical qualities.

AMPLITUDE MODULATION (AM) A means of applying intelligence to an electrical signal by varying its instantaneous amplitude. For example, imagine Morse characters being transmitted which in the space period had a value of 1 V and during the dot or dash period had a value of 2 V. The difference in the two levels carries the information, thus the signal is amplitude modulated in the simplest sense.

ANALOGUE Electronic circuitry which has linear operating conditions to produce an output signal directly analogous to its input.

ANTENNA See aerial.

ARRAY This can refer to any plurality of emitters or sensors that have been arranged with a spacing related to the wavelength of operation, the purpose of this arrangement being to define a particular beam pattern. Used with radio aerials, ultrasonic transducers, infra-red emitters, etc.

ATTENUATION The loss that occurs when transmitting intelligence. This can be electrical and occur in conductors, circuitry or atmosphere. It can also be associated with acoustic waves in whatever medium they may be travelling, i.e. liquid, solid or gas; or again it may be associated with mechanical losses in transmitting mechanical power from one point to another.

ATTENUATOR An electronic device for reducing the amplitude of an electrical signal, usually calibrated so that the precise signal reduction can be read from its scale.

AUDIO A term used in association with phenomena that are within the range of human hearing from the frequency aspect. This is typically in the range of 10 Hz to about 15 kHz.

AZIMUTH The bearing of an object measured in a horizontal plane with reference to a fixed direction.

BACKGROUND NOISE Spurious fluctuations in the output of an electronic device that are the result of natural or man-made electrical interference. It can also be generated within the circuitry and efforts are made to keep this to a minimum.

BALANCE POINT In marine automatic pilots this refers to a condition where no steering action is being called for, due to the electronic control unit being in a state whereby the error signal is precisely balanced by a proportional rudder signal.

BALANCED FEEDER A two-wire transmission system in which the electrical centre is at earth potential. It is terminated in a balanced load so that voltage due to stray fields cancel at the termination.

BALANCED MODULATOR An electronic circuit in which the carrier is applied in the same phase and the modulating wave is applied in anti-phase to opposing inputs. The net result is that the components, due to the carrier, cancel in the circuit output device. It is used in SSB equipment to remove the carrier signal.

BANDWIDTH The range of frequencies above and/or below the carrier frequency required for receiving a particular transmitted signal. The simpler the signal the narrower this may be.

BEACON A transmitting station used for navigational purposes. The frequency depends on the intended use; for instance most radar beacons send a coded identity reply on radar frequencies. DF beacons for marine use are usually in the band between 250 kHz and 500 kHz.

BEAM The path followed by electrons in a cathode ray tube or the path along which the energy from a directive aerial is accented. It is also used to describe the pressure pattern over the face of an ultrasonic transducer.

BEAMWIDTH The width of any transmitted beam measured at the half power points of the envelope, which is usually plotted on polar coordinates and expressed in degrees.

BLIND SECTOR A blank area on a radar or sonar screen caused by some obstruction to the radiation from the aerial or transducer.

BLOCKING DIODES These devices can be regarded as one-way valves for controlling the flow of electric current; i.e. current from two separate sources can be drawn on via these diodes to supply a common load, but each supply is 'blocked' from its counterpart by the one-way action.

BONDING A framework of conductors between metallic parts of a boat's structure, to bring these points of contact to a common potential, usually for the purpose of cathodic protection and interference suppression.

BRIGHT-UP PULSE In radar, sonar and other marine cathode ray presentations, the brightness of the trace is intensified at the start of the sweep. This has the effect of masking out the return of the spot to its origin at the end of the sweep period.

BROADBAND Any device that will work over a wide spectrum on either side of its mean tuning point. This could equally refer to an aerial or an amplifier or receiver, etc.

CADAN AXIS The axis of a device, which may be a gyroscope for example, through which a precise measurement is made.

CALIBRATOR A device used specifically to provide accurate measurement, for example the range rings on a radar or the internal depth standard on a survey echosounder.

CAPACITANCE (F) The ability to hold an electrical charge, displayed by two conductors separated by an insulating material usually referred to as a dielectric. The unit which indicates the quantity of charge any specific capacitor can hold is (for boating purposes) the microfarad (uF). This device has the ability to be charged and discharged while possessing an insulator between its terminals. It will, therefore, pass AC and block DC simultaneously.

CARDIOID A polar diagram which has the appearance of a heart, such as is obtained with the combined effect of a loop and vertical signal in a direction finder.

CARRIER WAVE (CW) The basic frequency of a radio transmission. Its purpose is to provide a primary signal against which sidebands may be created by the modulation process.

CATHODE RAY OSCILLOSCOPE An instrument for the specialised examination of electrical waveforms by displaying these phenomena on a cathode ray tube (CRT).

CAVITY A tuned circuit of special form for use at very short wavelengths.

CLUTTER Echoes arising from rain or waves which appear in random fashion on a radar or sonar screen.

COAXIAL CABLE A special screened cable manufactured to have a characteristic impedance and specific constants, used for transmission of radio frequency signals. In construction it is simply a central conducting core surrounded by a concentric layer of insulating material about which a conducting screen is disposed, also concentrically. This conductor system is then usually sheathed overall in PVC in order to prevent degradation by corrosion of the conductors.

CONVERTOR Any device for changing one form of energy or signal to another may be referred to by this term. Typical examples are power convertors which are employed to convert say 24 V ship's supply to 240 V AC 50 Hz for power tools, etc. Radio frequency convertors are used to change the frequency of a wave applied to the input to a convenient frequency for processing at the convertor output.

COSMIC NOISE The effect of random radiation from space which appears at the receiver aerial.

CROSS MODULATION A situation which may

arise in electronic circuits where a degree of non-linearity is present. Where more than one signal is present in the circuit the effect is for one to superimpose itself on the other.

D LAYER A weakly ionised stratum of the ionosphere about 60 km above the earth. This layer particularly enhances extremely long radio wave propagation by reflection.

DECIBEL (dB) A unit used for defining the ratio between two powers and may be

mathematically expressed as $10 \log \dfrac{\text{power 1}}{\text{power 2}}$

DECLINOMETER An instrument used to determine the local strength of the vertical component of the earth's field (declination) for the purposes of compass or sense unit site correction.

DELAY LINE An electrical device for causing a delay in an electrical signal. It has particular characteristics that enable it to be used for the generation of short pulses and is applied to this purpose in the latest small boat radars.

DEMODULATOR The device by which means the low frequency modulating wave is removed from the high frequency carrier wave.

DIFFRACTION Bending of the ground wave around the earth's curvature in the microwave region so that range is marginally extended beyond the line of sight condition.

DIGITAL Usually refers to circuitry which performs its specific function by using pulses or 'digits' of various rates or lengths and constant amplitude. The digital condition of 0 V corresponding usually to digital circuit condition '0' and another voltage level (often 5 V) corresponding to digital circuit condition 'I'.

DIP The earth's magnetic field has the appearance of an imaginary magnet of very short length placed at the centre of the earth with its poles roughly aligned with the terrestrial polar axis. This means that for places removed from the equator, the field pattern has a vertical component. The angle subtended by the resultant field to a line tangential with the earth's surface is called the angle of dip.

DIPLEXER A device for reducing interaction between two signals present on a common aerial.

DIPOLE An aerial used usually at VHF for marine purposes. It consists of two rods, one half wavelength long electrically fed at the centre, the whole assembly being enclosed in a fibre-glass cylinder.

DOPPLER EFFECT An effect made use of to measure speed by sensing the sideband produced by motion of either the transmitter or the receiver. As an upper sideband is produced when travelling in a manner to reduce the separating distance and a lower one is produced when the reverse is the case, it will be seen that the sense of direction may also be determined.

DUPLEXER A device which allows a transmitter and receiver to be used simultaneously on a common aerial.

E-BEND A waveguide bend in which the curve is created in the narrow wall of the wave-guide, so that the E plane is disposed radially in the curve.

E LAYER The Kennelly-Heaviside layer of the ionosphere, situated at a height of about 100 km.

ECHO BOX A resonant cavity with a very high Q to enable the radar operator to test the performance of the equipment during operation.

ELECTROLYTE Any compound that can be decomposed by the passage of an electric current, such as sea water or the sulphuric acid in a lead/acid battery.

ELECTROMAGNETIC DEFELECTION This normally refers to the means of deflecting the electron beam in a cathode ray tube. In normal operation this is achieved by coils disposed about the neck of the CRT. Stray magnetic fields also have the same effect to some extent, and this causes an unwanted deflection.

ELECTROSTATIC DEFLECTION A means of deflecting the beam within a cathode ray tube by means of imposing an electric field on the beam by means of plates.

ELECTROSTRICTIVE A device that constricts when subject to an electric field.

EMISSION The giving off of free electrons in a

valve or tube due to thermionic effects; or the radiation of electromagnetic waves in space.

F LAYER The ionised layer situated at a height of about 230 km above the earth. The F layer is relatively strongly ionised and so is of importance for the reflection of short waves in the region of 10 to 50 m.

FACSIMILE The transmission of pictures by means of telegraphy. Extensively used for news pictures and weather charts.

FIELD STRENGTH This can refer to either electric or magnetic fields. The electric field intensity at any point is measured in micro-volts per metre in an aerial of 1 metre. Magnetic field strength is measured in gauss, or for weak fields more conveniently gammas, i.e. 100,000 gammas = 1 gauss.

FILTER A device for rejecting or preventing the passage of a particular signal or current.

FIN A device used to produce righting torques in roll stabiliser equipments.

FLYBACK (OR RETRACE) The return of a scanning beam to its origin after the completion of the scanning period.

FREQUENCY (Hz or c/s) The number of times an alternating current goes through a complete cycle in each second.

FREQUENCY MODULATION (FM) A means of applying intelligence to an electrical signal by varying the instantaneous frequency of the carrier signal.

GAIN The amplification or magnification obtained within an electronic circuit.

GANGING A mechanical means of operating two or more variable circuit elements from a common control.

GATE A circuit with which a signal may be switched by the application of a control potential.

GONIOMETER A transformer with orthogonal stator windings used for coupling direction finder aerials of the Bellini-Tosi type. A rotable secondary disposed in the centre of the stator windings enables the direction of signal null to be identified.

GUNN EFFECT DEVICE A solid state micro-wave power source now used in small boat radars as a replacement for the klystron

formerly employed as a local oscillator.

H-BEND A waveguide bend in which the curve is created in the broad wall of the wave guide so that the H plane is disposed radially to the curve.

HARMONICS Frequencies appearing in an electrical circuit corresponding to multiples of the fundamental frequency.

HETERODYNE Resultant signals created by mixing two waves, these signals have frequencies equal to the sum and difference of the two mixed waves.

HORN A simple waveguide aerial in which one or both transverse dimensions increase toward the aperture.

HYPERBOLIC NAVIGATION Any system that depends for its operation on reception of a hyperbolic signal pattern. The signals may be characterised to suit the needs of the particular system; for example Loran signals are pulsed.

IMPEDANCE (ohm or Ω) The opposition presented to an alternating current within the circuit in which it flows. It is usually made up of a resistive and a reactive component which may be inductive or capacitive. For the purpose of measurement the unit ohm is employed.

INDUCTANCE (H) A circuit element which resists any change in the current flowing through it; for example any coil possesses inductance. Its unit of measurement is the henry (H).

INERTIA The natural reluctance of a body to change its state of rest or motion, in the absence of an external force.

INTEGRATOR In the electronic sense this is usually a resistance and capacitor network, with the object of making use of its time constant to allow the integration of circuit events.

INTERMEDIATE FREQUENCY (IF) The frequency produced when two electrical signals are mixed in a superheterodyne receiver. This frequency is created so that the sensitivity and selectivity parameter of signal circuits are more readily obtained.

INVERTOR In electronic circuitry the term is often applied to a device which is used to turn the applied signal upside down, or in other words reverse its phase. Can also refer to power convertors (see Convertor).

ION An atom with unequal numbers of electrons and protons.

IONISATION The liberation of electrons from molecules of gas or liquid.

IONOSPHERE The complex of ionised layers in the upper atmosphere under the influence of which radio waves are reflected, making long distance communication possible.

ISOCLINIC LINE A line on a chart joining places of equal magnetic dip angle.

ISOGONIC LINE A line on a chart joining places of equal magnetic variation.

ISOTROPIC A device having the same physical properties in all directions.

JAMMING Interference so strong that it renders a desired signal unreadable.

KEY A device by which a radio transmitter is switched to its operating condition. This may take the form of a conventional Morse key or may be some form of automatic keying device such as an auto-alarm.

KILOWATT (W) One thousand watts.

KLYSTRON A microwave generating valve often used as a local oscillator in radar receivers.

LIMITER An electronic circuit whose function is to limit to a predetermined level for the positive and/or negative voltage excursions of a waveform.

LINEAR AMPLIFIER An amplifier whose output is proportional to its input at all frequencies within its range. In SSB communications equipment it is usual to carry out signal processing at a low level in a unit called an exciter and to follow this stage with a linear amplifier of the power output required for the particular application.

LOCAL OSCILLATOR (LO) A continuous wave oscillator that is employed to produce a beat or heterodyne with the incoming signal in a receiver. The beat signal is the intermediate frequency.

LOCK PULSE A pulse derived from one part of an electronic circuit which is used to provide a trigger for some other circuit element, i.e.

the two circuit functions are locked together.

MAGNETIC DEFLECTION An electromagnetic field created by coils about the neck of a cathode ray tube which has the effect of deflecting the electron beam.

MAGNETOSTRICTION The contraction or expansion of metals such as nickel or permendum when subject to a magnetic field.

MAGNETRON A valve in which the fields of electron movement are partly coincident with a strong superimposed magnetic field. This device is used in the transmitting stage in marine radars because of its ability to produce very short high-power pulses of microwave energy.

MAGSLIP or SYNCHRO A device for transmitting angular position information; for example in a radar the position of the aerial is transmitted to the display.

METACENTRE The point in a floating body on the position of which its stability depends.

MICROWAVES Waves of between 30 cm and the infrared region, extensively used for radar.

MIXER The section of the receiver in which the local oscillator signal is combined with the incoming signal to produce the intermediate frequency.

MODULATION Variation of the amplitude, frequency or phase of a carrrier wave by impressing upon it the electrical equivalents of the information it is necessary to transmit.

NEGATIVE FEEDBACK The process of feeding back some part of the output of an amplifier to its earlier stages in such a manner as will reduce the output, the object being to improve the response curve and reduce distortion.

NODE The point in a standing waveform at which the voltage or current is at a minimum.

OCTANTAL ERROR Cyclic errors that occur in direction finders or other equipment in which the error changes sign at eight discrete points in the whole cycle of measurement.

OPTICAL ENCODER A device for converting circular or linear position or movement into electrical signals with characteristics that enable the position or movement to be sensed remotely.

PARABOLIC REFLECTOR A metal reflector of parabolic form used to tailor the radiation pattern of an aerial into a narrow beam.

PARALYSIS The overloading of a circuit by a signal. For example, many cheap echosounders are unable to produce an echo adjacent to the outgoing pulse as the energy in this pulse has paralysed the receiver for a period of time corresponding to several feet of depth.

PHASE LOCKED Two signals are said to be phase locked when at some instant a point on a cycle in each wave is coincidental due to some means of electrically controlling the phase of either or both signals.

PIEZO-ELECTRIC EFFECT The effect which produces mechanical strain, exhibited by some crystals and polarized ceramics when subject to an electric field. Typical materials are quartz, Rochelle salt, lead zinconate titanate and barium titanate. Mechanical strains also produce electrical charges within these materials, which may be used for microphones, echosounder transducers, etc.

PLAN POSITION INDICATOR (PPI) The form of radar display common to most marine radars, which presents a plan on the screen of all targets within a circular area in which the observer's craft is at the centre.

POLAR DIAGRAM A diagram showing the transmitted field strength of an aerial in polar co-ordinates. The radial distance represents the field strength and the angular coordinate represents the direction of the field.

POTENTIAL DIVIDER In DC terms this is a tapped resistance placed across a supply, used principally to improve stability in the relationships between the supply and the tapped-off voltage.

PUSH-PULL Two transistor valves or other devices connected so that when one is being driven into conduction, the other is taken toward cut-off.

QUADRANTAL ERROR An error which occurs with magnetic compasses and direction finders that is cyclic in character and has four maxima and minima in 360°.

QUARTZ CRYSTAL A small piece of quartz cut or ground to resonate at an exact frequency.

QUIESCENT A condition of rest between events in a circuit, such as the condition of a radar transmitter between pulses.

RACON A radar beacon that replies with an identifying code when it receives a signal from the radar on a boat.

RADOME A weatherproof cover, transparent to radar energy, used to house radar aerials.

RAMARK The ramark is a continuously transmitting beacon which will display a radial line of bearing on the radar screen. Sometimes the line is coded by dots.

REACTANCE That part of a circuit's impedance caused by inductance or capacitance.

REACTIVE LOAD A load which exhibits either capacitance or inductance, and as a result produces a phase shift between voltage and current.

RECTIFICATION The circuit process of converting an alternating current into a direct current.

REFRACTION Bending of the path of radio waves by either the atmosphere, the ionosphere, land, water or building masses.

RESISTANCE (ohm, Ω) A characteristic of electrical conductors and circuit elements that has the effect of impeding the flow of an electrical current.

RESISTIVE LOAD A load which is comprised of resistance only and does not therefore produce the phase shifts encountered with reactive loads.

RESONANCE The ability of a material or structure to respond at one frequency to a greater extent than others. The length of an aerial is chosen with this effect in mind so that it is more supportive to the signals it has to send or receive.

RIGHTING MOMENT The moment created about the metacentre of a boat by the action of its stabilisers.

RIPPLE An alternating current superimposed on a wave of lower frequency or a direct current.

SATURABLE REACTOR An inductor with a DC control winding usually wound on a centre limb where the AC fields are equal and opposite, with the object of varying the inductance or coupling of the AC coils by saturating the core with the field due to the control winding.

SCANNER In radar, the aerial assembly which is rotated to scan the area to be searched.

SCANNING A means of recording information by breaking it down into a series of lines which when reassembled are a reasonable facsimile of the original. The information may be associated with television, radar, echo-sounder, sonar, etc. and may employ a cathode ray tube or paper recorder to display the reassembled information.

SCREENING A metal absorber interposed between wires or circuits of radio apparatus, to prevent either radiation or reception of unwanted signals.

SEMICURCULAR ERROR An error which is cyclic and appears in radio direction finders. It has two maxima and minima in 360°, hence its name.

SHOCK EXCITATION Production of oscillations within a circuit by a pulse of energy.

SIDEBANDS (SB) A band of frequencies on either or one side of the carrier frequency in which radiation occurs due to modulation. In fact this part of the transmitted wave carries the signal intelligence.

SIDELOBES Small lobes of energy radiated by radar aerials on either side of the main beam.

STANDING WAVE Waves present in a conductor or waveguide created by an impedance mismatch in the system which reflects part of the energy so that depending on the phase of reflection the useful energy is reduced.

TIMEBASE A circuit for producing the scanning waveform in television, radar or other CRT display.

TOROID A coil in which the turns axis is itself circular.

TRF AMPLIFIER An amplifier where all amplification is at the signal frequency. Abbreviation means tuned radio frequency.

TR SWITCH OR CELL A device for excluding the transmitted pulse of a radar from the mixer of the receiver, which it would damage if not protected. In a radiotelephone this device limits all signals at the receiver input above a predetermined level.

UHF Ultra high frequency. Electromagnetic waves having frequencies between 300 and 3,000 megahertz (MHz).

ULTRASONIC Frequencies above the range of normal human hearing, i.e. above 15 kHz.

VELOCITY GYROSCOPE A gyroscope within a gimbal held captive by springs, so that an applied torque at right angles to the spin axis biases the gimbal against the springs to a degree proportional to the angular velocity of the applied torque.

VHF Very high frequency electromagnetic waves having frequencies between 30 and 300 megahertz (MHz).

VIDEO The signals in television or radar that appear after demodulation and are associated with information to be visually displayed.

WATT (W) The unit of measurement for electrical power or work done and equal to the product of the current and the voltage.

WAVEFORM The graphical representation of the changes in sign and amplitude of an electric current plotted against time.

WAVEGUIDE A precision extrusion, usually rectangular in section for marine purposes. The most popular size is WG16 which is $1 \times \frac{1}{2}$ in. outside. It is used as a feeder for microwave signals, for example to radar aerials.

WAVELENGTH The physical distance between an identical point on consecutive waves wavelength × frequency = velocity.

ZENER DIODE A device commonly used as a regulator or voltage reference. It is characterised by its ability to appear virtually open circuit until a critical voltage is reached and thereafter to conduct heavily.

Abbreviations

AF	Audio frequency
AGC	Automatic gain control
AM	Amplitude modulation
AVC	Automatic volume control
CRT	Cathode ray tube
CW	Carrier wave
Diff.	Differentiation
EHT	Extra high tension. Usually in kV, for example the supply for a CRT anode 8–20 kV.
FM	Frequency modulation
FTC	Fast time constant (rain clutter)
IF	Intermediate frequency
LO	Local oscillator
MCW	Modulated carrier wave
NM	Nautical miles
PM	Pulse modulation
PRF	Pulse repetition rate
RF	Radio frequency
RT or *R/T*	Radiotelephone
STC	Sensitivity time control (sea clutter)
UHF	Ultra high frequency
VHF	Very High Frequency
Ω	ohms

Prefixes

n	(nano) One thousand millionth or 10^{-9}
μ	(micro) One millionth or 10^{-6}
m	(milli) One thousandth or 10^{-3}
k	(kilo) One thousand or 10^{3}
M	(mega) One million or 10^{6}
G	(giga) One thousand million or 10^{9}

Index